Teen Health Series

Sexual Health Information For Teens, Fourth Edition

Sexual Health Information For Teens, Fourth Edition

Health Tips About Sexual Development,
Reproduction, Contraception, And
Sexually Transmitted Infections

Including Facts About Puberty, Sexuality,
Birth Control, HIV/AIDS, Human Papillomavirus,
Chlamydia, Gonorrhea, Herpes, And More

OMNIGRAPHICS
155 W. Congress, Suite 200
Detroit, MI 48226

Bibliographic Note
Because this page cannot legibly accommodate all the copyright notices, the Bibliographic Note portion of the
Preface constitutes an extension of the copyright notice.

* * *

Omnigraphics, Inc.
Editorial Services provided by Omnigraphics, Inc.,
a division of Relevant Information, Inc.
Keith Jones, *Managing Editor*

* * *

Library of Congress Cataloging-in-Publication Data

Names: Omnigraphics, Inc.

Title: Sexual health information for teens: health tips about sexual development, reproduction, contraception, and sexually transmitted infections including facts about puberty, sexuality, birth control, HIV/AIDS, human papillomavirus, chlamydia, gonorrhea, herpes, and more.

Description: Fourth edition. | Detroit, MI: Omnigraphics, Inc., [2016] |Series: Teen health reference series | Audience: Grade 9 to 12. Includes bibliographical references and index. | Description based on print version record and CIP data provided by publisher; resource not viewed.

Identifiers: LCCN 2015042867 (print) | LCCN 2015042291 (ebook) | ISBN 9780780813991 (ebook) | ISBN 9780780813854 (hardcover: alk. paper)

Subjects: LCSH: Teenagers--Health and hygiene. | Sexual health. | Reproductive health. | Puberty. | Sexually transmitted diseases--Prevention. | Sex instruction for teenagers.

Classification: LCC RA777 (print) | LCC RA777 .S47 2016 (ebook) | DDC 613.9071/2--dc23

LC record available at http://lccn.loc.gov/2015042867

Table of Contents

Preface

Part Four: For Guys Only

Part Five: Pregnancy Prevention

Part Six: Sexually Transmitted Diseases (STDs)

Part Seven: If You Need More Information

Preface

About This Book

As they mature and prepare for adulthood, teens face many academic and social challenges. In addition, they must deal with developing bodies, sexual pressures from peers, and alluring media messages. Irrespective of whether and when teens choose to enter sexual relationships, they need accurate information about how their choices can affect their health and well being.

Unplanned teen pregnancies, for example, can lead to multiple challenges. Teenagers who give birth are much more likely to deliver low birth weight or preterm infants than older women, and their babies are at elevated risk of dying in infancy. Only about 50% of teen mothers receive a high school diploma by 22 years of age, versus approximately 90% of women who had not given birth during adolescence. Furthermore, among sexually active teens and young adults, sexually transmitted infections continue to be problematic and the lack of proper sexual health information only makes the situation worse.

Sexual Health Information For Teens, Fourth Edition includes reliable information that can help teens navigate the often confusing, conflicting messages they receive about sex. It also offers updated facts about the sexual issues today's teens face. It describes reproductive anatomy and the physical and emotional changes that accompany puberty and emerging sexuality, including sensitive issues such as contraception, and sexual orientation. It offers facts about activities that can put teens at risk for unplanned pregnancies and sexually transmitted diseases. The long-term consequences of untreated, incurable sexually transmitted diseases—including cervical and other cancers, AIDS, liver disease, penile cancer, and syphilis—are also discussed. The book concludes with a directory of resources for further information.

How To Use This Book

This book is divided into parts and chapters. Parts focus on broad areas of interest; chapters are devoted to single topics within a part.

Part One: What To Expect As You Enter Puberty explains that confusing time in life when a person's body becomes sexually mature—a process known as puberty. It talks about male and female hormones, describes the specific changes that affect boys and girls in different ways, and provides facts about the mental changes and mood swings that often accompany puberty's physical transformations. It also discusses dating and healthy relationships, and issues related to emerging sexuality, such as body image, and sexual attraction.

Part Two: Protecting Your Sexual Health includes information on American teen's sexual and reproductive health, as well as factors that can impact a teen's sexual health, both in the short term and the long term. It discusses sexual choices and behaviors (including the physical and emotional risks of sexual activity) and provides facts about current sexual choices among teens. In addition, it includes chapters on sexual abuse and avoiding sexual predators.

Part Three: For Girls Only begins with an anatomical review of the female reproductive system. It addresses concerns girls often have about breast development, douching, and routine gynecological care. It also offers facts about female medical issues, including vaginal infections, pelvic inflammatory disease, and endometriosis. This part also provides information on preconception health and health care for women.

Part Four: For Guys Only begins with an anatomical review of the male reproductive system and male sexual development. It addresses concerns boys often have about sexual health. It also includes information about a variety of male medical issues, including testicular cancer, peyronie disease, penile cancer, and epididymitis.

Part Five: Teen Pregnancy offers facts about teen pregnancy and pregnancy prevention programs, including abstinence-based programs. It explains different kinds of contraceptives and how to use them correctly. It also provides information on their reliability and whether or not they protect against sexually transmitted diseases.

Part Six: Sexually Transmitted Diseases (STDs) includes information about chlamydia, gonorrhea, herpes, hepatitis, syphilis, HIV/AIDS, and other diseases that are spread by sexual contact. It describes how different types of infections are transmitted, the steps that can be taken to avoid them, symptoms that may accompany infection, available treatments, and the long-term consequences associated with untreated infections and diseases for which no cure currently exists.

Part Seven: If You Need More Information offers a directory of resources that provide information about sexual development, sexual health, and sexually transmitted diseases.

Bibliographic Note

This volume contains documents and excerpts from publications issued by the following government agencies: Centers for Disease Control and Prevention (CDC); National Cancer Institute (NCI); National Institute of Arthritis and Musculoskeletal and Skin Diseases (NIAMS); National Institute of Child Health and Human Development (NICHD); National Institute of Diabetes and Digestive and Kidney Diseases (NIDDK); National Institute on Drug Abuse (NIDA); National Institutes of Health (NIH); Office on Women's

Health (OWH); U.S. Department of Health and Human Services (HHS); U.S. Food and Drug Administration (FDA); and Youth.gov.

It may also contain original materials produced by Omnigraphics, Inc. and reviewed by medical consultants.

The photograph on the front cover is from © Moodboard/123RF.com.

Medical Review

Omnigraphics contracts with a team of qualified, senior medical professionals who serve as medical consultants for the *Teen Health Series*. As necessary, medical consultants review reprinted and originally written material for currency and accuracy. Citations including the phrase, Reviewed (month, year)" indicate material reviewed by this team. Medical consultation services are provided to the *Teen Health Series* editors by:

Dr. Vijayalakshmi, MBBS, DGO, MD

Dr. Senthil Selvan, MBBS, DCH, MD

About The *Teen Health Series*

At the request of librarians serving today's young adults, the *Teen Health Series* was developed as a specially focused set of volumes within Omnigraphics' *Health Reference Series*. Each volume deals comprehensively with a topic selected according to the needs and interests of people in middle school and high school. Teens seeking preventive guidance, information about disease warning signs, medical statistics, and risk factors for health problems will find answers to their questions in the *Teen Health Series*. The *Series*, however, is not intended to serve as a tool for diagnosing illness, in prescribing treatments, or as a substitute for the physician/patient relationship. All people concerned about medical symptoms or the possibility of disease are encouraged to seek professional care from an appropriate health care provider.

If there is a topic you would like to see addressed in a future volume of the *Teen Health Series*, please write to:

Editor
Teen Health Series
Omnigraphics, Inc.
155 W. Congress, Suite 200
Detroit, MI 48226

A Note About Spelling And Style

Teen Health Series editors use *Stedman's Medical Dictionary* as an authority for questions related to the spelling of medical terms and the *Chicago Manual of Style* for questions related to grammatical structures, punctuation, and other editorial concerns. Consistent adherence is not always possible, however, because the individual volumes within the *Series* include many documents from a wide variety of different producers and copyright holders, and the editor's primary goal is to present material from each source as accurately as is possible following the terms specified by each document's producer. This sometimes means that information in different chapters or sections may follow other guidelines and alternate spelling authorities.

Our Advisory Board

We would like to thank the following advisory board members for providing initial guidance to the development of this Series:

Dr. Lynda Baker, Associate Professor of Library and Information Science, Wayne State University, Detroit, MI

Nancy Bulgarelli, William Beaumont Hospital Library, Royal Oak, MI

Karen Imarisio, Bloomfield Township Public Library,

Bloomfield Township, MI

Karen Morgan, Mardigian Library,

University of Michigan-Dearborn, Dearborn, MI

Rosemary Orlando, St. Clair Shores Public Library,

St. Clair Shores, MI

Part One
What To Expect As You Enter Puberty

Chapter 1

Everything You Wanted To Know About Puberty

Puberty

Pimples. Growing breasts. Body hair. Moody moments. If any of this sounds familiar, you're likely on the path of puberty. It's a road everyone travels, and it certainly has its bumps. But it's also an amazing time.

Puberty is when you start making the change from being a child to being an adult. And it's when your body develops the ability to have a baby. It all happens thanks to changing hormones, or natural body chemicals.

With everything that's changing, life can feel a little overwhelming. But you can feel more in control if you take good care of your body. Knowing what to expect can help, too, so keep reading. (And don't forget that puberty also involves changes you can't see—like changes to your self-esteem and your feelings.)

Timing And Stages Of Puberty

Adolescence and puberty can be so confusing! Here's some info on what to expect and when:

- Puberty in girls usually starts between the ages of 8 and 13 and ends by around 14. For boys, puberty usually starts between 10 and 14, and ends by around 15 or 16.

About This Chapter: Information in this chapter is excerpted from "Puberty," Office on Women's Health (OWH), April 15, 2014; and information from "Talking With Teens," U.S. Department Of Health And Human Services (HHS), December 11, 2014.

- For girls, one of the first signs of puberty usually is their breasts starting to grow.

- Getting your period (menstruation) usually happens later, around two years after breast growth starts.

- In between, you'll probably start to see more hair in places like under your arms and in your pubic area.

- Puberty involves big changes to your shape, including getting taller (which stops when puberty ends).

Of course, it can be hard to have your body change at a slower or faster rate than your friends' bodies. If how fast or slow your body is changing is upsetting you, talk to an adult you trust.

If you're developing slower or faster than you think you should, your body may just be changing at its own natural rate. It's a good idea to let your doctor know if you start puberty before age 8. Also let your doctor know if you don't have any signs of puberty by the time you're 14. Your doctor can check whether a medical problem is involved.

Physical Changes Boys Experience During Puberty

- Boys usually start to show the physical changes of puberty between the ages of 11 and 14, which is slightly older than when girls start puberty.

- The male sex hormone called testosterone and other hormones cause the physical changes.

- A boy's brain is maturing while his body is changing.

- A boy's reproductive organs mature and become ready for reproduction.

- Height and weight increase.

- Body hair grows in the pubic area, under the arms, and on the face, and becomes thicker on the legs.

- His muscles become stronger.

- Vocal cords get thicker and longer and his voice deepens.

- His body develops an increased number of red blood cells.

- Sweat and oil glands become more active and his body odor changes.

- Acne can develop.

- Some boys develop small and temporary breast tissue.

- Reproductive system begins to work.

- He is then able to get a girl pregnant.

Physical Changes Girls Experience During Puberty

- Girls usually start to show the physical changes of puberty between the ages of 9 and 13, which is slightly sooner than boys.

- The female sex hormone called estrogen and other hormones cause the physical changes.

- Many girls are fully developed by the age of 16. Some girls will continue to develop through age 18.

- Her height and weight increase rapidly.

- Hair growth begins close to the pubic area and underarms.

- Breast buds appear; nipples become raised and this area may be tender.

- Sweat and oil glands become more active and her body odor changes.

- Acne can develop.

- Ovaries become larger and hormone production begins.

- Ovulation and menstruation (periods) begin.

- She is then able to get pregnant.

Your Feelings About Your Changing Body

During puberty your body may seem very different from what you're used to, and you might feel uncomfortable or shy about it. Remember that everyone goes through these changes—it's just part of life.

During puberty, it's common to struggle with body image, or how you feel about your body. This can be especially hard when models in magazines have bodies that seem "perfect." But a lot of what you see in magazines and online is either fake or unhealthy.

If you think you or a friend may have a problem with body image or an eating disorder, talk to a parent, a doctor, or another adult you trust. Help is available, and it's important to get treated. You can get better!

Remember, measure yourself by your great traits and loving heart—not by the size and shape of your body!

Chapter 2

Normal, Precocious, And Delayed Puberty

Normal Puberty

Puberty is the body's natural process of sexual maturation. Puberty's trigger lies in a small part of the brain called the hypothalamus, a gland that secretes gonadotropin-releasing hormone (GnRH). GnRH stimulates the pituitary gland, a pea-sized organ connected to the bottom of the hypothalamus, to emit two hormones: luteinizing hormone (LH) and follicle-stimulating hormone (FSH). These two hormones signal the female and male sex organs (ovaries and testes, respectively) to begin releasing the appropriate sex hormones, including estrogens and testosterone, which launch the other signs of puberty in the body.

Precocious Puberty

In approximately 90% of girls who experience precocious puberty, no underlying cause can be identified—although heredity and being overweight may contribute in some cases. When a cause cannot be identified, the condition is called idiopathic precocious puberty. In boys with precocious puberty, approximately 50% of cases are idiopathic. In the remaining 10% of girls and 50% of boys with precocious puberty, an underlying cause can be identified.

About This Chapter: Information in this chapter is excerpted from "What Causes Normal Puberty, Precocious Puberty, & Delayed Puberty?" Eunice Kennedy Shriver National Institute of Child Health and Human Development (NICHD), a component of the National Institutes of Health (NIH), December 16, 2013; and information from "Puberty And Precocious Puberty: Condition Information," Eunice Kennedy Shriver National Institute of Child Health and Human Development (NICHD), a component of the National Institutes of Health (NIH), December 16, 2013.

Sometimes the cause is an abnormality involving the brain. In other children, the signs of puberty occur because of a problem such as a tumor or genetic abnormality in the ovaries, testes, or adrenal glands, causing overproduction of sex hormones.

Precocious puberty can be divided into two categories, depending on where in the body the abnormality occurs—*central precocious puberty* and *peripheral precocious puberty*.

1. **Central Precocious Puberty**

   This type of early puberty, also known as gonadotropin-dependent precocious puberty, occurs when the abnormality is located in the brain. The brain signals the pituitary gland to begin puberty at an early age. Central precocious puberty is the most common form of precocious puberty and affects many more girls than boys. The causes of central precocious puberty include:

   • Brain tumors

   • Prior radiation to the brain

   • Prior infection of the brain

   • Other brain abnormalities

   Often, however, there is no identifiable abnormality in the brain; this is called *idiopathic central precocious puberty*.

2. **Peripheral Precocious Puberty**

   This form of early puberty is also called gonadotropin-independent precocious puberty. In peripheral precocious puberty, the abnormality is not in the brain but in the testicles, ovaries, or adrenal glands, causing overproduction of sex hormones, like testosterone and estrogens. Peripheral precocious puberty may be caused by:

   • Tumors of the ovary, testis, or adrenal gland

   • In boys, tumors that secrete a hormone called hCG, or human chorionic gonadotropin

   • Certain rare genetic syndromes, such as McCune-Albright syndrome or familial male precocious puberty

   • Severe hypothyroidism, in which the thyroid gland secretes abnormally low levels of hormones

   • Disorders of the adrenal gland, such as congenital adrenal hyperplasia

   • Exposure of the child to medicines or creams that contain estrogens or androgens

> Children affected by precocious puberty may experience problems such as:
>
> - Failure to reach their full height because their growth halts too soon
> - Psychological and social problems, such as anxiety over being "different" from their peers. However, many children do not experience major psychological or social problems, particularly when the onset of puberty is only slightly early.

Delayed Puberty

Many children with delayed puberty will eventually go through an otherwise normal puberty, just at a late age. Sometimes, this delay occurs because the child is just maturing more slowly than average, a condition called *constitutional delay of puberty*. This condition often runs in families.

Puberty can be delayed in children who have not gotten proper nutrition due to long-term illnesses. Also, some young girls who undergo intense physical training for a sport, such as running or gymnastics, start puberty later than normal.

In other cases, the delay in puberty is not just due to slow maturation but occurs because the child has a long-term medical condition known as hypogonadism, in which the sex glands (the testes in men and the ovaries in women) produce few or no hormones. Hypogonadism can be divided into two categories: *secondary hypogonadism* and *primary hypogonadism*.

- *Secondary hypogonadism* (also known as central hypogonadism or hypogonadotropic hypogonadism), is caused by a problem with the pituitary gland or hypothalamus (part of the brain). In secondary hypogonadism, the hypothalamus and the pituitary gland fail to signal the gonads to properly release sex hormones. Causes of secondary hypogonadism include:

  - Kallmann syndrome, a genetic problem that also diminishes the sense of smell

  - Isolated hypogonadotropic hypogonadism, a genetic condition that only affects sexual development but not the sense of smell

  - Prior radiation, trauma, surgery, or other injury to the brain or pituitary

  - Tumors of the brain or pituitary

- In *primary hypogonadism*, the problem lies in the ovaries or testes, which fail to make sex hormones normally. Some causes include:

9

- Genetic disorders, especially Turner syndrome (in women) and Klinefelter syndrome (in men)

- Certain autoimmune disorders

- Developmental disorders

- Radiation or chemotherapy

- Infection

- Surgery

What Are The Symptoms Of Puberty, Precocious Puberty, And Delayed Puberty?

Normal Puberty

In Girls

The signs of puberty include:

- Growth of pubic and other body hair

- Growth spurt

- Breast development

- Onset of menstruation (after puberty is well advanced)

- Acne

In Boys

The signs of puberty include:

- Growth of pubic hair, other body hair, and facial hair

- Enlargement of testicles and penis

- Muscle growth

- Growth spurt

- Acne

- Deepening of the voice

Precocious Puberty

The symptoms of precocious puberty are similar to the signs of normal puberty but they manifest earlier—before the age of 8 in girls and before age 9 in boys.

Delayed Puberty

Delayed puberty is characterized by the lack of onset of puberty within the normal range of ages.

How Many Children Are Affected By/At Risk Of Precocious Puberty?

Precocious puberty affects about 1% of the U.S. population (roughly 3 million children). Many more girls are affected than boys. One study suggests that African American girls have some early breast development or some early pubic hair more often than white girls or Hispanic girls.

Who Is At Risk?

There is a greater chance of being affected by precocious puberty if a child is:

- Female

- African American

- Obese

Chapter 3
Seeing The Doctor

As you get older, it's a good idea to get more involved in taking care of your own health. Getting involved with your health will not only help protect your body—it can make you feel really proud of yourself!

Of course, you don't have to take care of your health by yourself. Work together with caring adults like your parents or guardians to protect your great, growing body.

Work closely with your doctor—and not just when you're sick but also to prevent any problems. Your doctor will tell you how often you should come in for a checkup, which is usually once a year. Learn more about:

- People who provide health care

- Why you might see a gynecologist

- Ways to work well with people who provide health care

Your doctor or other health care provider can help you with everything from sports injuries to immunizations. You can start getting more involved by asking the doctor for tips in areas like nutrition, exercise, and safety.

People Who Provide Health Care

Caring for your health is an important part of growing up. If you notice changes that you are not sure are normal, ask your parents or a trusted adult to help you make an

---

About This Chapter: Information in this chapter is excerpted from "Seeing The Doctor," Office on Women's Health (OWH), April 15, 2014.

Tough Topics

Your doctor can be a great resource on teen health topics that can be a little rough for you. These might include:

- How fast your body should develop during puberty
- Feeling unhappy for no obvious reason
- Worries about your eating habits
- The whole complicated topic of sex
- Pressure to smoke, drink alcohol, or use drugs

You may feel a little embarrassed to raise these issues, but doctors and nurses have heard about all this before—and they want to give you the support you need to stay healthy and happy.

appointment with a doctor or other health care provider. Health care providers you can see include:

- **A pediatrician.** This is a doctor who cares for children and teens. Some pediatricians have special training in reproductive health issues like problems with periods, but not all do.

- **A family practitioner.** This is a doctor who does not focus on a specific medical specialty but works on various medical areas in patients of all ages.

- **A gynecologist.** A gynecologist is a doctor who focuses on women's reproductive health. Some gynecologists specialize in taking care of teenagers.

- **An adolescent specialist.** This type of doctor specializes in caring for teenagers. Most adolescent medicine doctors take care of reproductive health in addition to general health.

- **A nurse practitioner (NP).** A nurse practitioner is a registered nurse with special training. If your clinic or doctor's office has an NP, he or she can do many of the things a doctor can do and will work with the doctor if you need special tests or medicines.

- **A certified nurse midwife.** This is a nurse who is trained to care for the general and gynecological health of women and their babies.

Working With Doctors And Nurses

Answering questions, filling out papers, getting poked and prodded—going to the doctor may stress you out! If it does, remember that you'll get used to working with doctors, nurses, and other health professionals.

Making An Appointment

As you get more involved in your own health care, you may want or need to make your own appointments. You may feel a little nervous, but calling will be easier if you have a list of questions to ask, such as:

- How much will my visit cost?
- If I have insurance, do you work with my plan?
- What times is the doctor available?
- Can I see the same doctor each time?
- Do I have to bring anything with me when I come?
- What will happen during the visit?
- If I want, can the visit be kept confidential?
- Is it okay if someone comes with me to the exam?
- If I don't have much money, do you have a "sliding scale" based on my ability to pay?

What Questions Will The Doctor Or Nurse Ask?

It's a good idea to know what questions you may be asked. That way, you can think about the answers and make sure to take any necessary info with you to your appointment.

You may be asked about:

- What kind of help you might want or need
- Allergies to medicines
- Any medicines you are taking
- Concerns you have about your general health, including your emotional health
- If you or your family has a history of certain medical problems
- Your period, such as how long it normally lasts, how old you were when you first got it, and the first day of your last period
- Whether you have ever had sex
- If you've ever been forced to have sex
- If you smoke, drink alcohol, or use drugs
- How things are going at home and at school

It is important to be honest so that the doctor or other health care provider has all the right information about your health and body.

Tips For Teaming With Your Doctor Or Nurse

You may feel a little nervous when talking with a health care professional like a doctor. After all, you need this person's help. But remember—it's the doctor's job to help you! Here are some suggestions that can make working with your doctor easier:

- **Write down any questions in advance.** It's hard to remember everything, especially when you may be feeling a little nervous. And ask what to do if more questions come up after the appointment.

- **Bring a family member or trusted friend with you.** That person can take notes, offer support, and help you remember information.

- **Be honest.** Even if you're embarrassed, make sure to tell the doctor everything he or she may need to know in order to help you. Your doctor probably has seen or heard it all before!

- **If the doctor gives you medication, make sure you know exactly how to take it and for how long.** Also ask about any possible side effects and what to do if you have a problem.

You want to feel like you can trust and work well with your doctor or nurse. If you don't, then maybe you need to think about finding someone else.

What If I Don't Want My Parents To Know?

- It's a good idea to get your parents' or guardians' support around any health concerns even if it's hard, but sometimes that may just not feel possible. If so, here are some key points:

- Keep in mind that often your doctor's visit can be kept confidential. That means anything you say will be secret, even if you're getting birth control or sexually transmitted disease (STD) testing. It's best to ask about the doctor's policy before you begin.

- Some states have laws to make sure visits for STDs are confidential.

- Even if your doctor keeps your visit confidential, your parents may get a bill or insurance papers that list the services you got. Ask your doctor's office about that. They may have ways to stop some services from being listed.

- If your doctor's office can't offer confidentiality, ask where you can go to get confidential care.

- If you go to a family planning clinic for services like birth control counseling, your privacy definitely will be protected. Plus, the visit likely will cost less or be free. Often, you can find a family planning clinic External link pretty easily.

Paying For Care

Paying for doctor visits and other health care causes confusion and worry in some families. Understanding a few key points will help.

Your family may already have private health insurance.

You or your family will need to get information from the insurance company. This includes:

- What medical services it pays for

- How it pays

- How much it pays

In the United States, the Affordable Care Act (ACA) requires insurance companies to pay for the whole cost of certain services, including some vaccines, STD tests, and types of birth control.

If your family doesn't have health insurance (or isn't happy with what it has), the ACA is making it easier to get health insurance.

If your family can't afford insurance, you may be able to get Medicaid. This is basically insurance from the government for people with low incomes.

If your family earns too much money to get Medicaid, they may be able to get CHIP for you. CHIP, or Children's Health Insurance Program, is low-cost health insurance for kids.

You may be able to get free or lower-cost care at certain places in your community. These include community health clinics, free clinics, public hospitals, school-based health centers, and public housing primary care centers. You can search online for centers.

If you have certain disabilities, you may be able to get Medicare. This is another kind of insurance from the government.

Paying for care can be confusing and stressful. Definitely try to work with a trusted adult on this. Take notes, and keep all bills, insurance information, and important papers together in case you need them again.

Chapter 4
Body Image And Self-Esteem

Having Body Image Issues

Do you wish you could lose weight, get taller, or develop faster? It's pretty common to worry a little about how your body looks, especially when it's changing. You can learn about body image and ways to take control of yours.

What Is Body Image?

Body image is how you think and feel about your body. It includes whether you think you look good to other people.

Body image is affected by a lot of things, including messages you get from your friends, family, and the world around you. Images we see in the media definitely affect our body image even though a lot of media images are changed or aren't realistic.

Why does body image matter? Your body image can affect how you feel about yourself overall. For example, if you are unhappy with your looks, your self-esteem may start to go down. Sometimes, having body image issues or low self-esteem may lead to depression, eating disorders, or obesity.

How Can I Deal With Body Image Issues?

Everyone has something they would like to change about their bodies. But you'll be happier if you focus on the things you like about your body—and your whole self. Need some help?

About This Chapter: Information in this chapter is excerpted from "Having Body Image Issues," Office on Women's Health (OWH), January 7, 2015; and information from "Self-Esteem And Self-Confidence," Office on Women's Health (OWH), January 7, 2015.

Check out some tips:

- **List your great traits.** If you start to criticize your body, tell yourself to stop. Instead, think about what you like about yourself, both inside and out.

- **Know your power.** Hey, your body is not just a place to hang your clothes! It can do some truly amazing things. Focus on how strong and healthy your body can be.

- **Treat your body well.** Eat right, sleep tight, and get moving. You'll look and feel your best—and you'll be pretty proud of yourself too.

- **Give your body a treat.** Take a nice bubble bath, do some stretching, or just curl up on a comfy couch. Do something soothing.

- **Mind your media.** Try not to let models and actresses affect how you think you should look. They get lots of help from makeup artists, personal trainers, and photo fixers. And advertisers often use a focus on thinness to get people to buy stuff. Don't let them mess with your mind!

- **Let yourself shine.** A lot of how we look comes from how we carry ourselves. Feeling proud, walking tall, and smiling big can boost your beauty—and your mood.

- **Find fab friends.** Your best bet is to hang out with people who accept you for you! And work with your friends to support each other.

If you can't seem to accept how you look, talk to an adult you trust. You can get help feeling better about your body.

What Do You See?

A lot of our body image comes from pics we see in the media or on social media sites. But those images can be unhealthy, fixed up, or faked. Focusing on inner beauty makes more sense. As one teen says, "**My brilliance shines from the inside**, from my heart. I reflect a life full of experience, full of love and anger. **My beauty overpowers a room**, not just the magazine page."

Stressing About Body Changes

During puberty and your teen years, your body changes a lot. All those changes can be hard to handle. They might make you worry about what other people think of how you look and about whether your body is normal. If you have these kinds of concerns, you are not alone.

Here are some common thoughts about changing bodies.

- Why am I taller than most of the boys my age?

- Why haven't I grown?

- Am I too skinny?

- Am I too fat?

- Will others like me now that I am changing?

- Are my breasts too small?

- Are my breasts too large?

- Why do I have acne?

- Do my clothes look right on my body?

- Are my hips getting bigger?

If you are stressed about your body, you may feel better if you understand why you are changing so fast—or not changing as fast as your friends.

During puberty, you get taller and see other changes in your body, such as wider hips and thighs. Your body will also start to have more fat compared to muscle than before. Each young woman changes at her own pace, and all of these changes are normal.

What Are Serious Body Image Problems?

If how your body looks bothers you a lot and you can't stop thinking about it, you could have body dysmorphic disorder, or BDD.

People with BDD think they look ugly even if they have a small flaw or none at all. They may spend many hours a day looking at flaws and trying to hide them. They also may ask friends to reassure them about their looks or want to have a lot of cosmetic surgery. If you or a friend may have BDD, talk to an adult you trust, such as a parent or guardian, school counselor, teacher, doctor, or nurse. BDD is an illness, and you can get help.

Self-Esteem And Self-Confidence

You may have heard a lot about self-esteem and self-confidence. But what exactly are they, and how do you get them?

What Is Self-Esteem?

Self-esteem has to do with the **value** and **respect** you have for yourself. Simply put, it's your opinion of yourself.

If you have healthy self-esteem, you feel good about yourself and are proud of what you can do. Having healthy self-esteem can help you feel positive overall. And it can make you

21

brave enough to tackle some serious challenges, like trying out for a school play or standing up to a bully.

If you have low self-esteem, you may not think very highly of yourself. Of course, it's normal to feel down about yourself sometimes. But if you feel bad about yourself more often than good, you may have low self-esteem.

How can low self-esteem hurt? Low self-esteem may stop you from doing things you want to do or from speaking up for yourself. Low self-esteem may even lead you to try to feel better in unhealthy ways, like using drugs or alcohol. Also, some people may start to feel so sad or hopeless about themselves that they develop mental health problems like depression and eating disorders.

A lot of things can affect self-esteem. These include how others treat you, your background and culture, and experiences at school. For example, being put down by your boyfriend, classmates, or family or being bullied can affect how you see yourself. But one of the biggest influences on your self-esteem is … you!

What Is Self-Confidence?

Self-confidence is a little different from self-esteem. Self-confidence has to do with what you think about your skills and abilities.

Self-confidence often comes from trying new things, like speaking more in class or trying out for an afterschool activity. Does that sound a little stressful? That's normal! As you try new things, you will gain confidence in spite of your fears. In fact, that's what real self-confidence is—your belief that you will be fine even in the face of obstacles.

Rate Your Self-Esteem And Self-Confidence

If you have healthy self-esteem and self-confidence, you probably will agree with some or most of the following statements:

- I feel good about who I am.

- I am proud of what I can do, but don't need to show off.

- I know there are some things that I'm good at and some things I need to improve.

- I feel it is okay if I win or if I lose.

- I usually think, "I can do this," before I do something.

- I am eager to learn new things.

- I can handle criticism.

- I like to try to do things without help, but I don't mind asking for help if I need it.

- I like myself.

If some of the items on this checklist are true for you, congrats! You're on the right track.

If you have low self-esteem and self-confidence, you probably will agree with some or most of the following statements:

- I can't do anything well.

- I have no friends.

- I do not like to try new things.

- I get really upset about making mistakes.

- I'm not as nice, pretty, or smart as the others in my class.

- I don't like it when people say nice things about me.

- I get very upset when people criticize me.

- I feel better if I put other people down.

- I don't know what I'm good at.

- I usually think, "I can't do this," before I do something.

- I don't like myself.

If many of the items on this list apply to you, try some ways to raise your self-esteem. It's no fun to be hard on yourself, and you can work to stop. Remember, everyone brings something unique to the world.

Chapter 5
Dating And Sexual Feelings

Thinking about romance, starting to date, and feeling attraction all can be incredibly cool—and a little intense.

As you start dating, think about what you're looking for. A solid relationship comes from being with someone who supports you, trusts you, and appreciates you for who you are. You want someone who deserves you!

As you start thinking about love and sex, don't forget to focus on feeling good about yourself. Take good care of your body. See a doctor if you are having sex. Talk to your parent or guardian, doctor, or another trusted adult if you have questions.

When it comes to deciding about kissing and more, remember that so much of what you see on TV and hear in songs is not real or healthy. And remember that there are lots of ways to show affection other than sex. Don't do anything that makes you uncomfortable. You'll probably remember these exciting days for many years, and you want to remember them happily!

What Teens Are Saying About Sex

You may get lots of messages about sex in everything from music lyrics to religious rules. Here's what some young people are saying about waiting, staying safe, and respecting their bodies.

"I don't want to get pregnant at a young age, nor do I want to do something that I will regret later in life. Even if you don't end up getting pregnant, you can still be left very hurt emotionally."

About This Chapter: Information in this chapter is excerpted from "Dating And Sexual Feelings," Office on Women's Health (OWH), April 15, 2014.

"I think you should wait until you find the right guy—the guy that really loves you back, the one that is special. Once you find the right guy, of course you should wait for the right age also. If I choose to have sex, I will use birth control."

"It is best to wait. The guy may tell people about it, and the girl will be labeled a nasty name. And don't let your boyfriend ever pressure you. A guy like that does not respect you."

"My boyfriend and I decided we are both ready to have sex. We know the consequences, we love each other, and it did not change anything. He would still love me just as much if I didn't want to have sex anymore. We are using condoms because we don't want to risk anything happening. However, we discussed what to do *if* a condom fails, and we both know that we will get through it together."

"I have decided not to have sex at a young age because I would never want to have a child while I am still one."

"The best way to not get pregnant or STDs is to stay abstinent. Abstinence is a harder promise to keep as you get older because there's so much pressure to be sexually active. Talk to your parents and guidance counselors. They'll help you keep your promise."

Talking With Your Partner About Sex

Anyone you're seriously thinking about having sex with should be someone you can talk to about it. Talk about what kind of birth control you would use to protect yourselves from pregnancy and STDs (sexually transmitted diseases, also called sexually transmitted infections).

Are you worried that you'll sound like you're accusing your partner of having an STD? You can focus instead on protecting your health and respecting each other's feelings.

It's a good idea to talk about all this at a time and in a place where you're comfortable and won't be interrupted. It's a great idea to do this while your clothes are still on!

It's Not Too Late To Stop Having Sex

Some people feel like once they've had sex there's no turning back. That's not true. You don't have to feel bad about yourself if you regret having sex. Everybody makes mistakes—that's just part of learning. But it doesn't make sense to keep doing something that feels wrong to you.

Could I Be Gay?

If you're having feelings of romantic or physical attraction to other girls, you may wonder if you are gay. It's natural as you develop to wonder about these feelings, and it may take time to figure out whether you are attracted to guys, girls, or both. Keep in mind that being attracted to girls is normal. Also, keep in mind that having a gay or lesbian parent or sibling doesn't mean you are gay.

If you're feeling concerned about your sexual orientation, talk to someone you trust. Also, if you're feeling stressed about telling others you're gay or if you're being bullied about being gay, you can get help. If you feel like you are going to hurt yourself, reach out right away to an adult, a friend, or a counselor. Things can get better. You can visit The Trevor Project (http://www.thetrevorproject.org) or call 866-488-7386 for help.

If you are going to have sex with another girl, keep in mind that women who have sex with women are at risk for many of the same STDs as women who have sex with men. Also, if you are a lesbian, it's a good idea to talk to your doctor about protecting your overall health. Lesbians are more likely to have certain health problems, like obesity, smoking, and depression, so make sure you learn how to stay healthy and strong.

Dating Older Guys

If you date someone even a few years older than you, the chances go up that your partner will want to have sex before you feel ready. Also, if you have sex with a man who is legally an adult and you're underage, he could go to jail. Laws for this are different in each state.

Staying Safe When Dating

You should always feel physically and emotionally safe in a dating relationship. Consider some of the advice below to take good care of yourself.

Remember that you deserve to make your own decisions about sex and not feel rushed or pressured. You don't owe anyone sex, whether they pressure you by being nasty or by being nice! Sometimes in an unhealthy relationship a partner may try to get you pregnant even though you're not ready. Remember that it's your body and your future!

When you go out on a date, take your cell phone and cab money with you. That way you can leave if you start to feel uncomfortable. It is also a good idea to make an agreement with your parents that you can call them at any time, no questions asked, if you need help or are feeling unsafe.

Sex you don't agree to is rape, whether it's with a stranger or a date. Rape includes forcing a body part or object into your vagina, rectum (bottom), or mouth. If someone forces you to do anything sexually, tell a trusted adult or call the National Sexual Assault Hotline at 800-656-4673 (HOPE).

To stay safe in a dating situation, it's a good idea to avoid drugs and alcohol. They make it more likely you'll do something you would never otherwise do, like have unprotected sex. And remember that someone can slip a date rape drug into your drink, so keep it with you at all times.

Protect yourself on the Internet and in text messages. You may think "sexting," or sending sexy photos or messages, is private. But messages can be traced back to you, and you can even get in legal trouble for sending or forwarding them. Whatever you send can get passed around and can stay out there forever. Keep in mind that your parents, classmates, teachers, and possible future employers could wind up seeing it. If someone dares you to send this kind of message, think about why they're doing it—and what you have to lose!

Treat your body with the respect it deserves—and make sure others do, too!

What About Masturbation?

You may have heard about or tried masturbation (which basically means giving yourself sexual pleasure). There are lots of opinions about masturbation. From a medical point of view, experts say it's almost always not a problem—unless it's interfering with your responsibilities or your social life. Plus, they say, it can be a way to release tension and learn about your body.

Chapter 6
Sexual Attraction And Orientation

Sexual Orientation

During your teen years, your sexual feelings will develop. These sexual feelings are part of the body and of the mind. It is normal and natural to have sexual feelings, even though you may feel embarrassed by them sometimes. Many teens feel confused by their new sexual feelings. If you feel that way, you are not alone.

The term "sexual orientation" means the kind of person to whom you are romantically and physically drawn to. There are three main kinds of sexual orientation:

- **Heterosexual.** People who are heterosexual are attracted to members of the opposite sex. Heterosexual boys are attracted to girls, and heterosexual girls are attracted to boys. Heterosexuals are sometimes called "straight."

- **Homosexual.** People who are homosexual are attracted to people of the same sex. Girls who are attracted to other girls are lesbian; boys who are attracted to other boys are often known as gay. (The term gay is sometimes also used to describe homosexual individuals of either gender.)

- **Bisexual.** People who are bisexual are romantically and physically attracted to members of both sexes.

Lesbian, Gay, And Bisexual

Lesbian, gay, and bisexual describe a person's sexual orientation—emotional, romantic, or sexual feelings toward other people.

About This Chapter: Information in this chapter is excerpted from "Sexual Orientation," Office on Women's Health (OWH), October 31, 2013; text from "Supporting Your LGBTQ Youth: A Guide For Foster Parents," Child Welfare Information Gateway, May 2013; and text from "LGBT Youth," Centers for Disease Control and Prevention (CDC), November 12, 2014.

Lesbian refers specifically to women who love women, while *gay* can refer to any person who is attracted to people of the same sex. (The term homosexual is considered outdated and offensive by many gay people.)

Bisexual people are attracted to men or women regardless of their anatomy. People do not need to have any particular sexual experience (or any sexual experience at all) to identify as bisexual, gay, or lesbian, because sexual orientation and sexual behavior are not the same thing.

Transgender refers to a person's gender identity—an internal understanding of one's own gender. A transgender person's gender identity does not match the sex (a biological characteristic) assigned to him or her at birth. Many, but not all, transgender people choose to alter their bodies hormonally and/or surgically to match their gender identity. Some people's experience, perception, or expression of their gender evolves and changes over time.

Gender identity and sexual orientation are separate aspects of a person's identity: A transgender person may be bisexual, gay, or straight (or may identify in some other way).

Some youth (and adults) identify as *questioning* when they start to recognize that they may be part of the LGBT community.

This does not mean that sexual orientation or gender identity is a choice. These youth may need time to process what being LGBT means for them; to reconcile any anti-LGBT stereotypes they have internalized; and to decide if, when, and how they should identify themselves as lesbian, gay, bisexual, or transgender to others.

Some people's gender expression (meaning, the ways in which they express their gender identity to others) does not conform to society's expectations for their sex. This might include choices in clothing, mannerisms, names, hairstyles, friends, and hobbies. It is important to understand that society's gender expectations are cultural, not biological, and they change over time (for example, women used to be expected to wear only dresses; now teens of both genders wear jeans, sweatshirts, and tennis shoes). In any case, not all gender-variant (or gender non-conforming) youth will continue to express themselves this way into adulthood, and many will never identify as gay, lesbian, bisexual, or transgender.

LGBTQ Youth Are No More Likely Than Other Youth To Be Mentally Ill Or Dangerous.

Gay or transgender people are not more likely than heterosexuals or gender-conforming people to molest or otherwise pose a threat to children. And although it is true that LGBTQ people experience higher rates of anxiety, depression, and related behaviors (including alcohol and drug abuse) than the general population, studies show that this is a result of the stress of being LGBTQ in an often-hostile environment, rather than a factor of a person's LGBTQ identity itself. Professional mental health organizations agree that homosexuality is not a mental disorder and is a natural part of the human condition.

LGBT Youth

Most lesbian, gay, bisexual, transgender, and questioning (LGBTQ) youth are happy and thrive during their adolescent years. Going to a school that creates a safe and supportive learning environment for all students and having caring and accepting parents are especially important. This helps all youth achieve good grades and maintain good mental and physical health. However, some LGBTQ youth are more likely than their heterosexual peers to experience difficulties in their lives and school environments, such as violence.

Experiences With Violence

Negative attitudes toward lesbian, gay, and bisexual (LGB) people put these youth at increased risk for experiences with violence, compared with other students. Violence can include behaviors such as bullying, teasing, harassment, physical assault, and suicide-related behaviors.

According to data from Youth Risk Behavior Surveys (YRBS) conducted during 2001–2009 in seven states and six large urban school districts, the percentage of LGB students (across the sites) who were threatened or injured with a weapon on school property in the prior year ranged from 12% to 28%. In addition, across the sites?

- 19% to 29% of gay and lesbian students and 18% to 28% of bisexual students experienced dating violence in the prior year.

- 14% to 31% of gay and lesbian students and 17% to 32% of bisexual students had been forced to have sexual intercourse at some point in their lives.

LGBTQ youth are also at increased risk for suicidal thoughts and behaviors, suicide attempts, and suicide. A nationally representative study of adolescents in grades 7–12 found that lesbian, gay, and bisexual youth were more than twice as likely to have attempted suicide as their heterosexual peers. More studies are needed to better understand the risks for suicide among transgender youth. However, one study with 55 transgender youth found that about 25% reported suicide attempts.

Another survey of more than 7,000 seventh- and eighth-grade students from a large Midwestern county examined the effects of school (social) climate and homophobic bullying on lesbian, gay, bisexual, and questioning (LGBQ) youth and found that

- LGBQ youth were more likely than heterosexual youth to report high levels of bullying and substance use;

- Students who were questioning their sexual orientation reported more bullying, homophobic victimization, unexcused absences from school, drug use, feelings of depression, and suicidal behaviors than either heterosexual or LGB students;

- LGB students who did not experience homophobic teasing reported the lowest levels of depression and suicidal feelings of all student groups (heterosexual, LGB, and questioning students); and

- All students, regardless of sexual orientation, reported the lowest levels of depression, suicidal feelings, alcohol and marijuana use, and unexcused absences from school when they were

  - In a positive school climate and
  - Not experiencing homophobic teasing.

Effects On Education And Health

Exposure to violence can have negative effects on the education and health of any young person. However, for LGBT youth, a national study of middle and high school students shows that LGBT students (61.1%) were more likely than their non-LGBT peers to feel unsafe or uncomfortable as a result of their sexual orientation. According to data from CDC's YRBS, the percentage of gay, lesbian, and bisexual students (across sites) who did not go to school at least one day during the 30 days before the survey because of safety concerns ranged from 11% to 30% of gay and lesbian students and 12% to 25% of bisexual students.

The stresses experienced by LGBT youth also put them at greater risk for depression, substance use, and sexual behaviors that place them at risk for HIV and other sexually transmitted diseases (STDs). For example, HIV infection among young men who have sex with men aged 13?24 years increased by 26% over 2008–2011.

What Schools Can Do

For youth to thrive in their schools and communities, they need to feel socially, emotionally, and physically safe and supported. A positive school climate has been associated with decreased depression, suicidal feelings, substance use, and unexcused school absences among LGBQ students.

Schools can implement clear policies, procedures, and activities designed to promote a healthy environment for all youth. For example, research has shown that in schools with LGB support groups (such as gay-straight alliances), LGB students were less likely to experience threats of violence, miss school because they felt unsafe, or attempt suicide than those students in schools without LGB support groups. A recent study found that LGB students had fewer suicidal thoughts and attempts when schools had gay-straight alliances and policies prohibiting expression of homophobia in place for 3 or more years.

To help promote health and safety among LGBTQ youth, schools can implement the following policies and practices:

- Encourage respect for all students and prohibit bullying, harassment, and violence against all students.

- Identify "safe spaces," such as counselors' offices, designated classrooms, or student organizations, where LGBTQ youth can receive support from administrators, teachers, or other school staff.

- Encourage student-led and student-organized school clubs that promote a safe, welcoming, and accepting school environment (e.g., gay-straight alliances, which are school clubs open to youth of all sexual orientations).

- Ensure that health curricula or educational materials include HIV, other STD, or pregnancy prevention information that is relevant to LGBTQ youth (such as, ensuring that curricula or materials use inclusive language or terminology).

- Encourage school district and school staff to develop and publicize trainings on how to create safe and supportive school environments for all students, regardless of sexual orientation or gender identity, and encourage staff to attend these trainings.

- Facilitate access to community-based providers who have experience providing health services, including HIV/STD testing and counseling, to LGBTQ youth.

- Facilitate access to community-based providers who have experience in providing social and psychological services to LGBTQ youth.

What Parents Can Do

How parents respond to their LGB teen can have a tremendous impact on their adolescent's current and future mental and physical health. Supportive reactions can help youth cope with the challenges of being an LGBTQ teen. However, some parents react negatively to learning that they may have an LGBTQ daughter or son. In some cases, parents no longer allow their teens to remain in the home. In other situations, stress and conflict at home can cause some youth to run away. As a result, LGB youth are at greater risk for homelessness than their heterosexual peers.

To be supportive, parents should talk openly with their teen about any problems or concerns and be watchful of behaviors that might indicate their child is a victim of bullying or violence?or that their child may be victimizing others. If bullying, violence, or depression is suspected, parents should take immediate action, working with school personnel and other adults in the community.

Ways Parents Can Influence The Health Of Their LGB Youth

More research is needed to better understand the associations between parenting and the health of LGB youth. Following are selected research-based steps parents can take to support the health and well-being of their LGB teen:

Talk and listen. Parents who talk with and listen to their teen in a way that invites an open discussion about sexual orientation can help their teen feel loved and supported. Parents should have honest conversations with their teens about sex, and about how to avoid risky behavior and unsafe or high-risk situations.

Provide support. Parents who take time to come to terms with how they feel about their teen's sexual orientation will be more able to respond calmly and use respectful language. Parents should develop common goals with their teen, including being healthy and doing well in school.

Stay involved. Parents who make an effort to know their teen's friends and know what their teen is doing can help their teen stay safe and feel cared about.

Be proactive. Parents can access many organizations and online information resources to learn more about how they can support their LGB teen, other family members, and their teen's friends.

Chapter 7
Healthy Relationships

During adolescence, young people learn how to form safe and healthy relationships with friends, parents, teachers, and romantic partners. Both boys and girls often try on different identities and roles during this time, and relationships contribute to their development. Peers, in particular, play a big role in identity formation, but relationships with caring adults —including parents, mentors or coaches—are also important for adolescent development. Often, the parent-adolescent relationship is the one relationship that informs how a young person handles other relationships. Unfortunately, adolescents sometimes develop unhealthy relationships, and experience or exhibit bullying or dating violence.

Dating Violence

Some adolescents get involved in unhealthy dating relationships. One in 10 adolescents reported being hit or physically hurt on purpose by a boyfriend or girlfriend at least once in the previous year. Controlling and demanding behaviors often happen before violence occurs. For example, one partner may tell another what to wear and who to spend time with. Over time, controlling and demanding behavior may become increasingly violent and that violence can have negative effects on physical and mental health throughout life (including lower self-esteem, eating disorders and suicidal thoughts). Adults can help by paying attention and talking to adolescents about how to build healthy, respectful relationships.

About This Chapter: Information in this chapter is excerpted from "Healthy Relationships," U.S. Department of Health and Human Services (HHS), May 11, 2015; and information from "Characteristics of Healthy & Unhealthy Relationships," Youth.gov, February 7, 2012.

LGBT

Among adolescents ages 18 to 19, just under eight percent of females and just under three percent of males identify as homosexual or bisexual. Many lesbian, gay, bisexual, and transgender (LGBT) adolescents are happy and thrive during their teenage years. As a group they are more likely than their heterosexual peers to experience difficulties: LGBT adolescents are at increased risk for suicide attempts, being homeless, alcohol use and risky sex. How a parent responds to their LGBT adolescent can have a tremendous impact on an adolescent's current and future mental and physical health. Parental response to their LGBT adolescent can have a tremendous impact on the child's current and future mental and physical health. Supportive reactions can help adolescents cope and thrive.

Bullying

Bullying is a serious problem, but it can be prevented or stopped when those involved know how to address it. Many adolescents have experienced bullying, whether they were bullied, bullied someone else, or saw someone being bullied. Although definitions vary, bullying usually involves an imbalance of power, an intent to hurt, and repetition of the behavior. Adolescents who bully use their power to control or harm, and those being bullied sometimes feel powerless to defend themselves. Many schools and communities have anti-bullying initiatives in place; new resources are being developed by the federal government and other institutions to help adolescents, parents, and others understand bullying and cyberbullying.

Friendships

Friendships play a major role in the lives of adolescents. A circle of caring and supportive friends can help adolescents transition to adulthood. Parents, teachers, and other adult role models can help young people learn how to make and keep good friends. Still, forming and maintaining friendships during adolescence can be challenging. Peer pressure – good and bad – often affects decisions young people make. Adults can set good examples, teach interpersonal skills, and help adolescents nurture positive friendships. One important lesson is that friends can say "no" to each other and remain friends.

Characteristics Of Healthy And Unhealthy Relationships

Respect for both oneself and others is a key characteristic of healthy relationships. In contrast, in unhealthy relationships, one partner tries to exert control and power over the other physically, sexually, and/or emotionally.

Healthy relationships share certain characteristics that teens should be taught to expect. They include:

- *Mutual respect.* Respect means that each person values who the other is and understands the other person's boundaries.

- *Trust.* Partners should place trust in each other and give each other the benefit of the doubt.

- *Honesty.* Honesty builds trust and strengthens the relationship.

- *Compromise.* In a dating relationship, each partner does not always get his or her way. Each should acknowledge different points of view and be willing to give and take.

- *Individuality.* Neither partner should have to compromise who he/she is, and his/her identity should not be based on a partner's. Each should continue seeing his or her friends and doing the things he/she loves. Each should be supportive of his/her partner wanting to pursue new hobbies or make new friends.

- *Good communication.* Each partner should speak honestly and openly to avoid miscommunication. If one person needs to sort out his or her feelings first, the other partner should respect those wishes and wait until he or she is ready to talk.

- *Anger control.* We all get angry, but how we express it can affect our relationships with others. Anger can be handled in healthy ways such as taking a deep breath, counting to ten, or talking it out.

- *Fighting fair.* Everyone argues at some point, but those who are fair, stick to the subject, and avoid insults are more likely to come up with a possible solution. Partners should take a short break away from each other if the discussion gets too heated.

- *Problem solving.* Dating partners can learn to solve problems and identify new solutions by breaking a problem into small parts or by talking through the situation.

- *Understanding.* Each partner should take time to understand what the other might be feeling.

- *Self-confidence.* When dating partners have confidence in themselves, it can help their relationships with others. It shows that they are calm and comfortable enough to allow others to express their opinions without forcing their own opinions on them.

- *Being a role model.* By embodying what respect means, partners can inspire each other, friends, and family to also behave in a respectful way.

- *Healthy sexual relationship.* Dating partners engage in a sexual relationship that both are comfortable with, and neither partner feels pressured or forced to engage in sexual activity that is outside his or her comfort zone or without consent.

Unhealthy Relationships

Unhealthy relationships are marked by characteristics such as disrespect and control. It is important for youth to be able to recognize signs of unhealthy relationships before they escalate. Some characteristics of unhealthy relationships include:

- *Control.* One dating partner makes all the decisions and tells the other what to do, what to wear, or who to spend time with. He or she is unreasonably jealous, and/or tries to isolate the other partner from his or her friends and family.

- *Hostility.* One dating partner picks a fight with or antagonizes the other dating partner. This may lead to one dating partner changing his or her behavior in order to avoid upsetting the other.

- *Dishonesty.* One dating partner lies to or keeps information from the other. One dating partner steals from the other.

- *Disrespect.* One dating partner makes fun of the opinions and interests of the other partner or destroys something that belongs to the partner.

- *Dependence.* One dating partner feels that he or she "cannot live without" the other. He or she may threaten to do something drastic if the relationship ends.

- *Intimidation.* One dating partner tries to control aspects of the other's life by making the other partner fearful or timid. One dating partner may attempt to keep his or her partner from friends and family or threaten violence or a break-up.

- *Physical violence.* One partner uses force to get his or her way (such as hitting, slapping, grabbing, or shoving).

- *Sexual violence.* One dating partner pressures or forces the other into sexual activity against his or her will or without consent.

It is important to educate youth about the value of respect and the characteristics of healthy and unhealthy relationships before they start to date. Youth may not be equipped with the necessary skills to develop and maintain healthy relationships, and may not know how to break up in an appropriate way when necessary. Maintaining open lines of communication may help them form healthy relationships and recognize the signs of unhealthy relationships, thus preventing the violence before it starts.

Part Two
Protecting Your Sexual Health

Chapter 8

Facts On American Teens' Sexual And Reproductive Health

Adolescent Sexual Behavior

- Dating plays a part in adolescents' healthy development. But when teens are dating exclusively (going steady), they are more likely to have sex earlier.

- The proportion of adolescents who have ever had sex has declined since the early 1990s.

- Adolescents who have sex early are less likely to use contraception, putting them at greater risk of pregnancy and STDs.

- Many adolescents are engaging in sexual behaviors other than vaginal intercourse. Nearly half have had oral sex and just over one in 10 have had anal sex.

- Not all sexually active adolescents take part in high-risk sexual behaviors. Thirty-nine percent of females and 33 percent of males who have ever had sex have only had one partner.

- The likelihood of sex increases with each school grade level, from 32 percent in ninth grade to 62 percent in 12th grade.

- Between 2006 and 2008, 14 percent of female adolescents and 25 percent of male adolescents had sex for the first time with someone they had just met or with whom they were "just friends."

- Many adolescents are engaging in oral sex prior to having sexual intercourse. About 51 percent of 15- to 24-year-olds had oral sex before they first had sexual intercourse.

About This Chapter: Information in this chapter is excerpted from "Adolescent Sexual Behavior," Office of Adolescent Health, July 8, 2015; and text from "Reproductive Health," U.S. Department Of Health And Human Services (HHS), July 8, 2015.

- New media play an important role in adolescents' dating and sexual relationships. More than one-third of adolescents say they have sent or posted sexually suggestive messages by text, IM, or e-mail.

Reproductive Health

Adolescence marks the period between childhood and adulthood when hormonal changes transform boys and girls into young men and women able to have children of their own. The percent of adolescents who are having sex at earlier ages has decreased since 1988 and contraceptive use has increased since the 1990s. Together these two factors have contributed to the U.S. reaching its lowest teen pregnancy and birth rates in years. Still, almost half of all high school students reported that they had had sexual intercourse in 2013 and one in eight adolescent females will become pregnant before turning 20. Condom and contraceptive use is critical for adolescents to prevent pregnancy and sexually transmitted diseases. Among sexually active adolescents, male high school students were more likely to use a condom the last time they had sex than were females (66 percent vs. 53 percent).

Dating And Sexual Relationship

Dating during adolescence is common and can be part of healthy development. However, serious and exclusive dating relationships can lead adolescents to have sex earlier than they would have otherwise. Those who have sex at an early age are more likely to engage in risky sexual behaviors. Overall, the proportion of adolescents who have ever had sex has declined substantially since the early 1990s. Of adolescents who have had sex, approximately one-third has had just one partner. Sixteen percent has had two partners, 32 percent has had three to five partners, and 20 percent has had six or more partners. Many adolescents are engaging in sexual behaviors other than vaginal intercourse: nearly one-half have had oral sex, and just over one in 10 have had anal sex.

Teen Pregnancy And Childbearing

Latest estimates reveal that more than 614,000 teen girls in the United States learn they are pregnant each year. Although this number is the lowest in U.S. history, it is still higher than many other developed countries, including Canada and the U.K. teen parents face multiple risks for poor life outcomes: often, they fail to finish high school and are more likely to be poor as adults. In all, one in eight adolescent females will give birth by her 20th birthday and this number is higher for black and Hispanic adolescents. Children born to adolescents face particular challenges—they are more likely to have poorer educational, behavioral, and health outcomes throughout their lives, as compared to children born to older parents. Teen pregnancy is an issue that many people are working to address.

Sexually Transmitted Diseases

Adolescents account for about half of all STDs diagnosed every year, even though they make up a much smaller percentage of the sexually active population. Today, four in 10 sexually active teen girls have had an STD that can cause infertility and even death. Also, though rates of HIV are very low among adolescents, males make up more than three-quarters of HIV diagnoses among 13- to 19-year-olds. STDs often have no obvious sign or physical symptom, so regular screenings are critical. The most effective way to prevent STDs is to abstain from sexual activity; if teens are having sex, they should be using a condom correctly and with every sexual act.

Contraceptive And Condom Use

Rates of teen pregnancy are higher in the U.S. than in other countries. Hormonal methods of birth control (such as the pill) and barrier methods (such as condoms) can reduce the risk of pregnancy, and condom use with every sexual act can greatly reduce—though not eliminate— the risk of STDs. Condom and contraceptive use among adolescents has increased since the 1990s, but many adolescents are inconsistent users: of those who had sex in the past month, almost one in four males and almost 4 in 10 females did not use a condom.

Chapter 9
Risky Sexual Behaviors

Many young people engage in sexual risk behaviors that can result in unintended health outcomes. For example, among U.S. high school students surveyed in 2013,

- 47% had ever had sexual intercourse.

- 34% had had sexual intercourse during the previous 3 months, and, of these

- 41% did not use a condom the last time they had sex.

- 15% had had sex with four or more people during their life.

- Only 22% of sexually experienced students have ever been tested for HIV.

Sexual risk behaviors place adolescents at risk for HIV infection, other sexually transmitted diseases (STDs), and unintended pregnancy, such as,

- Nearly 10,000 young people (aged 13-24) were diagnosed with HIV infection in the United States in 2013.

- Young gay and bisexual men (aged 13-24) accounted for an estimated 19% (8,800) of all new HIV infections in the United States, and 72% of new HIV infections among youth in 2010.

- Nearly half of the 20 million new STDs each year were among young people, between the ages of 15 to 24.

- Approximately 273,000 babies were born to teen girls aged 15–19 years in 2013.

About This Chapter: Information in this chapter is excerpted from "Sexual Risk Behaviors: HIV, STD, & Teen Pregnancy Prevention," Centers for Disease Control and Prevention (CDC), September 1, 2015; and text from "Lower Your Sexual Risk of HIV," U.S. Department of Health and Human Services (HHS), August 13, 2015.

Lower Your Sexual Risk Of HIV

Figure 9.1. Lower Your Sexual Risk Of HIV

No-Risk Sexual Activities

These activities carry no risk of HIV transmission:

- Non-sexual massage

- Casual or dry kissing

- Phone sex, cyber sex, sexy talk

- Masturbation (without your partner's body fluids)

- Frottage—also known as "dry humping" or body-to-body rubbing

You can still contract other STDs, like herpes, HPV, or pubic lice ("crabs") if you have bare skin-to-skin contact with your partner.

Using Condoms

When used consistently and correctly, condoms are highly effective in preventing HIV. They are also effective at preventing STDs transmitted through body fluids, like gonorrhea, chlamydia, and HIV. However, they provide less protection against STDs spread through skin-to-skin contact like human papillomavirus (genital warts), genital herpes, and syphilis.

Taking HIV Medicines To Prevent HIV

As noted above, there are ways to prevent getting HIV by taking some of the medicines used to treat HIV. These methods are PrEP (taking HIV medicine daily to prevent HIV infection) and PEP (taking medicine to prevent HIV after a possible exposure).

What Is Male Circumcision?

Male circumcision is the surgical removal of some or all of the foreskin (or prepuce) from the penis.

Circumcision

Male circumcision reduces the risk that a man will get HIV from an infected female partner, and also lowers the risk of other STDs, penile cancer, and infant urinary tract infection. Studies have not consistently shown that it prevents HIV among men who have sex with men. Circumcision is only partly effective and should be used with other prevention measures. Men who are considering circumcision should weigh its risks and costs against its potential benefits.

In December 2014, CDC issued a request for public comment on draft counseling recommendations about elective male circumcision for the prevention of HIV, STDs, and other health outcomes in the United States. The guidance is designed to help health care providers provide accurate information to individual men, as well as to parents, to help them make informed decisions about circumcision.

Abstinence from vaginal, anal, and oral intercourse is the only 100% effective way to prevent HIV, other STDs, and pregnancy. The correct and consistent use of male latex condoms can reduce the risk of STD transmission, including HIV infection. However, no protective method is 100% effective, and condom use cannot guarantee absolute protection against any STD or pregnancy.

Chapter 10
Abuse And Rape

What Are Rape And Sexual Assault?

Rape is sex you don't agree to, including forcing a body part or an object into your vagina, rectum (bottom), or mouth. In the United States, almost one in five women has been raped during her lifetime.

Sexual assault or abuse is any type of sexual activity that a person does not agree to, including:

- Rape or attempted rape

- Touching your body or making you touch someone else's

- Incest or sexual contact with a child

- Someone watching or photographing you in sexual situations

- Someone exposing his or her body to you

Sometimes, sexual violence is committed by a stranger. Most often, though, it is committed by someone you know, including a date or an intimate partner like a husband, ex-husband, or boyfriend. Sexual violence is always wrong, and a person who is sexually abused does not ever "cause" the attack.

About This Chapter: Information in this chapter is excerpted from "Violence Against Women," Office on Women's Health (OWH), September 30, 2015; and information from "What Are Date Rape Drugs and How Do You Avoid Them?" NIDA for Teens, a component of National Institute on Drug Abuse (NIDA), March 16, 2015.

Keep in mind that there are times when a person is not able to agree to sex, such as if they are drunk or have been drugged with a date rape drug, or if they are underage.

Women who are sexually abused may suffer serious health problems, such as sexually transmitted infections, stomach problems, and ongoing pain. They also are at risk for emotional problems, like depression, anxiety, and post-traumatic stress disorder. If you or someone you know has been sexually abused, it is important to get help as soon as possible.

Getting Help For Sexual Assault

Take steps right away if you have been assaulted:

- Get away from the attacker and find a safe place as fast as you can. Call 911.

- Call someone you trust or a hotline, such as the National Sexual Assault Hotline at 800-656-HOPE (4673).

- Protect any evidence. Do not clean any part of your body or comb your hair. Do not change clothes. Try not to touch anything at the crime scene.

- Go to your nearest hospital emergency room right away. You need to be examined and treated for injuries you may not even know you have. Ask to be screened for sexually transmitted infections (STIs) and for emergency contraception to help prevent pregnancy. The hospital also can collect evidence like hairs, saliva, semen, or clothing fiber that the attacker may have left behind.

- Discuss filing a police report. If you're not sure whether you want to file a report, ask hospital staff if they can collect evidence without filing a report. It is best to collect evidence as soon as possible.

After a sexual assault, you may need a lot of emotional support. Every woman responds differently, but reactions can include feeling terribly shocked, confused, and afraid. Some women experience denial or feeling emotionally numb. Whatever your experience, reach out to people who care about you and get help from a mental health professional. The hospital usually can put you in touch with a counselor or support group. Even if a long time has passed since you were abused, you still can get help.

If someone you know has been abused or assaulted you can help by listening and offering comfort. If the person wants, you also can go along to the police station, the hospital, or counseling sessions. Make sure the person knows the abuse is not his or her fault, and that it is natural to feel angry and ashamed.

Staying Safe From Sexual Assault

Steps you can take to reduce your chances of being sexually assaulted include:

- Making sure you don't drink too much alcohol, so you can keep yourself safe
- Parking in well-lit areas
- Not leaving a social event with someone you just met
- Keeping your car and home doors locked
- Having your key ready as you approach your door

One important way to stay safe at clubs and parties is to learn more about date rape drugs. These are drugs that have no smell or taste that can be slipped into drinks. They are used to make it hard for a person to fight off a rape or to remember what happened.

Another important way to avoid sexual abuse is to leave a relationship that is becoming unhealthy. Remember, no one has a right to pressure you into doing sexual things you do not want to do.

What Are Date Rape Drugs And How Do You Avoid Them?

You may have been warned that sometimes people secretly slip drugs into other people's drinks to take advantage of them sexually. These drugs are called "date rape drugs."

Date rape, also known as "drug-facilitated sexual assault," is any type of sexual activity that a person does not agree to. It may come from someone you know, may have just met, and/or thought you could trust.

Date rape drugs can make people become physically weak or pass out. This is why people who want to rape someone use them, because they leave individuals unable to protect themselves.

Many of these drugs have no color, smell, or taste, and people often do not know that they've taken anything. Many times people (usually girls or women, but not always) who have been drugged are unable to remember what happened to them.

The Dangerous Three

The three most common date rape drugs are Rohypnol® (flunitrazepam), GHB (gamma hydroxybutryic acid), and ketamine.

- **Rohypnol** (also known as roofies, forget-me-pill, R-2) is a type of prescription pill known as a benzodiazepine—it's chemically similar to drugs such as Valium or Xanax, but unlike these drugs, it is not approved for medical use in this country.

  - It has no taste or smell and is sometimes colorless when dissolved in a drink.

  - People who take it can feel very sleepy and confused and forget what happens after its effects kick in.

  - It can also cause weakness, trouble breathing, and make it difficult for those who have taken it to move their body.

  - The effects of Rohypnol can be felt within 30 minutes of being drugged and can last for several hours.

- **GHB** (also known as cherry meth, scoop, goop) is a type of drug that acts as a central nervous system depressant and is prescribed for the treatment of narcolepsy (a sleep disorder).

  - It can cause people to throw up, slow their heart rate, and make it hard to breathe.

  - At high doses, it can result in a coma or death.

  - It is a tasteless, odorless drug that can be a powder or liquid. It's colorless when dissolved in a drink.

  - Mixing it with alcohol makes these effects worse.

  - GHB can take effect in 15 to 30 minutes, and the effects may last for 3 to 6 hours.

- **Ketamine** (also known as cat valium, k-hole, purple) is a dissociative anesthetic, so called because it distorts perceptions of sight and sound and produces feelings of detachment from the environment and self. It also reduces pain and overall feeling. Like other anesthetic drugs, it is used during surgical procedures in both humans and animals.

  - It is a tasteless, odorless drug that can be a powder or liquid.

  - It can cause hallucinations and make people feel totally out of it.

  - It can also increase heartbeat, raise blood pressure, and cause nausea.

  - The effects of ketamine may last for 30 to 60 minutes.

To prevent misuse of Rohypnol, the manufacturer recently changed the pill to look like an oblong olive green tablet with a speckled blue core. When dissolved in light-colored drinks, the new pills dye the liquid blue and alert people that their drink has been tampered with. Unfortunately, generic versions of Rohypnol may not contain the blue dye.

All Drugs Lower Your Defenses

It's important to remember that all drugs affect how well your mind and body operate. In fact, alcohol is linked to far more date rapes than the drugs we've mentioned here. And nearly all drugs of abuse make people vulnerable to being taken advantage of by impairing judgment, reducing reaction time, and clouding a person's thinking.

And as disgusting as it is, when you don't have your wits about you, someone may take that as an opportunity to push themselves on you.

So What Can You Do To Avoid Date Rape Drugs?

If you are at a party where people are drinking alcohol, you should be aware that there could be predators hoping to make you drunk or vulnerable. No matter what you are drinking, even if it's sodas or juice, people can slip drugs in your drinks—so pour all drinks yourself and never leave them unattended (even if you have to take them into the bathroom with you).

Also, be sure to stick with your friends—there's safety in numbers.

But even if you leave your drink or leave your friends behind, know this for certain: if you are drugged and taken advantage of, it's not your fault.

Bottom line
People who date rape other people are committing a crime.

Chapter 11

Protecting Yourself From Online Sexual Predators

Safety In Online Communities

You probably connect with people online a lot and love it. Just remember to be smart about what you share. Even with privacy settings your info and photos can wind up being seen by lots of people, including your parents/guardians, your teachers, bosses, and strangers, some of whom could be dangerous. Even information that seems harmless, such as where you went to dinner last night, could be used by a stranger to find you.

Scam artists have been known to use personal information to pose as a friend, in hopes that you will give them more personal information, such as your credit card or cell phone numbers.

- **Before joining an "online community" or writing in a blog, think about who might be able to see your profile.** Some sites will let only certain users see your posted content; others let everyone see postings.

- **Think about keeping some control over the information you post.** If you can, limit access to your page to a select group of people, such as your friends from school, your club, your team, your community groups, or your family. Keep in mind, though, this does not always mean that other people can't see your page.

- **Keep your information to yourself.** Don't post your full name, Social Security number, address, phone number, or bank and credit card account numbers—and don't post other people's information, either. Be careful about posting information that could be used to

About This Chapter: Information in this chapter is excerpted from "Safety In Online Communities," Office on Women's Health (OWH), November 26, 2014.

identify you or locate you at home or school. This could include the name of your school, sports team, clubs, and where you work, live, or hang out. In some instances, you may be asked to supply your birthday or other information. For example, Facebook requests your full name, birthday, and gender in order to set up a page about yourself. In this case, Facebook requests your birthday to protect young people from 'adult' content. Be sure to have an adult, like a parent or guardian, review any web site that may request this kind of information before you post it. If you do receive permission from your parent or guardian to post this kind of information, be sure to limit the people who can view your information to close friends and family.

- **Make sure your screen name doesn't say too much about you.** Don't use your name, your age, or your hometown. It doesn't take a genius to combine clues to figure out who you are and where you can be found.

- **Post only information that you are comfortable with others seeing—and knowing— about you.** Many people can see your page, including your parents/guardians, your teachers, the police, the college you might want to apply to next year, or the job you might want to apply for in five years.

- **Remember that once you post information online, you can't take it back.** Even if you delete the information from a site, older versions exist on other people's computers.

- **Don't post your photo.** It can be changed and spread around in ways you may not be happy about.

- **Don't flirt with strangers online.** Because some people lie about who they really are, you never really know who you're dealing with.

- **Don't meet someone you met online in person.** If someone you met online wants to meet you in person, tell your parents/guardians or a trusted adult right away.

- **Trust your gut if you have suspicions.** If you feel threatened by someone or uncomfortable because of something online, tell your parents/guardians or an adult you trust and report it to the police and the web site. You could end up protecting someone else.

- **Choose your words wisely.** Some websites where you can chat with your friends have rules about what you can say. You can get kicked out if you break those rules.

Is It Okay To Share My Password With My Best Friend?

No. You should not share your password with any of your friends, even your best friend. The only people who should know your Internet or email password are your parents/guardians and you! If you let someone else know what your password is, then they can read anything that you may want to keep private. Another person could use bad language or go to sites you shouldn't be visiting under your name.

One teenager found out the hard way that others can still get to your supposedly "private" page. He created his page when he was 18 years old and starting college. It included photos, a blog, and other personal information. Now he was 20 years old and searching for an internship. Even though the information on his page seemed harmless, his mother, who worked in a Career Services office, urged him to make his page private and he did.

Finally, he got a call from an agency and went in for an interview. He was ready to answer the typical interview questions, but instead, the interviewer began asking questions about what was on his supposedly "private" page.

Is There Anything That I Shouldn't Tell Someone On The Internet?

Yes! Just like you wouldn't walk up to a stranger and give out your phone number or share your name, where you live, or where you go to school, you shouldn't share this kind of information online either. It is very important that you don't email or IM anyone that you don't know or share any information that can identify you.

Remember:
- Don't post your photo on the Internet or send it to someone you don't know.
- Don't post or send personal information, including:
  - full name
  - address
  - phone number
  - login name, IM screen name, passwords
  - school name
  - school location
  - sports teams
  - clubs
  - city you live in

- Social Security number
- financial information (credit card numbers and bank account numbers)
- where you work or hang out
- names of family members

Chapter 12
Sexual Choices

Talking To Your Parents About Sex

It can be really helpful to talk to your parents or guardians about sex and healthy relationships. It can be tough being a teen, and your parents and caregivers can be a great source of love and support.

Before getting started, think about what you want from the conversation. Do you want basic info, advice, or help getting birth control? Knowing what you want can make it easier to get it. You might even take some notes or write down some questions.

Not sure how to get the conversation started? Consider these tips for talking to your parents about sex:

- Use a TV show or movie as a way into the topic.

- Start out with less awkward questions, like "What age did you start dating?" Then work your way up to the complicated ones, such as "When did you and your friends first start talking about sex?"

- Use girlshealth.gov as a starting point to talk to your parents. You might show them what you've read or send them a link.

- Think about what you might say before starting to talk, so you don't get tongue-tied. Find a time when you're both not busy and distracted.

About This Chapter: Information in this chapter is excerpted "Talking To Your Parents About Sex," Office on Women's Health (OWH), April 15, 2014; and from "Deciding About Sex," Office on Women's Health (OWH), April 15, 2014.

- Cut the stress by saying honestly that you feel a little uncomfortable.

- If it's easier, get started with a text, email, or IM.

Do you think your parents or guardians don't want to talk about sex? You may just find out they're happy to have the chance to support you and help you figure out what's best for you.

What Is sex?

Here are some key points about sex and "fooling around":

- When people say "sex," they usually mean sexual intercourse, or a man putting his penis in a woman's vagina.

- There are other types of sexual contact, like touching a partner's genitals. These also are very personal acts and are worth thinking about in a serious way.

- It's possible to get pregnant if a guy ejaculates ("comes") on the outside of your vagina.

- You can get some STDs (sexually transmitted diseases, also called sexually transmitted infections or STIs) from giving or receiving oral sex or from genital-to-genital contact that isn't intercourse. Using a condom can help protect you.

- Above all, don't do anything sexual that doesn't feel right to you!

R-E-S-P-E-C-T

In one study, young women were more likely than young men to do something sexual that their partner wanted to do **even though they didn't like doing it.** What's up with that? You can say "no" and take control of your body!

Ways To decide If You're Ready For Sex

If you are deciding about sex, you've got a lot to think about. And it makes sense to do your thinking in advance—not when you're swept up in the excitement of the moment.

Think about your values, deepest feelings, and future goals. Remember that having sex with someone is no guarantee that you'll stay together. Not even having a baby together guarantees that. And as much as you care what the other person thinks, it's what you think that really matters!

For teens, not having sex—abstinence—makes good sense. That's partly because your chances of staying safe from unplanned pregnancy and HIV and other STDs are better if you wait. It's also partly because being older can help you handle the strong emotional aspects of sex. Just because your body seems ready doesn't mean that you are!

Questions To Ask Yourself About Sex

Here are some questions you can ask yourself to help decide about sex:

- Do you really feel ready to have sex and not just excited about the idea?

- Do you really trust and feel safe with your partner?

- Are you feeling pressure—from friends, your partner, or even yourself—or is this something that's really right for you?

- Are you doing this because you think everyone else is? (More than half of high schoolers haven't had sex yet.)

- Do you feel really nervous—not just a little worried but really concerned or scared?

- Can you talk to your partner about preventing pregnancy and STDs?

- Do you know what to do help prevent pregnancy and STDs?

- Do you know what you would do if you got pregnant?

- How would you feel if other people found out you had sex?

Remember, you're in charge of your body and your life!

Chapter 13

Why Waiting To Have Sex Makes Sense

You may hear so many messages suggesting that it's a good idea to have sex, from songs on the radio to talk at school. You may also feel curious about sex or have a strong attraction to someone.

Deciding to have sex is a big deal, though, so think it through. You could wind up with an unplanned pregnancy. You could also catch an STD, or sexually transmitted disease (also known as an STI, or sexually transmitted infection).

Having sex before you're ready can seriously hurt your relationship—and your feelings. Few people regret waiting to have sex, but many wish they hadn't started early.

Keep in mind that even if you've already had sex, you can still choose to stop. Read on to see why abstinence—not having sex—makes a lot of good sense.

> ## Facts vs. Fiction
> STDs can mess with your health and your life. Know the facts first before having sex.

Unplanned Pregnancy

Three out of 10 teen girls in the United States get pregnant before they turn 20. And most teen pregnancies are not planned.

About This Chapter: Information in this chapter is excerpted from "Why Waiting To Have Sex Makes Sense," Office on Women's Health (OWH), April 15, 2014.

Getting pregnant before you're ready can be a huge shock. The emotional stress and money worries of raising a baby can be a lot even for an older couple. Imagine what your life would be like if you had to get up with a baby in the night and take care of it every day!

Abstinence is the safest way to prevent the challenges that come with teen pregnancy. Check out some of these facts about teen pregnancy:

- Teen mothers are less likely to finish high school.

- Teen moms are more likely to be—and stay—single parents.

- Babies born to teen moms face greater health risks.

- Teen moms face health risks, too, including possibly being obese later in life.

- Teen moms are at a higher risk of being poor.

- Kids of teen moms are more likely to have problems in school and with the police.

If you do get pregnant, remember that you need to take care of yourself. Be sure to see a doctor. Get help from a trusted adult, like your parents, grandparents, or school counselor.

Sexually Transmitted Diseases (STDs)

Sexually transmitted diseases, or STDs (also known as sexually transmitted infections or STIs) are a huge problem among young people.

Consider some reasons that abstinence makes sense in staying safe from STDs:

- One in 4 teen girls has an STD.

- Condoms decrease the risk of STDs, but they are not 100 percent effective. This is especially true for STDs that can spread just by skin-to-skin contact, such as herpes, which has no cure.

- Having an STD increases your chances of getting HIV, too, and there is no cure for HIV.

- Some STDs have no symptoms, so you can't know if your partner is infected. A partner with no symptoms can still give the STD to you, though.

- Some STDs have no symptoms, so you can't know if you have them, but they can cause serious health problems. These problems include trouble getting pregnant when you are ready to have a baby.

What If I Don't Have "Real" Sex?

Different people may have different definitions of abstinence. Some think it means not having sexual intercourse, but others think it means avoiding other sexual acts, too. Experts say complete abstinence—not having vaginal, oral, and anal sex—is safest. Consider these facts:

- Even if you don't have intercourse but semen (cum) gets in your vagina, there's a chance you could get an STD or get pregnant.

- You can get some STDs from oral sex.

- It's easier to get some STDs from anal sex than from vaginal sex.

Avoiding intimate sexual contact, including skin-to-skin genital contact, is the only sure way to prevent all STDs and pregnancy. If you are having sexual contact, though, it's super-smart to use a condom.

Also keep in mind that acts like oral sex are intimate acts. Try to think about whether you want to do something intimate before you do it. Think about having respect for yourself and having the respect of your partner.

Stats On Sex

As you consider whether abstinence is right for you, consider some research on what teens think about sex.

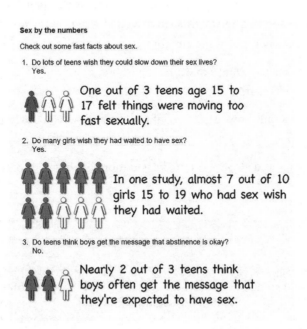

Sex by the numbers

Check out some fast facts about sex.

1. Do lots of teens wish they could slow down their sex lives? Yes.

One out of 3 teens age 15 to 17 felt things were moving too fast sexually.

2. Do many girls wish they had waited to have sex? Yes.

In one study, almost 7 out of 10 girls 15 to 19 who had sex wish they had waited.

3. Do teens think boys get the message that abstinence is okay? No.

Nearly 2 out of 3 teens think boys often get the message that they're expected to have sex.

Figure 13.1. Sex Stats

Ways To Stick To Abstinence

It's not always easy to abstain from sex. It can help to make a plan ahead of time and get support from people you trust. You might try talking with your parents/guardians about sex to see if they have advice. You also might keep in mind the reasons you made the choice to be abstinent.

Don't be afraid to take a stand with your partner. If you are close enough with someone to consider having sex, you should be close enough to talk about the decision. If you and your partner can't agree, then you might think about whether you'd be better off with someone whose beliefs are closer to your own.

Your own body may tell you to give up on abstinence. Remember that your body is not in charge! Remind yourself of the possible physical, emotional, and financial costs of having sex before you're really ready.

Consider These Tips For Staying Abstinent:

- **Get involved.** Some people find it helps to get involved in activities that let them focus on something other than sex, like volunteering or joining a sports team.

- **Get together.** When you hang out with your date, it can help to hang out in a group. Also, try not to spend a lot of time in secluded places with no one else around or at someone's house when no adults are home.

- **Get out.** Always take a cell phone and cab or bus money in case you want to get out of an uncomfortable situation.

- **Practice.** Think about how to say "no" ahead of time, so you don't have to come up with replies on the spot.

- **Stay sober.** Drugs and alcohol can make you more likely to do something you otherwise never would.

> ## Sex Talk
>
> Maybe your partner says, "If you love me, you'll have sex with me." It's just not true. You don't have to have sex with someone to prove you care. Sharing time, thoughts, feelings, and mutual respect are what make a relationship strong. And don't ever feel like you owe your date anything sexually because that person spent money on you. You don't owe that person anything—except "thank you"!

Part Three
For Girls Only

Chapter 14

The Female Reproductive System

How The Female Reproductive System Works

The female reproductive system is all the parts of your body that help you reproduce, or have babies. And it is quite amazing! Consider these two fabulous facts:

- Your body likely has hundreds of thousands of eggs that could grow into a baby. And you have them from the time you're born.

- Right inside you is a perfect place for those eggs to meet with sperm and grow a whole human being!

What's Inside The Female Reproductive System?

The **ovaries** are two small organs. Before puberty, it's as if the ovaries are asleep. During puberty, they "wake up." The ovaries start making more estrogen and other hormones, which cause body changes. One important body change is that these hormones cause you to start getting your period, which is called menstruating.

Once a month, the ovaries release one egg (ovum). This is called ovulation.

The **fallopian tubes** connect the ovaries to the uterus. The released egg moves along a fallopian tube.

The **uterus**—or womb—is where a baby would grow. It takes several days for the egg to get to the uterus.

About This Chapter: Information in this chapter is excerpted from "How The Female Reproductive System Works," Office on Women's Health (OWH), April 15, 2014.

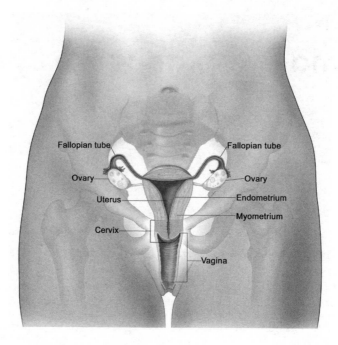

Figure 14.1. Female Reproductive System

As the egg travels, estrogen makes the lining of the uterus (called the endometrium) thick with blood and fluid. This makes the uterus a good place for a baby to grow. You can get pregnant if you have sex with a male without birth control and his sperm joins the egg (called fertilization) on its way to your uterus.

If the egg doesn't get fertilized, it will be shed along with the lining of your uterus during your next period. But don't look for the egg—it's too small to see!

The blood and fluid that leave your body during your period passes through your cervix and vagina.

The **cervix** is the narrow entryway in between the vagina and uterus. The cervix is flexible so it can expand to let a baby pass through during childbirth.

The **vagina** is like a tube that can grow wider to deliver a baby that has finished growing inside the uterus.

The **hymen** covers the opening of the vagina. It is a thin piece of tissue that has one or more holes in it. Sometimes a hymen may be stretched or torn when you use a tampon or during a first sexual experience. If it does tear, it may bleed a little bit.

What's Outside The Vagina?

The **vulva** covers the entrance to the vagina. The vulva has five parts: mons pubis, labia, clitoris, urinary opening, and vaginal opening.

The **mons pubis** is the mound of tissue and skin above your legs, in the middle. This area becomes covered with hair when you go through puberty.

The **labia** are the two sets of skin folds (often called lips) on either side of the opening of the vagina.

The **labia majora** are the outer lips, and the **labia minora** are the inner lips. It is normal for the labia to look different from each other.

The **clitoris** is a small, sensitive bump at the bottom of the mons pubis that is covered by the labia minora.

The **urinary opening**, below the clitoris, is where your urine (pee) leaves the body.

The **vaginal opening** is the entry to the vagina and is found below the urinary opening.

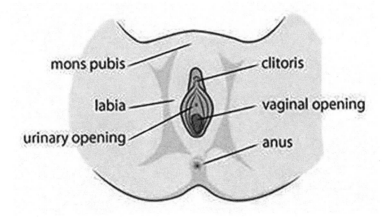

Figure 14.2. Outside The Vagina

Chapter 15

Getting Your Period (Menstruation)

Starting your period—or menstruation—is a major part of puberty and means your body now can make a baby. It also means lots of other changes are going on throughout the month.

Some girls find getting their periods very exciting, and others feel uncomfortable about it. It definitely can take a little getting used to! But lots of women come to see their periods as a wonderful sign that their bodies are healthy and working the way they're supposed to.

What Is Your Period?

What comes out during your period is the blood and tissue that build up as the lining of your uterus each month.

Your period flow can be light, heavy, or in between. Sometimes menstrual blood also will be different shades of red, from light to dark. You may see some dark **clumps or clots** of blood, which is normal.

Your period may be heavy the first day or so each time and then decrease on later days.

Periods usually last between three and five days. It is normal to have periods that are shorter or longer, up to seven days. It is also normal if your periods are not the same number of days each month, especially in the first years.

About This Chapter: Information in this chapter is excerpted from "Getting Your Period," Office on Women's Health (OWH), April 15, 2014.

At What Age Do You Get Your First Period?

Usually, girls get their periods between ages 12 and 14, but it can happen years before or after that. Don't worry if you get your period later or earlier than your friends get theirs—that happens a lot. If you haven't gotten your period by age 15 (or within three years of when your breasts started to grow), talk to your parents or guardians, your doctor, or another adult you trust.

What Causes Your Period?

Natural body chemicals, or hormones, cause your ovaries to release one egg about once a month. Most months, the egg and the lining of your uterus come out of your vagina as your period. This is part of your menstrual cycle.

This cycle is what makes it possible for a woman to have a baby. During sexual intercourse, the egg can get fertilized by a male's sperm and then attach to the lining of the uterus (endometrium) and grow into a baby.

Does Your Period Come Each Month?

Menstrual cycles take place over about one month (around 21 to 34 days), but each woman's cycle is different. Many women have a cycle that lasts 28 days. The cycle includes not just your period, but the rise and fall of hormones and other body changes that take place over the month.

Keep in mind that your periods may not be regular at first. You may have two in one month, or have a month without a period at all. Periods will become more regular in time.

To learn about your own pattern, it's a good idea to keep track of your periods on a calendar. Why? A period calendar lets you:

- Get a sense of when to expect your next period

- Know if you missed a period (if it comes on a regular schedule)

- Have a record of your period schedule and when your last one came to share with your gynecologist or other health care provider

When you chart your cycle, remember that it starts with the first day of one period and goes until the first day of the next period.

Chapter 16
Problems With Your Period

It's common to have cramps or feel uncomfortable when you have your period. And it's common to sometimes have periods that don't come on a regular schedule when you first start getting them. So how do you know when there's a problem?

Signs Of Period Problems

One way to know if you may be having period problems is to learn what's usual for you. Consider these questions:

- **How painful are your cramps each month?** Are they usually the same each time? If they get much worse, they may be a sign of a problem.

- **How often do you get your period?** How long does it last?

- **What is your stress level like when you get your period?** Are you just a little more stressed, or do you feel like you can't cope at all?

- **How heavy is your blood flow?** You can tell how heavy it is by how many times you have to change your pads or tampons.

If you see changes from what your period is usually like or if you need help with heavy bleeding, pain, or uncomfortable feelings, talk with your parents or guardians about seeing your doctor. Having answers to the questions above also can help when you talk to your doctor.

About This Chapter: Information in this chapter is excerpted from "Problem Periods," Office on Women's Health (OWH), April 15, 2014.

What Can Affect Your Period

- **Stress.** If you are under a lot of stress, your periods might stop for a bit, but they usually begin again when your stress goes down.

- **Exercise.** Too much physical activity can cause your body fat to be very low, which can cause your periods to stop. This can happen if you are training hard for sports or if you work out a lot on your own. Being active usually is good for you, but if you are over-tired or get injured often, you may be overdoing it.

- **Hormone problems.** In a normal menstrual cycle, your hormones—or natural body chemicals—go up and down. Sometimes there are problems with hormones. One common hormone condition that causes period problems is PCOS, or polycystic ovary syndrome. Read our information on PCOS for teens, and see your doctor if you think you may have PCOS.

- **Major weight loss.** Girls who have anorexia will often stop having periods.

When To See A Doctor

You should talk to your doctor or other trusted adult if any of the items on the list below are true for you. You may need to see your doctor.

- You have not gotten your period by the age of 15 or within three years of when your breasts started to grow

- It has been three months or more since your last period and you haven't gotten it again

- You are bleeding for more days than usual or more than seven days

- Your bleeding is very heavy

- You suddenly feel sick after using tampons

- You bleed in between periods or with sex (more than just a few drops)

- You have very bad pain during your period

You should contact your doctor about period problems—and not just so you can feel more comfortable. Consider that:

- Period problems could be a sign of an important health issue. For example, strong pain during your period could be a sign of endometriosis, which happens when tissue from your uterus grows outside the uterus.

- Missing your period a few times in a row could be a sign of a serious problem. One type of problem affects your bones, since your bone health is related to hormones.

- If you're sexually active, missing your period could be a sign of pregnancy. It's important to go to the doctor right away if you think you might be pregnant.

Chapter 17
Breast Health

Changes To Your Breasts

It's natural for girls to wonder about their breasts: Are they too big? Too small? If your breasts are large, they may get you unwanted attention. If they're small, you may worry that they'll never grow. Remember that your breasts don't need to look like your friend's breasts or a magazine model's breasts. The world would be boring if everyone looked the same!

Here's some more info on your changing breasts:

What Happens To Breasts During Puberty?

Throughout puberty, you will experience changes in your breasts. The first change is developing a very small bump under the nipple. Early on, you may also notice that your breasts feel a little itchy or achy. Later on, they also may feel tender or sore during your period.

Keep in mind that it is very common for your two breasts to be different sizes, especially as they first start to grow. Other people can't tell that your breasts are different sizes. Give your body time to grow at its own rate and in its own way. Vitamins, herbal teas, and creams—even exercises—won't change the size of your breasts.

Should I Wear A Bra?

Wearing a bra can help support and protect your breasts. If you find that exercise is not as comfortable when your breasts start to grow, try wearing a sports bra with a snug fit for support.

About This Chapter: Information in this chapter is excerpted from "Changes To Your Breasts," Office on Women's Health (OWH), April 15, 2014; information from "Mammograms Fact Sheet," Office On Women's Health (OWH), June 21, 2013; and information from "Cosmetic surgery," Office on Women's Health (OWH), April 15, 2014.

Are you having a hard time finding a bra that fits well? Often, you can get help in a department store or special bra store. There are certain steps people there can take for measuring your body to get a good fit.

What About Lumps And Other Changes?

Most of the changes your breasts will go through are normal. Let your doctor know if you find a lump or have a pain that you are not sure about. Although lumps are common in young women, keep in mind that it is very rare for the lumps to be cancer.

Mammograms

What Is A Mammogram?

A mammogram is a low-dose X-ray exam of the breasts to look for changes that are not normal. The results are recorded on X-ray film or directly into a computer for a doctor called a radiologist to examine.

A mammogram allows the doctor to have a closer look for changes in breast tissue that cannot be felt during a breast exam. It is used for women who have no breast complaints and for women who have breast symptoms, such as a change in the shape or size of a breast, a lump, nipple discharge, or pain. Breast changes occur in almost all women. In fact, most of these changes are not cancer and are called "benign," but only a doctor can know for sure. Breast changes can also happen monthly, due to your menstrual period.

What Is The Best Method Of Detecting Breast Cancer As Early As Possible?

A high-quality mammogram plus a clinical breast exam, an exam done by your doctor, is the most effective way to detect breast cancer early. Finding breast cancer early greatly improves a woman's chances for successful treatment.

Like any test, mammograms have both benefits and limitations. For example, some cancers can't be found by a mammogram, but they may be found in a clinical breast exam.

Checking your own breasts for lumps or other changes is called a breast self-exam (BSE). Studies so far have not shown that BSE alone helps reduce the number of deaths from breast cancer. BSE should not take the place of routine clinical breast exams and mammograms.

If you choose to do BSE, remember that breast changes can occur because of pregnancy, aging, menopause, menstrual cycles, or from taking birth control pills or other hormones.

It is normal for breasts to feel a little lumpy and uneven. Also, it is common for breasts to be swollen and tender right before or during a menstrual period. If you notice any unusual changes in your breasts, contact your doctor.

Cosmetic Surgery

Teens might have cosmetic surgery for a number of reasons, including to remove acne scars, change their noses, and make their breasts smaller or bigger. But if there's something you don't like about your body, your best bet is to try to work on how you feel about it. Your attitude can make a big difference. Try to focus on what you like about yourself. And remember that you've got lots more to offer the world than just how you look.

What Are The Risks Of Cosmetic Surgery?

People who have cosmetic surgery face many of the same risks as anyone having surgery. These include:

- Infection

- Not healing well

- Damage to nerves

- Bleeding

- Not being happy with the results

- Risks from anesthesia, such as lung problems

You face additional concerns if you're considering surgery to make your breasts bigger through breast implants. (Keep in mind that you usually can't have this surgery until you're 18.)

For one, these surgeries usually need to be done over at some point. Also, breast implant risks include dimples and wrinkles that won't go away, pain, and an implant breaking. There are other possible problems, too, including that you might not be able to breastfeed when you have a baby and it could be harder to see signs of breast cancer in a mammogram (breast X-ray).

Chapter 18
Why See A Gynecologist

Going to see a gynecologist—a doctor who focuses on women's reproductive health—means you're taking responsibility for your body in new ways. It can be very exciting to know you're making sure all is going well with puberty, your reproductive system, and more.

Keep in mind that other doctors also can help with gynecological issues. For example, an adolescent medicine specialist, family doctor, or pediatrician can answer questions and may be able to examine your vagina, too.

Of course, it can be stressful to deal with a whole new type of doctor's visit, but learning more can help you know what to expect.

Seeing A Gynecologist Can:

- Help you understand your body and how to care for it
- Give you and the doctor a sense of what is normal for you so you can notice any problem changes, like signs of a vaginal infection
- Let the doctor find problems early so they can be treated
- Explain what a normal vaginal discharge should look like and what could be a sign of a problem
- Teach you how to protect yourself if you have sex

About This Chapter: Information in this chapter is excerpted from "Why see a gynecologist?" Office on Women's Health (OWH), April 15, 2014.

Your gynecologist can answer any questions you have about the many changes that may be happening to your body. It's great to build a relationship with your gynecologist over the years so he or she understands your health and what matters to you.

When Do I Need To Go?

The American College of Obstetricians and Gynecologists recommends that teenage girls start seeing a gynecologist between the ages of 13 and 15.

If you don't go at that time, you should **make sure to visit a gynecologist**, adolescent health specialist, or other health professional who can take care of women's reproductive health if:

- You have ever had sex (vaginal, oral, or anal) or intimate sexual contact

- It has been three months or more since your last period and you haven't gotten it again

- You have stomach pain, fever, and fluid coming from your vagina that is yellow, gray, or green with a strong smell—all of which are possible signs of a serious condition called pelvic inflammatory disease (PID) that needs immediate treatment

- You are having problems with your period, like a lot of pain, bleeding heavily, or bleeding for longer than usual, or it has stopped coming regularly

- You have not gotten your period by the age of 15 or within three years of when your breasts started to grow

- You've had your period for two years and it's still not regular or comes more than once a month

- You were having sex and missed your period

What Will Happen At The Visit?

It's understandable if you're nervous about your first visit. Keep in mind that part of the time will be spent just talking. Your doctor may ask questions about you and your family to learn if you have a history of illnesses. And you can ask the doctor any questions you might have. Don't worry—your doctor probably has already heard every question imaginable! You can talk about any concerns you have, including:

- Cramps and questions about periods

- Acne

- Weight issues

- Feeling depressed

- Sexually transmitted diseases or STDs (also known as sexually transmitted infections or STIs)

- Drinking, using drugs, or smoking

Stay Safe

If you are sexually active, tell your doctor. You likely will need to be tested for sexually transmitted diseases (STDs) like HIV and chlamydia. STDs (also called STIs or sexually transmitted infections) are common among young people. Plus, you can have an STD without having any symptoms. Don't let any possible embarrassment put your health—or your life—at risk.

During your visit, your doctor will probably go through some of the usual items on a doctor's checkup checklist, like weighing you and measuring your blood pressure. He or she also may check the outside of your genitals and do a breast exam. It's common for young women to have some lumpiness in their breasts, but your doctor may want to make sure you don't have problem lumps or pain.

You may have heard of Pap tests and pelvic exams and wonder if you need them. Most likely you won't need either of these until you're 21. If you are sexually active or have symptoms like an unusual vaginal fluid or a history of problems, there's a chance your doctor may choose to do one or both of these. It's helpful, then, to know what to expect.

A pelvic exam usually involves the doctor examining the outside of your genital area (the vulva). It may also involve the doctor using a tool called a speculum to look inside your vagina and check to make sure your cervix is healthy. Frequently, he or she also will feel inside to make sure organs like your ovaries and uterus feel okay. You probably will feel pressure, but it shouldn't hurt. Try to relax—breathing deeply can help.

A Pap test is done by gently taking some cells from your cervix. These cells are checked for changes that could be cancer or that could turn into cancer.

If you haven't already had the HPV vaccine, ask your doctor about it. It helps guard against the human papillomavirus, which can cause genital warts and is the major cause of cervical cancer.

You have options to make your visit more comfortable:

- During the exam, if the doctor is a man, a female nurse or assistant should also be in the room. You can also ask if you can see a female doctor.

- You can ask to have your mom, sister, or a friend stay in the room with you during the visit if that would help.

- You can ask questions about what's going to happen so you know what to expect.

- You can ask the doctor about keeping things you discuss private.

Taking care of your health is a huge sign that you are growing up. Be proud of yourself for learning information that can protect your health.

Chapter 19

Pap Test

The Pap test (or Pap smear) looks for cancers and precancers in the cervix (the lower part of the uterus that opens into the vagina). Precancers are cell changes that might become cancer if they are not treated the right way. Most health insurance plans must cover Pap tests or cervical cancer screening at no cost to you.

What Is A Pap Test?

A Pap test checks the cervix for abnormal cell changes. The cervix is the lower part of the uterus (womb), which opens into the vagina. Cell changes can develop on the cervix that, if not found and treated, can lead to cervical cancer. Cervical cancer can almost always be prevented, and having regular Pap tests is the key.

Why Do I Need A Pap Test?

A Pap test checks the cervix for abnormal cell changes. The cervix is the lower part of the uterus (womb), which opens into the vagina. Cell changes can develop on the cervix that, if not found and treated, can lead to cervical cancer. Cervical cancer can almost always be prevented, and having regular Pap tests is the key.

Do All Women Need Pap Tests?

A Pap test can save your life. It can find early signs of cervical cancer. If caught early, the chance of successful treatment of cervical cancer is very high. Pap tests can also find abnormal

About This Chapter: Information in this chapter is excerpted from "Pap Test," Office on Women's Health (OWH), January 3, 2014.

cervical cells before they turn into cancer cells. Treating these abnormal cells can help prevent most cases of cervical cancer from developing. Getting a Pap test is one of the best things you can do to prevent cervical cancer.

Who Does Not Need A Regular Pap Test?

The only women who do not need regular Pap tests are:

- Women ages 65 and older who have had three normal Pap tests in a row and no abnormal test results in the last 10 years, and have been told by their doctors that they don't need to be tested anymore.

- Women who do not have a cervix (usually because of a hysterectomy) and who do not have a history of cervical cancer or abnormal Pap results.

All women should speak to a doctor before stopping regular Pap tests.

How Often Do I Need To Get A Pap Test?

It depends on your age and health history. Talk with your doctor about what is best for you. Most women can follow these guidelines:

- If you are between ages 21 and 29, you should get a Pap test every 3 years.

- If you are between ages 30 and 64, you should get a Pap test and human papillomavirus (HPV) test together every 5 years or a Pap test alone every 3 years.

- If you are 65 or older, ask your doctor if you can stop having Pap tests.

Some women may need more frequent Pap tests. You should talk to your doctor about getting a Pap test more often if:

- You have a weakened immune system because of organ transplant, chemotherapy, or steroid use.

- Your mother was exposed to diethylstilbestrol (DES) while pregnant.

- You have had treatment for abnormal Pap results or cervical cancer in the past.

- You are HIV-positive. Women who are living with HIV, the virus that causes AIDS, are at a higher risk of cervical cancer and other cervical diseases. The U.S. Centers for Disease Control and Prevention (CDC) recommends that all HIV-positive women get an initial Pap test, and get re-tested 6 months later. If both Pap tests are normal, HIV-positive women can get yearly Pap tests in the future.

How Can I Prepare For A Pap Test?

Some things can cause incorrect Pap test results.

For two days before the test do not:

- Use tampons

- Use vaginal creams, suppositories, or medicines

- Use vaginal deodorant sprays or powders

- Have sex

- Douche

Should I Get A Pap Test When I Have My Period?

No. Doctors suggest you schedule a Pap test when you do not have your period. The best time to be tested is 10 to 20 days after the first day of your period.

How Is A Pap Test Done?

Your doctor can do a Pap test during a pelvic exam. It is a simple and quick test. You will lie down on an exam table. Your doctor will put an instrument called a speculum into your vagina and will open it to see your cervix. He or she will then use a special stick or brush to take a few cells from the surface of and inside the cervix. The cells are placed on a glass slide and sent to a lab for testing. A Pap test may be mildly uncomfortable but should not be painful. You may have some spotting afterwards.

When Will I Get The Results Of My Pap Test?

Usually it takes one to three weeks to get Pap test results. Most of the time, test results are normal. If the test shows that something might be wrong, your doctor will contact you to schedule more tests. There are many reasons for abnormal Pap test results. Abnormal Pap test results do not always mean you have cancer.

My Pap Test Was "Abnormal." What Happens Now?

It can be scary to hear that your Pap test results are "abnormal." But abnormal Pap test results usually do not mean you have cancer. Most often there is a small problem with the cervix. If results of the Pap test are unclear or show a small change in the cells of the cervix, your doctor may repeat the Pap test immediately, in 6 months, or a year, or he or she may run more tests.

Some abnormal cells will turn into cancer. Treating abnormal cells that don't go away on their own can prevent almost all cases of cervical cancer. If you have abnormal results, talk with your doctor about what they mean. Your doctor should answer any questions you have and explain anything you don't understand. Treatment for abnormal cells is often done in a doctor's office during a routine appointment.

If the test finds more serious changes in the cells of the cervix, the doctor will suggest more tests. Results of these tests will help your doctor decide on the best treatment.

My Pap Test Result Was A "False Positive." What Does This Mean?

Pap tests are not always perfect. False positive and false negative results can happen. This can be upsetting and confusing.

- **False positive.** A false positive Pap test occurs when a woman is told she has abnormal cervical cells, but the cells are not actually abnormal or cancerous. If your doctor says your Pap results were a false positive, there is no problem.

- **False negative.** A false negative Pap test is when a woman is told her cells are normal, but there is a problem with the cervical cells that was missed. False negatives delay the discovery and treatment of unhealthy cells of the cervix. But having regular Pap tests boosts your chances of finding any problems. Cervical cancers usually take many years to develop. If abnormal cells are missed at one time, they will probably be found on your next Pap test.

How Can I Reduce My Chances Of Getting Cervical Cancer?

You can reduce your chances of getting cervical cancer in several ways:

- **Get regular Pap tests.** Regular Pap tests help your doctor find and treat any abnormal cells before they turn into cancer.

- **Get an HPV vaccine** (if you are 26 or younger). Most cases of cervical cancer are caused by a type of HPV that is passed from person to person through genital contact. Most women never know they have HPV. It usually stays hidden. While it sometimes goes away on its own, it can cause changes in the cells of the cervix. Pap tests usually find these changes.

- **Be monogamous.** Having sex with just one partner can also lower your risk. Be faithful to each other. That means that you only have sex with each other and no one else.

- **Use condoms.** The best way to prevent any sexually transmitted infection (STI), including HPV, the cause of most cases of cervical cancer, is to not have vaginal, oral, or anal sex. If you do have sex, use condoms. Condoms lower your risk of getting HPV and other STIs. Although HPV can also occur in female and male genital areas that are not protected by condoms, research shows that condom use is linked to lower cervical cancer rates. Protect yourself with a condom every time you have vaginal, anal, or oral sex.

How Can I Get A Free Or Low-Cost Pap Test?

Pap tests are covered under the Affordable Care Act, the health care law passed in 2010. Most insurance plans now cover Pap tests at no cost to you.

- If you have insurance, check with your insurance provider to find out what's included in your plan.

- If you don't have insurance, find a program near you that offers free or low-cost Pap tests.

- If you have Medicare, find out how often Medicare covers Pap tests and pelvic exams.

- If you have Medicaid, the benefits covered are different in each state, but certain benefits must be covered by every Medicaid program. Check with your state's program to find out what's covered.

Chapter 20

Getting The HPV Vaccine

HPV Vaccine Information For Young Women

Three vaccines are available to prevent the human papillomavirus (HPV) types that cause most cervical cancers as well as some cancers of the anus, vulva (area around the opening of the vagina), vagina, and oropharynx (back of throat including base of tongue and tonsils). Two of these vaccines also prevent HPV types that cause most genital warts. HPV vaccines are given in 3 shots over 6 months.

Why Is The HPV vaccine important?

Genital HPV is a common virus that is passed from one person to another through direct skin-to-skin contact during sexual activity. Most sexually active people will get HPV at some time in their lives, though most will never even know it. HPV infection is most common in people in their late teens and early 20s. There are about 40 types of HPV that can infect the genital areas of men and women. Most HPV types cause no symptoms and go away on their own. But some types can cause cervical cancer in women and other less common cancers—like cancers of the anus, penis, vagina, and vulva and oropharynx. Other types of HPV can cause warts in the genital areas of men and women, called genital warts. Genital warts are not life-threatening. But they can cause emotional stress and their treatment can be very uncomfortable. Every year, about 12,000 women are diagnosed with cervical cancer and 4,000 women die from this disease in the U.S. About 1% of sexually active adults in the United States have visible genital warts at any point in time.

About This Chapter: Information in this chapter is excerpted from "Human Papillomavirus (HPV)," Centers for Disease Control and Prevention (CDC), March 26, 2015.

Which Girls/Women Should Receive HPV Vaccination?

HPV vaccination is recommended for 11- and 12-year-old girls. It is also recommended for girls and women age 13 through 26 years of age who have not yet been vaccinated or completed the vaccine series; HPV vaccine can also be given to girls beginning at age 9 years.

Will Sexually Active Females Benefit From The Vaccine?

Ideally females should get the vaccine before they become sexually active and exposed to HPV. Females who are sexually active may also benefit from vaccination, but they may get less benefit. This is because they may have already been exposed to one or more of the HPV types targeted by the vaccines. However, few sexually active young women are infected with all HPV types prevented by the vaccines, so most young women could still get protection by getting vaccinated.

Can Pregnant Women Get The Vaccine?

The vaccines are not recommended for pregnant women. Studies show that HPV vaccines do not cause problems for babies born to women who were vaccinated while pregnant, but more research is still needed. A pregnant woman should not get any doses of either HPV vaccine until her pregnancy is completed.

Getting the HPV vaccine when pregnant is not a reason to consider ending a pregnancy. If a woman realizes that she got one or more shots of an HPV vaccine while pregnant, she should do two things:

- Wait until after her pregnancy to finish the remaining HPV vaccine doses.
- Call the pregnancy registry [877-888-4231 for Gardasil, 800-986-8999 for Gardasil 9, or 888-825-5249 for Cervarix].

Should Girls And Women Be Screened For Cervical Cancer Before Getting Vaccinated?

Girls and women do not need to get an HPV test or Pap test to find out if they should get the vaccine. However it is important that women continue to be screened for cervical cancer, even after getting all 3 shots of either HPV vaccine. This is because neither vaccine protects against ALL types of cervical cancer.

How Effective Are The HPV Vaccines?

All HPV vaccines target the HPV types that most commonly cause cervical cancer and can cause some cancers of the vulva, vagina, anus, and oropharynx. Two of the vaccines also protect against the HPV types that cause most genital warts. HPV vaccines are highly effective in preventing the targeted HPV types, as well as the most common health problems caused by them.

The vaccines are less effective in preventing HPV-related disease in young women who have already been exposed to one or more HPV types. That is because the vaccines prevent HPV before a person is exposed to it. HPV vaccines do not treat existing HPV infections or HPV-associated diseases.

How Long Does Vaccine Protection Last?

Research suggests that vaccine protection is long-lasting. Current studies have followed vaccinated individuals for ten years, and show that there is no evidence of weakened protection over time.

What does the vaccine not protect against?

The vaccines do not protect against all HPV types—so they will not prevent all cases of cervical cancer. Since some cervical cancers will not be prevented by the vaccines, it will be important for women to continue getting screened for cervical cancer. Also, the vaccines do not prevent other sexually transmitted infections (STIs). So it will still be important for sexually active persons to lower their risk for other STIs.

Will Girls And Women Be Protected Against HPV And Related Diseases, Even If They Don't Get All 3 Doses?

It is not yet known how much protection girls and women get from receiving only one or two doses of an HPV vaccine. So it is important that girls and women get all 3 doses.

How Safe Are The HPV Vaccines?

All three HPV vaccines have been licensed by the Food and Drug Administration (FDA). The CDC has approved these vaccines as safe and effective. The vaccines were studied in thousands of people around the world, and these studies showed no serious safety concerns. Side effects reported in these studies were mild, including pain where the shot was given, fever, dizziness, and nausea. Vaccine safety continues to be monitored by CDC and the FDA. More than 60 million doses of HPV vaccine have been distributed in the United States as of March 2014.

Fainting, which can occur after any medical procedure, has also been noted after HPV vaccination. Fainting after any vaccination is more common in adolescents. Because fainting can cause falls and injuries, adolescents and adults should be seated or lying down during HPV vaccination. Sitting or lying down for about 15 minutes after a vaccination can help prevent fainting and injuries.

What Vaccinated Girls/Women Need To Know: Will Girls/Women Who Have Been Vaccinated Still Need Cervical Cancer Screening?

Regular cervical cancer screening (Pap and HPV tests) and follow-up can prevent most cases of cervical cancer. The Pap test can detect cell changes in the cervix before they turn into cancer. The HPV test looks for the virus that can cause these cell changes. Screening can detect most, but not all, cervical cancers at an early, treatable stage. Most women diagnosed with cervical cancer in the U.S. have either never been screened, or have not been screened in the last 5 years.

Are There Other Ways To Prevent Cervical Cancer?

Yes, vaccinated women will still need regular cervical cancer screening because the vaccines protect against most but not all HPV types that cause cervical cancer. Also, women who got the vaccine after becoming sexually active may not get the full benefit of the vaccine if they had already been exposed to HPV.

Are There Other Ways To Prevent HPV?

For those who are sexually active, condoms may lower the chances of getting HPV, if used with every sex act, from start to finish. Condoms may also lower the risk of developing HPV-related diseases (genital warts and cervical cancer). But HPV can infect areas that are not covered by a condom—so condoms may not fully protect against HPV.

People can also lower their chances of getting HPV by being in a faithful relationship with one partner; limiting their number of sex partners; and choosing a partner who has had no or few prior sex partners. But even people with only one lifetime sex partner can get HPV. And it may not be possible to determine if a partner who has been sexually active in the past is currently infected. That's why the only sure way to prevent HPV is to avoid all sexual activity.

Chapter 21
Douching

What Is Douching?

The word "douche" means to wash or soak. Douching is washing or cleaning out the inside of the vagina with water or other mixtures of fluids. Most douches are sold in stores as pre-packaged mixes of water and vinegar, baking soda, or iodine. The mixtures usually come in a bottle or bag. You squirt the douche upward through a tube or nozzle into your vagina. The water mixture then comes back out through your vagina.

Douching is different from washing the outside of your vagina during a bath or shower. Rinsing the outside of your vagina with warm water will not harm your vagina. But, douching can lead to many different health problems.

> Most doctors recommend that women do not douche.

How Common Is Douching?

In the United States, almost one in four women 15 to 44 years old douche.

More African-American and Hispanic women douche than white women. Douching is also common in teens of all races and ethnicities.

Studies have not found any health benefit to douching. But, studies have found that douching is linked to many health problems.

About This Chapter: Information in this chapter is excerpted from "Douching Fact Sheet," Office on Women's Health (OWH), January 19, 2015.

Why Should Women Not Douche?

Most doctors recommend that women do not douche. Douching can change the necessary balance of vaginal flora (bacteria that live in the vagina) and natural acidity in a healthy vagina.

A healthy vagina has good and harmful bacteria. The balance of bacteria helps maintain an acidic environment. The acidic environment protects the vagina from infections or irritation.

Douching can cause an overgrowth of harmful bacteria. This can lead to a yeast infection or bacterial vaginosis. If you already have a vaginal infection, douching can push the bacteria causing the infection up into the uterus, fallopian tubes, and ovaries. This can lead to pelvic inflammatory disease, a serious health problem.

Douching is also linked to other health problems.

What Health Problems Are Linked To Douching?

Health problems linked to douching include:

- Bacterial vaginosis (BV), which is an infection in the vagina. Women who douche often (once a week) are five times more likely to develop BV than women who do not douche.
- Pelvic inflammatory disease, an infection in the reproductive organs that is often caused by an STI
- Problems during pregnancy, including preterm birth and ectopic pregnancy
- STIs, including HIV
- Vaginal irritation or dryness

Researchers are studying whether douching causes these problems or whether women at higher risk for these health problems are more likely to douche.

Should I Douche To Get Rid Of Vaginal Odor Or Other Problems?

No. You should not douche to try to get rid of vaginal odor or other vaginal problems like discharge, pain, itching, or burning.

Douching will only cover up odor for a short time and will make other problems worse. Call your doctor or nurse if you have:

- Vaginal discharge that smells bad
- Vaginal itching and thick, white, or yellowish-green discharge with or without an odor

- Burning, redness, and swelling in or around the vagina
- Pain when urinating
- Pain or discomfort during sex

These may be signs of a vaginal infection, or an STI. Do not douche before seeing your doctor or nurse. This can make it hard for the doctor or nurse to find out what may be wrong.

Should I Douche To Clean Inside My Vagina?

No. Doctors recommend that women do not douche. You do not need to douche to clean your vagina. Your body naturally flushes out and cleans your vagina. Any strong odor or irritation usually means something is wrong.

Douching also can raise your chances of a vaginal infection or an STI. If you have questions or concerns, talk to your doctor.

What Is The Best Way To Clean My Vagina?

It is best to let your vagina clean itself. The vagina cleans itself naturally by making mucous. The mucous washes away blood, semen, and vaginal discharge.

If you are worried about vaginal odor, talk to your doctor or nurse. But you should know that even healthy, clean vaginas have a mild odor that changes throughout the day. Physical activity also can give your vagina a stronger, muskier scent, but this is still normal.

Keep your vagina clean and healthy by:

- Washing the outside of your vagina with warm water when you bathe. Some women also use mild soaps. But, if you have sensitive skin or any current vaginal infections, even mild soaps can cause dryness and irritation.
- Avoiding scented tampons, pads, powders, and sprays. These products may increase your chances of getting a vaginal infection.

Can douching before or after sex prevent STIs?

No. Douching before or after sex **does not** prevent STIs. In fact, douching removes some of the normal bacteria in the vagina that protect you from infection. This can actually increase your risk of getting STIs, including HIV, the virus that causes AIDS.

Should I Douche If I Had Sex Without Using Protection Or If The Condom Broke?

No. Douching removes some of the normal bacteria in the vagina that protect you from infection. This can increase your risk of getting STIs, including HIV. Douching also does not protect against pregnancy.

If you had sex without using protection or if the condom broke during sex, see a doctor right away. You can get medicine to help prevent HIV and unwanted pregnancy.

Should I Douche If I Was Sexually Assaulted?

No, you should not douche, bathe, or shower. As hard as it may be to not wash up, you may wash away important evidence if you do. Douching may also increase your risk of getting STIs, including HIV.

Go to the nearest hospital emergency room as soon as possible. The National Sexual Assault Hotline at 800-656-HOPE (4673) can help you find a hospital able to collect evidence of sexual assault. Your doctor or nurse can help you get medicine to help prevent HIV and unwanted pregnancy.

Can douching after sex prevent pregnancy?

No. Douching **does not** prevent pregnancy. It should never be used for birth control. If you had sex without using birth control or if your birth control method did not work correctly (failed), you can use emergency contraception to keep from getting pregnant.

If you need birth control, talk to your doctor or nurse about which type of birth control method is best for you.

How Does Douching Affect Pregnancy?

Douching can make it harder to get pregnant and can cause problems during pregnancy:

- **Trouble getting pregnant.** Women who douched at least once a month had a harder time getting pregnant than those women who did not douche.

- **Higher risk of ectopic pregnancy.** Douching may increase a woman's chance of damaged fallopian tubes and ectopic pregnancy. Ectopic pregnancy is when the fertilized egg attaches to the inside of the fallopian tube instead of the uterus. If left untreated, ectopic pregnancy can be life-threatening. It can also make it hard for a woman to get pregnant in the future.

- **Higher risk of early childbirth.** Douching raises your risk for premature birth. One study found that women who douched during pregnancy were more likely to deliver their babies early. This raises the risk for health problems for you and your baby.

Chapter 22
Vaginal Infections

Signs that you may have a vaginal infection include itching, burning, pain in or around your vagina, or a problem with your vaginal discharge (fluid). If you've had sexual contact with someone, these signs may mean that you have a sexually transmitted disease (also known as an STD or STI, which means sexually transmitted infection). Not all vaginal infections are caused by sexual contact. Keep in mind that any time you have itching, burning, or pain in or around your vagina, you need to see a doctor to get treated.

Help For Infections

If you have pain, itching, or other symptoms around your vagina, don't try to treat them yourself. Don't risk your health. See a doctor or other health care professional who can figure out the cause and right treatment.

Abnormal Discharge

You may wonder if the fluid, or discharge, that comes out of your vagina is a sign of infection. Discharge changes throughout your menstrual cycle, but it normally may look clear, cloudy white, or yellowish. There is no need to worry if you have normal-looking discharge. Signs of possible problems include discharge that is:

- Green or gray

- Smelly

- Foamy or lumpy

About This Chapter: Information in this chapter is excerpted from "Vaginal Infections," Office on Women's Health (OWH), April 15, 2014.

Problems with your discharge may be a sign of infection. Keep reading to learn more about vaginal infections and how to prevent them.

Types Of Vaginal Infections

Two common vaginal infections are **bacterial vaginosis** and **yeast infections**.

Bacterial vaginosis (BV) happens when a certain kind of bacteria (a type of germ) that's in your vagina grows too much. Possible symptoms include:

• A bad smell from your vagina that might seem "fishy"

• More discharge (fluid) than you usually have and that is gray or white

• Itching around your vagina

It's important to see your doctor if you have symptoms. BV can be treated with antibiotics. If BV is not treated, it sometimes may cause serious health problems, such as pelvic inflammatory disease (though this is rare).

BV usually happens to people who have sex, but you can also get it without having sex. Experts don't know exactly what causes BV. The best way to avoid BV is to avoid having sex. If you are having sex, use a condom to protect your health. Douching also increases the chances that you'll get BV.

Yeast infections happen when a fungus (a type of germ) that's usually in the vagina grows too much. Possible symptoms include:

• Burning, redness, and swelling of the vagina and the vulva

• Pain when you urinate (pee)

• Pain during sex

• A thick, white discharge that looks like cottage cheese and does not have a bad smell

• A red rash on the outside of your vagina (this is rare)

Lots of women think they have a yeast infection when they really have something else. Before trying to treat yourself with an over-the-counter medicine, it's important to talk with a doctor. That's especially true if you've never had a yeast infection before or if you have them often.

Sometimes you may have symptoms that make you believe you have a vaginal infection, but you instead have a urinary tract infection.

Urinary tract infections (UTIs) happen when bacteria get inside the parts of your body that make, store, or remove urine, like your bladder. Symptoms of a urinary tract infection include:

- Burning when you urinate (pee)
- Feeling a need to urinate often
- Feeling a strong need to urinate but only a little urine comes out
- Back or stomach pain
- Cloudy or dark urine
- Fever and chills—if that happens, tell a doctor right away
- Blood in your urine—if that happens, tell a doctor right away

Most UTIs are not serious, but some can lead to serious problems, including kidneys that don't work well. UTIs can be cured with antibiotics.

Ways To Avoid Vaginal Infections

You can't always prevent vaginal infections. But you can take steps to help keep your vagina (and your bladder) healthy:

- **Keep your genital area clean.** Wash the outside of your vagina and bottom every day with mild soap. When you go to the bathroom, wipe from the front of your body toward the back, not the other way.

- **Keep your vagina cool.** Bacteria love the heat! Avoid tight underwear or clothes made of synthetic fibers like rayon and polyester that can trap heat. Wear cotton or cotton-crotch underwear.

- **Change out of wet bathing suits and exercise clothes as soon as possible.** Bacteria like wet places, too!

- **Don't douche.** Putting water or other products into your vagina removes some of the normal bacteria that protect you from infection.

- **Change your underwear every day**, so you don't let germs near your vagina.

- **Drink enough liquids.** This can help wash out your urinary tract and help prevent infections there. You'll know that you're drinking enough if your urine (pee) is light yellow or almost clear.

- **Avoid scented hygiene products** like bubble bath, sprays, scented pads, and scented tampons. They can be irritating.

Having sex may increase your odds of some infections even if they're not considered sexually transmitted infections. Abstinence is the safest way to avoid infections.

Chapter 23
Pelvic Inflammatory Disease (PID)

Untreated sexually transmitted diseases (STDs) can cause pelvic inflammatory disease (PID), a serious condition, in women. 1 in 8 women with a history of PID experience difficulties getting pregnant. You can prevent PID if you know how to protect yourself.

What Is PID?

Pelvic inflammatory disease is an infection of a woman's reproductive organs. It is a complication often caused by some STDs, like chlamydia and gonorrhea. Other infections that are not sexually transmitted can also cause PID.

How Do I Get PID?

You are more likely to get PID if you

- Have an STD and do not get treated;
- Have more than one sex partner;
- Have a sex partner who has sex partners other than you;
- Have had PID before;
- Are sexually active and are age 25 or younger;
- Douche;
- Use an intrauterine device (IUD) for birth control.

About This Chapter: Information in this chapter is excerpted from "Pelvic Inflammatory Disease (PID)—CDC Fact Sheet," Centers for Disease Control and Prevention (CDC), January 29, 2014.

How Can I Reduce My Risk Of Getting PID?

The only way to avoid STDs is to not have vaginal, anal, or oral sex.

If you are sexually active, you can do the following things to lower your chances of getting PID:

- Being in a long-term mutually monogamous relationship with a partner who has been tested and has negative STD test results;

- Using latex condoms the right way every time you have sex.

How Do I Know If I Have PID?

There are no tests for PID. A diagnosis is usually based on a combination of your medical history, physical exam, and other test results. You may not realize you have PID because your symptoms may be mild, or you may not experience any symptoms. However, if you do have symptoms, you may notice

- Pain in your lower abdomen;

- Fever;

- An unusual discharge with a bad odor from your vagina;

- Pain and/or bleeding when you have sex;

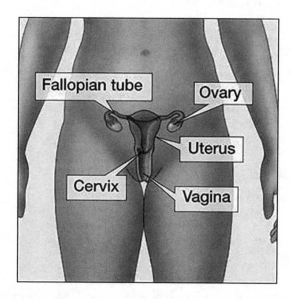

Figure 23.1. Female Anatomy

- Burning sensation when you urinate; or

- Bleeding between periods.

You should

- Be examined by your doctor if you notice any of these symptoms;

- Promptly see a doctor if you think you or your sex partner(s) have or were exposed to an STD;

- Promptly see a doctor if you have any genital symptoms such as an unusual sore, a smelly discharge, burning when peeing, or bleeding between periods;

- Get a test for chlamydia every year if you are sexually active and 25 years of age or younger;

- Have an honest and open talk with your health care provider if you are sexually active and ask whether you should be tested for other STDs.

Can PID Be Cured?

Yes, if PID is diagnosed early, it can be treated. However, treatment won't undo any damage that has already happened to your reproductive system. The longer you wait to get treated, the more likely it is that you will have complications from PID. While taking antibiotics, your symptoms may go away before the infection is cured. Even if symptoms go away, you should finish taking all of your medicine. Be sure to tell your recent sex partner(s), so they can get tested and treated for STDs, too. It is also very important that you and your partner both finish your treatment before having any kind of sex so that you don't re-infect each other.

You can get PID again if you get infected with an STD again. Also, if you have had PID before, you have a higher chance of getting it again.

What Happens If I Don't Get Treated?

If diagnosed and treated early, the complications of PID can be prevented. Some of the complications of PID are

- Formation of scar tissue both outside and inside the fallopian tubes that can lead to tubal blockage;

- Ectopic pregnancy (pregnancy outside the womb);

- Infertility (inability to get pregnant);

- Long-term pelvic/abdominal pain.

Chapter 24

Ovarian Cysts

Ovarian cysts are fluid-filled sacs in the ovary. They are common and usually form during ovulation. Ovulation happens when the ovary releases an egg each month. Many women with ovarian cysts don't have symptoms. The cysts are usually harmless.

What Are Ovarian Cysts?

A cyst is a fluid-filled sac. It can form in many places in the body. Ovarian cysts form in or on the ovaries.

What Are The Different Types Of Ovarian Cysts?

The most common types of ovarian cysts (called functional cysts) form during the menstrual cycle. They are usually benign (not cancerous).

The two most common types of cysts are:

- **Follicle cysts.** In a normal menstrual cycle, the ovaries release an egg each month. The egg grows inside a tiny sac called a follicle. When the egg matures, the follicle breaks open to release the egg. Follicle cysts form when the follicle doesn't break open to release the egg. This causes the follicle to continue growing into a cyst. Follicle cysts often have no symptoms and go away in one to three months.

- **Corpus luteum cysts.** Once the follicle breaks open and releases the egg, the empty follicle sac shrinks into a mass of cells called corpus luteum. Corpus luteum makes hor-

About This Chapter: Information in this chapter is excerpted from "Ovarian Cysts," Office on Women's Health (OWH), November 19, 2014.

mones to prepare for the next egg for the next menstrual cycle. Corpus luteum cysts form if the sac doesn't shrink. Instead, the sac reseals itself after the egg is released, and then fluid builds up inside. Most corpus luteum cysts go away after a few weeks. But, they can grow to almost four inches wide. They also may bleed or twist the ovary and cause pain. Some medicines used to cause ovulation can raise the risk of getting these cysts.

Other types of benign ovarian cysts are less common:

- **Endometriomas** are caused by endometriosis. Endometriosis happens when the lining of the uterus (womb) grows outside of the uterus.

- **Dermoids** come from cells present from birth and do not usually cause symptoms.

- **Cystadenomas** are filled with watery fluid and can sometimes grow large.

In some women, the ovaries make many small cysts. This is called polycystic ovary syndrome (PCOS). PCOS can cause problems with the ovaries and with getting pregnant.

Malignant (cancerous) cysts are rare. They are more common in older women. Cancerous cysts are ovarian cancer. For this reason, ovarian cysts should be checked by your doctor. Most ovarian cysts are not cancerous.

Who Gets Ovarian Cysts?

Ovarian cysts are common in women with regular periods. In fact, most women make at least one follicle or corpus luteum cyst every month. You may not be aware that you have a cyst unless there is a problem that causes the cyst to grow or if multiple cysts form. About 8% of premenopausal women develop large cysts that need treatment.

Ovarian cysts are less common after menopause. Postmenopausal women with ovarian cysts are at higher risk for ovarian cancer.

At any age, see your doctor if you think you have a cyst. See your doctor also if you have symptoms such as bloating, needing to urinate more often, pelvic pressure or pain, or abnormal (unusual) vaginal bleeding. These can be signs of a cyst or other serious problem.

What Causes Ovarian Cysts?

The most common causes of ovarian cysts include:

- **Hormonal problems.** Functional cysts usually go away on their own without treatment. They may be caused by hormonal problems or by drugs used to help you ovulate.

- **Endometriosis.** Women with endometriosis can develop a type of ovarian cyst called an endometrioma. The endometriosis tissue may attach to the ovary and form a growth. These cysts can be painful during sex and during your period.

- **Pregnancy.** An ovarian cyst normally develops in early pregnancy to help support the pregnancy until the placenta forms. Sometimes, the cyst stays on the ovary until later in the pregnancy and may need to be removed.

- **Severe pelvic infections.** Infections can spread to the ovaries and fallopian tubes and cause cysts to form.

What Are The Signs And Symptoms Of Ovarian Cysts?

Most ovarian cysts are small and don't cause symptoms.

If a cyst does cause symptoms, you may have pressure, bloating, swelling, or pain in the lower abdomen on the side of the cyst. This pain may be sharp or dull and may come and go.

If a cyst ruptures, it can cause sudden, severe pain.

If a cyst causes twisting of an ovary, you may have pain along with nausea and vomiting.

Less common symptoms include:

- Pelvic pain
- Dull ache in the lower back and thighs
- Problems emptying the bladder or bowel completely
- Pain during sex
- Unexplained weight gain
- Pain during your period
- Unusual (not normal) vaginal bleeding
- Breast tenderness
- Needing to urinate more often

How Are Ovarian Cysts Found?

If you have symptoms of ovarian cysts, talk to your doctor. Your doctor may do a pelvic exam to feel for swelling of a cyst on your ovary.

If a cyst is found, your doctor will either watch and wait or order tests to help plan treatment. Tests include:

- **Ultrasound.** This test uses sound waves to create images of the body. With ultrasound, your doctor can see the cyst's:
  - Shape
  - Size
  - Location
  - Mass (whether it is fluid-filled, solid, or mixed)
- **Pregnancy test** to rule out pregnancy
- **Hormone level tests** to see if there are hormone-related problems
- **Blood test.** If you are past menopause, your doctor may give you a test to measure the amount of cancer-antigen 125 (CA-125) in your blood. The amount of CA-125 is higher with ovarian cancer. In premenopausal women, many other illnesses or diseases besides cancer can cause higher levels of CA-125.

Are Ovarian Cysts Ever An Emergency?

Yes, sometimes. If your doctor told you that you have an ovarian cyst and you have any of the following symptoms, get medical help right away:

- Pain with fever and vomiting
- Sudden, severe abdominal pain
- Faintness, dizziness, or weakness
- Rapid breathing

These symptoms could mean that your cyst has broken open, or ruptured. Sometimes, large, ruptured cysts can cause heavy bleeding.

Will My Ovarian Cyst Require Surgery?

Maybe. The National Institutes of Health (NIH) estimates that 5% to 10% of women have surgery to remove an ovarian cyst. Only 13% to 21% of these cysts are cancerous.

Your cyst may require surgery if you are past menopause or if your cyst:

- Does not go away after several menstrual cycles
- Gets larger

- Looks unusual on the ultrasound

- Causes pain

If your cyst does not require surgery, your doctor may:

- Talk to you about pain medicine. Your doctor may recommend over-the-counter medicine or prescribe stronger medicine for pain relief.

- Prescribe hormonal birth control if you have cysts often. Hormonal birth control, such as the pill, vaginal ring, shot, or patch, help prevent ovulation. This may lower your chances of getting more cysts.

What Types Of Surgeries Remove Ovarian Cysts?

If your cyst requires surgery, your doctor will either remove just the cyst or the entire ovary.

Surgery can be done in two different ways:

- **Laparoscopy.** With this surgery, the doctor makes a very small cut above or below your belly button to look inside your pelvic area and remove the cyst. This is often recommended for smaller cysts that look benign (not cancerous) on the ultrasound.

- **Laparotomy.** Your doctor may choose this method if the cyst is large and may be cancerous. This surgery uses a larger cut in the abdomen to remove the cyst. The cyst is then tested for cancer. If it is likely to be cancerous, it is best to see a gynecologic oncologist, who may need to remove the ovary and other tissues, like the uterus.

Can Ovarian Cysts Lead To Cancer?

Yes, some ovarian cysts can become cancerous. But most ovarian cysts are not cancerous.

The risk for ovarian cancer increases as you get older. Women who are past menopause with ovarian cysts have a higher risk for ovarian cancer. Talk to your doctor about your risk for ovarian cancer. Screening for ovarian cancer is not recommended for most women. This is because testing can lead to "false positives." A false positive is a test result that says a woman has ovarian cancer when she does not.

Can Ovarian Cysts Make It Harder To Get Pregnant?

Typically, no. Most ovarian cysts do not affect your chances of getting pregnant. Sometimes, though, the illness causing the cyst can make it harder to get pregnant. Two conditions that cause ovarian cysts and affect fertility are:

- **Endometriosis,** which happens when the lining of the uterus (womb) grows outside of the uterus. Cysts caused by endometriosis are called endometriomas.

- **Polycystic ovary syndrome (PCOS),** one of the leading causes of infertility (problems getting pregnant). Women with PCOS often have many small cysts on their ovaries.

How Do Ovarian Cysts Affect Pregnancy?

Ovarian cysts are common during pregnancy. Typically, these cysts are benign (not cancerous) and harmless. Ovarian cysts that continue to grow during pregnancy can rupture or twist or cause problems during childbirth. Your doctor will monitor any ovarian cyst found during pregnancy.

Can I Prevent Ovarian Cysts?

No, you cannot prevent functional ovarian cysts if you are ovulating. If you get ovarian cysts often, your doctor may prescribe hormonal birth control to stop you from ovulating. This will help lower your risk of getting new cysts.

Chapter 25

Endometriosis

Endometriosis happens when the lining of the uterus (womb) grows outside of the uterus. It affects about 5 million American women. The most common symptom is pain. The pain happens most often during your period, but it can also happen at other times. Endometriosis may also make it harder to get pregnant. Several different treatment options can help manage the symptoms and improve your chances of getting pregnant.

What Is Endometriosis?

Endometriosis, sometimes called "endo," is a common health problem in women. It gets its name from the word endometrium, the tissue that normally lines the uterus or womb. Endometriosis happens when this tissue grows outside of your uterus and on other areas in your body where it doesn't belong.

Most often, endometriosis is found on the:

- Ovaries

- Fallopian tubes

- Tissues that hold the uterus in place

- Outer surface of the uterus

Other sites for growths can include the vagina, cervix, vulva, bowel, bladder, or rectum. Rarely, endometriosis appears in other parts of the body, such as the lungs, brain, and skin.

About This Chapter: Information in this chapter is excerpted from "Endometriosis," Office on Women's Health (OWH), December 5, 2014.

What Are The Symptoms Of Endometriosis?

Symptoms of endometriosis can include:

- **Pain.** This is the most common symptom. Women with endometriosis may have many different kinds of pain. These include:

  - Very painful menstrual cramps. The pain may get worse over time.

  - Chronic (long-term) pain in the lower back and pelvis

  - Pain during or after sex. This is usually described as a "deep" pain and is different from pain felt at the entrance to the vagina when penetration begins.

  - Intestinal pain

  - Painful bowel movements or pain when urinating during menstrual periods. In rare cases, you may also find blood in your stool or urine.

- **Bleeding or spotting** between menstrual periods. This can be caused by something other than endometriosis. If it happens often, you should see your doctor.

- **Infertility,** or not being able to get pregnant.

- **Stomach (digestive) problems.** These include diarrhea, constipation, bloating, or nausea, especially during menstrual periods.

Why Does Endometriosis Cause Pain And Health Problems?

Endometriosis growths are benign (not cancerous). But they can still cause problems.

Endometriosis happens when tissue that is normally on the inside of your uterus or womb grows outside of your uterus or womb where it doesn't belong. Endometriosis growths bleed in the same way the lining inside of your uterus does every month—during your menstrual period. This can cause swelling and pain because the tissue grows and bleeds in an area where it cannot easily get out of your body.

The growths may also continue to expand and cause problems, such as:

- Blocking your fallopian tubes when growths cover or grow into your ovaries. Trapped blood in the ovaries can form cysts.

- Inflammation (swelling)

- Forming scar tissue and adhesions (type of tissue that can bind your organs together). This scar tissue may cause pelvic pain and make it hard for you to get pregnant.

- Problems in your intestines and bladder

How Common Is Endometriosis?

Endometriosis is a common health problem for women. At least 5 million women in the United States have endometriosis. Many other women probably have endometriosis but don't have any symptoms.

What Causes Endometriosis?

No one knows for sure what causes this disease. Researchers are studying possible causes:

- **Problems with menstrual period flow.** Retrograde menstrual flow is the most likely cause of endometriosis. Some of the tissue shed during the period flows through the fallopian tube into other areas of the body, such as the pelvis.

- **Genetic factors.** Because endometriosis runs in families, it may be inherited in the genes.

- **Immune system problems.** A faulty immune system may fail to find and destroy endometrial tissue growing outside of the uterus. Immune system disorders and certain cancers are more common in women with endometriosis.

- **Hormones.** The hormone estrogen appears to promote endometriosis. Research is looking at whether endometriosis is a problem with the body's hormone system.

- **Surgery.** During a surgery to the abdominal area, such as a Cesarean (C-section) or hysterectomy, endometrial tissue could be picked up and moved by mistake. For instance, endometrial tissue has been found in abdominal scars.

How Can I Prevent Endometriosis?

You can't prevent endometriosis. But you can reduce your chances of developing it by lowering the levels of the hormone estrogen in your body. Estrogen helps to thicken the lining of your uterus during your menstrual cycle.

To keep lower estrogen levels in your body, you can:

- **Talk to your doctor about hormonal birth control methods,** such as pills, patches or rings with lower doses of estrogen.

- **Exercise regularly** (more than 4 hours a week). This will also help you **keep a low percentage of body fat.** Regular exercise and a lower amount of body fat help decrease the amount of estrogen circulating through the body.

- **Avoid large amounts of alcohol.** Alcohol raises estrogen levels. No more than one drink per day is recommended for women who choose to drink alcohol.

- **Avoid large amount of drinks with caffeine.** Studies show that drinking more than one caffeinated drink a day, especially sodas and green tea, can raise estrogen levels.

How Is Endometriosis Treated?

There is no cure for endometriosis, but treatments are available for the symptoms and problems it causes. Talk to your doctor about your treatment options.

Medicine

If you are not trying to get pregnant, hormonal birth control is generally the first step in treatment. This may include:

- Extended-cycle (you have only a few periods a year) or continuous cycle (you have no periods) birth control. These types of hormonal birth control are available in the pill or the shot and help stop bleeding and reduce or eliminate pain.

- Intrauterine device (IUD) to help reduce pain and bleeding. The hormonal IUD protects against pregnancy for up to 7 years. But the hormonal IUD may not help your pain and bleeding due to endometriosis for that long.

Hormonal treatment works only as long as it is taken and is best for women who do not have severe pain or symptoms.

If you are trying to get pregnant, your doctor may prescribe a gonadotropin-releasing hormone (GnRH) agonist. This medicine stops the body from making the hormones responsible for ovulation, the menstrual cycle, and the growth of endometriosis. This treatment causes a temporary menopause, but it also helps control the growth of endometriosis. Once you stop taking the medicine, your menstrual cycle returns, but you may have a better chance of getting pregnant.

Surgery

Surgery is usually chosen for severe symptoms, when hormones are not providing relief or if you are having fertility problems. During the operation, the surgeon can locate any areas of endometriosis and may remove the endometriosis patches. After surgery, hormone treatment is often restarted unless you are trying to get pregnant.

Other treatments you can try, alone or with any of the treatments listed above, include:

- **Pain medicine.** For mild symptoms, your doctor may suggest taking over-the-counter medicines for pain. These include ibuprofen (Advil and Motrin) or naproxen (Aleve).

- **Complementary and alternative medicine (CAM) therapies.** Some women report relief from pain with therapies such as acupuncture, chiropractic care, herbs like cinnamon twig or licorice root, or supplements, such as thiamine (vitamin B1), magnesium, or omega-3 fatty acids.

Can I Get Pregnant If I Have Endometriosis?

Yes. Many women with endometriosis get pregnant. But, you may find it harder to get pregnant. Endometriosis affects about one-half (50%) of women with infertility.

No one knows exactly how endometriosis might cause infertility. Some possible reasons include:

- Patches of endometriosis block off or change the shape of the pelvis and reproductive organs. This can make it harder for the sperm to find the egg.

- The immune system, which normally helps defend the body against disease, attacks the embryo.

- The endometrium (the layer of the uterine lining where implantation happens) does not develop as it should.

If you have endometriosis and are having trouble getting pregnant, talk to your doctor. He or she can recommend treatments, such as surgery to remove the endometrial growths.

Chapter 26

Polycystic Ovary Syndrome (PCOS)

What Is Polycystic Ovary Syndrome (PCOS)?

Polycystic ovary syndrome (PCOS) is a health problem that can affect a woman's:

- Menstrual cycle

- Ability to have children

- Hormones

- Heart

- Blood vessels

- Appearance

With PCOS, women typically have:

- High levels of androgens. These are sometimes called male hormones, though females also make them.

- Missed or irregular periods (monthly bleeding)

- Many small cysts (sists) (fluid-filled sacs) in their ovaries

How Many Women Have PCOS?

Between 1 in 10 and 1 in 20 women of childbearing age has PCOS. As many as 5 million women in the United States may be affected. It can occur in girls as young as 11 years old.

About This Chapter: Information in this chapter is excerpted from "Polycystic Ovary Syndrome (PCOS) Fact Sheet," Office on Women's Health (OWH), December 23, 2014.

What Causes PCOS?

The cause of PCOS is unknown. But most experts think that several factors, including genetics, could play a role. Women with PCOS are more likely to have a mother or sister with PCOS.

A main underlying problem with PCOS is a hormonal imbalance. In women with PCOS, the ovaries make more androgens than normal. Androgens are male hormones that females also make. High levels of these hormones affect the development and release of eggs during ovulation.

Researchers also think insulin may be linked to PCOS. Insulin is a hormone that controls the change of sugar, starches, and other food into energy for the body to use or store. Many women with PCOS have too much insulin in their bodies because they have problems using it. Excess insulin appears to increase production of androgen. High androgen levels can lead to:

- Acne

- Excessive hair growth

- Weight gain

- Problems with ovulation

What Are The Symptoms Of PCOS?

The symptoms of PCOS can vary from woman to woman. Some of the symptoms of PCOS include:

- Infertility (not able to get pregnant) because of not ovulating. In fact, PCOS is the most common cause of female infertility.

- Infrequent, absent, and/or irregular menstrual periods

- Hirsutism—increased hair growth on the face, chest, stomach, back, thumbs, or toes

- Cysts on the ovaries

- Acne, oily skin, or dandruff

- Weight gain or obesity, usually with extra weight around the waist

- Male-pattern baldness or thinning hair

- Patches of skin on the neck, arms, breasts, or thighs that are thick and dark brown or black

- Skin tags—excess flaps of skin in the armpits or neck area

- Pelvic pain

- Anxiety or depression

- Sleep apnea—when breathing stops for short periods of time while asleep

Why Do Women With PCOS Have Trouble With Their Menstrual Cycle And Fertility?

The ovaries, where a woman's eggs are produced, have tiny fluid-filled sacs called follicles or cysts. As the egg grows, the follicle builds up fluid. When the egg matures, the follicle breaks open, the egg is released, and the egg travels through the fallopian tube to the uterus (womb) for fertilization. This is called ovulation.

In women with PCOS, the ovary doesn't make all of the hormones it needs for an egg to fully mature. The follicles may start to grow and build up fluid but ovulation does not occur. Instead, some follicles may remain as cysts. For these reasons, ovulation does not occur and the hormone progesterone is not made. Without progesterone, a woman's menstrual cycle is irregular or absent. Plus, the ovaries make male hormones, which also prevent ovulation.

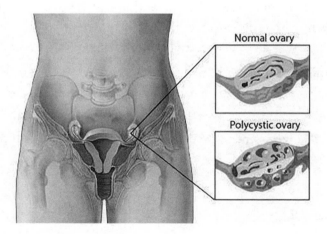

Figure 26.1. Normal Ovary And Polycystic Ovary

How Do I Know If I Have PCOS?

There is no single test to diagnose PCOS. Your doctor will take the following steps to find out if you have PCOS or if something else is causing your symptoms.

Medical history. Your doctor will ask about your menstrual periods, weight changes, and other symptoms.

Physical exam. Your doctor will want to measure your blood pressure, body mass index (BMI), and waist size. He or she also will check the areas of increased hair growth. You should try to allow the natural hair to grow for a few days before the visit.

Pelvic exam. Your doctor might want to check to see if your ovaries are enlarged or swollen by the increased number of small cysts.

Blood tests. Your doctor may check the androgen hormone and glucose (sugar) levels in your blood.

Vaginal ultrasound (sonogram). Your doctor may perform a test that uses sound waves to take pictures of the pelvic area. It might be used to examine your ovaries for cysts and check the endometrium (lining of the womb). This lining may become thicker if your periods are not regular.

How Is PCOS Treated?

Because there is no cure for PCOS, it needs to be managed to prevent problems. Treatment goals are based on your symptoms, whether or not you want to become pregnant, and lowering your chances of getting heart disease and diabetes. Many women will need a combination of treatments to meet these goals. Some treatments for PCOS include:

Lifestyle modification. Many women with PCOS are overweight or obese, which can cause health problems. You can help manage your PCOS by eating healthy and exercising to keep your weight at a healthy level.

Birth control pills. For women who don't want to get pregnant, birth control pills can:

- Control menstrual cycles
- Reduce male hormone levels
- Help to clear acne

Diabetes medications. The medicine metformin (Glucophage) is used to treat type 2 diabetes. It has also been found to help with PCOS symptoms, though it isn't approved by the U.S Food and Drug Administration (FDA) for this use.

Fertility medications. Lack of ovulation is usually the reason for fertility problems in women with PCOS. Several medications that stimulate ovulation can help women with PCOS become pregnant. Even so, other reasons for infertility in both the woman and man should be ruled out before fertility medications are used. Also, some fertility medications increase the risk for multiple births (twins, triplets).

Surgery. "Ovarian drilling" is a surgery that may increase the chance of ovulation. It's sometimes used when a woman does not respond to fertility medicines. The doctor makes a very small cut above or below the navel (belly button) and inserts a small tool that acts like a telescope into the abdomen (stomach). This is called laparoscopy. The doctor then punctures the ovary with a small needle carrying an electric current to destroy a small portion of the ovary. This procedure carries a risk of developing scar tissue on the ovary. This surgery can lower male hormone levels and help with ovulation. But, these effects may only last a few months. This treatment doesn't help with loss of scalp hair or increased hair growth on other parts of the body.

Medicine for increased hair growth or extra male hormones. Medicines called anti-androgens may reduce hair growth and clear acne. Spironolactone (Aldactone), first used to treat high blood pressure, has been shown to reduce the impact of male hormones on hair growth in women. Finasteride (Propecia), a medicine taken by men for hair loss, has the same effect. Anti-androgens are often combined with birth control pills. These medications should not be taken if you are trying to become pregnant.

Before taking Aldactone, tell your doctor if you are pregnant or plan to become pregnant. Do not breastfeed while taking this medicine. Women who may become pregnant should not handle Propecia.

Other options include:

- Vaniqa cream to reduce facial hair
- Laser hair removal or electrolysis to remove hair
- Hormonal treatment to keep new hair from growing

Other treatments. Some research has shown that bariatric (weight loss) surgery may be effective in resolving PCOS in morbidly obese women. Morbid obesity means having a BMI of more than 40, or a BMI of 35 to 40 with an obesity-related disease. The drug troglitazone was shown to help women with PCOS. But, it was taken off the market because it caused liver problems. Similar drugs without the same side effect are being tested in small trials.

How Does Pcos Affect A Woman While Pregnant?

Women with PCOS appear to have higher rates of:

- Miscarriage
- Gestational diabetes

- Pregnancy-induced high blood pressure (preeclampsia)

- Premature delivery

Babies born to women with PCOS have a higher risk of spending time in a neonatal intensive care unit or of dying before, during, or shortly after birth. Most of the time, these problems occur in multiple-birth babies (twins, triplets).

Researchers are studying whether the diabetes medicine metformin can prevent or reduce the chances of having problems while pregnant. Metformin also lowers male hormone levels and limits weight gain in women who are obese when they get pregnant.

Metformin is an FDA pregnancy category B drug. It does not appear to cause major birth defects or other problems in pregnant women. But, there have only been a few studies of metformin use in pregnant women to confirm its safety. Talk to your doctor about taking metformin if you are pregnant or are trying to become pregnant. Also, metformin is passed through breastmilk. Talk with your doctor about metformin use if you are a nursing mother.

Does PCOS Put Women At Risk For Other Health Problems?

Women with PCOS have greater chances of developing several serious health conditions, including life-threatening diseases. Recent studies found that:

- More than 50 percent of women with PCOS will have diabetes or pre-diabetes (impaired glucose tolerance) before the age of 40.

- The risk of heart attack is 4 to 7 times higher in women with PCOS than women of the same age without PCOS.

- Women with PCOS are at greater risk of having high blood pressure.

- Women with PCOS have high levels of LDL (bad) cholesterol and low levels of HDL (good) cholesterol.

- Women with PCOS can develop sleep apnea. This is when breathing stops for short periods of time during sleep.

Women with PCOS may also develop anxiety and depression. It is important to talk to your doctor about treatment for these mental health conditions.

Women with PCOS are also at risk for endometrial cancer. Irregular menstrual periods and the lack of ovulation cause women to produce the hormone estrogen, but not the hormone progesterone. Progesterone causes the endometrium (lining of the womb) to shed each month as a menstrual period. Without progesterone, the endometrium becomes thick, which can cause heavy or irregular bleeding. Over time, this can lead to endometrial hyperplasia, when the lining grows too much, and cancer.

I Have PCOS. What Can I Do To Prevent Complications?

If you have PCOS, get your symptoms under control at an earlier age to help reduce your chances of having complications like diabetes and heart disease. Talk to your doctor about treating all your symptoms, rather than focusing on just one aspect of your PCOS, such as problems getting pregnant. Also, talk to your doctor about getting tested for diabetes regularly. Other steps you can take to lower your chances of health problems include:

- Eating right
- Exercising
- Not smoking

How Can I Cope With The Emotional Effects Of PCOS?

Having PCOS can be difficult. You may feel:

- Embarrassed by your appearance
- Worried about being able to get pregnant
- Depressed

Getting treatment for PCOS can help with these concerns and help boost your self-esteem. You may also want to look for support groups in your area or online to help you deal with the emotional effects of PCOS. You are not alone and there are resources available for women with PCOS.

Chapter 27
Primary Ovarian Insufficiency (POI)

What Is Primary Ovarian Insufficiency (POI)?

Health care providers use the term POI when a woman's ovaries stop working normally before she is 40 years of age.

Many women naturally experience reduced fertility when they are around 40 years old. This age may mark the start of irregular menstrual periods that signal the onset of menopause. For women with POI, irregular periods and reduced fertility occur before the age of 40, sometimes as early as the teenage years.

In the past, POI used to be called "premature menopause" or "premature ovarian failure," but those terms do not accurately describe what happens in a woman with POI. A woman who has gone through menopause will never have another normal period and cannot get pregnant. A woman with POI may still have periods, even though they might not come regularly, and she may still get pregnant.

What Are The Symptoms Of POI?

The first sign of POI is usually menstrual irregularities or missed periods, which is sometimes called amenorrhea.

In addition, some women with POI have symptoms similar to those experienced by women who are going through natural menopause, including:

- Hot flashes

- Night sweats

About This Chapter: Information in this chapter is excerpted from "Primary Ovarian Insufficiency (POI): Condition Information," National institute of Child and Human Development (NICHD), April 12, 2013.

- Irritability

- Poor concentration

- Decreased sex drive

- Pain during sex

- Vaginal dryness

For many women with POI, trouble getting pregnant or infertility is the first symptom they experience and is what leads them to visit their health care provider. This is sometimes called "occult" (hidden) or early POI.

How Many People Are Affected By Or At Risk For POI?

Estimates suggest that about 1% of women and teenage girls in the United States have POI. Researchers estimate that, categorized by age, POI affects:

- 1 in 10,000 women by age 20

- 1 in 1,000 women by age 30

- 1 in 250 women by age 35

- 1 in 100 women by age 40

Several factors can affect a woman's risk for POI:

- **Family history.** Women who have a mother or sister with POI are more likely to have the disorder. About 10% to 20% of women with POI have a family history of the condition.

- **Genes.** Some changes to genes and genetic conditions put women at higher risk for POI. Research suggests that these disorders and conditions cause as much as 28% of POI cases.

- **Other factors**. Autoimmune diseases, viral infections, chemotherapy, and other treatments also may put a woman at higher risk of POI.

What Causes POI?

In about 90% of cases, the exact cause of POI is a mystery.

Research shows that POI is related to problems with the follicles—the small sacs in the ovaries in which eggs grow and mature.

Follicles start out as microscopic seeds called primordial follicles. These seeds are not yet follicles, but they can grow into them. Normally, a woman is born with approximately 2 million primordial follicles, typically enough to last until she goes through natural menopause, usually around age 50.

For a woman with POI, there are problems with the follicles:

- **Follicle depletion.** A woman with follicle depletion runs out of working follicles earlier than normal or expected. In the case of POI, the woman runs out of working follicles before natural menopause occurs around age 50. Presently there is no safe way for scientists today to make primordial follicles.

- **Follicle dysfunction.** A woman with follicle dysfunction has follicles remaining in her ovaries, but the follicles are not working properly. Scientists do not have a safe and effective way to make follicles start working normally again.

Although the exact cause is unknown in a majority of cases, some causes of follicle depletion and dysfunction have been identified:

- **Genetic and chromosomal disorders.** Disorders such as Fragile X syndrome and Turner syndrome can cause follicle depletion.

- **Low number of follicles.** Some women are born with fewer primordial follicles, so they have a smaller pool of follicles to use throughout their lives. Even though only one mature follicle releases an egg each month, less mature follicles usually develop along with that mature follicle and egg. Scientists don't understand exactly why this happens, but these "supporting" follicles seem to help the mature follicle function normally. If these extra follicles are missing, the main follicle will not mature and release an egg properly.

- **Autoimmune diseases.** Typically, the body's immune cells protect the body from invading bacteria and viruses. However, in autoimmune diseases, immune cells turn on healthy tissue. In the case of POI, the immune system may damage developing follicles in the ovaries. It could also damage the glands that make the hormones needed for the ovaries and follicles to work properly. Recent studies suggest that about 20% of women with POI have an autoimmune disease.

- **Chemotherapy or radiation therapy.** These strong treatments for cancer may damage the genetic material in cells, including follicle cells.

- **Metabolic disorders.** These disorders affect the body's ability to create, store, and use the energy it needs. For example, galactosemia affects how your body processes galactose, a type of sugar. More than 80% of women and girls with galactosemia also have POI.

- **Toxins.** Cigarette smoke, chemicals, and pesticides can speed up follicle depletion. In addition, viruses have been shown to affect follicle function.

What Are The Treatments For POI?

Currently, there is no proven treatment to restore normal function to a woman's ovaries. But there are treatments for some of the symptoms of POI, as well as treatments and behaviors to reduce health risks and conditions associated with POI.

It is also important to note that between 5% and 10% of women with POI get pregnant without medical intervention after they are diagnosed with POI. Some research suggests that these women go into what is known as "spontaneous remission" of POI, meaning that the ovaries begin to function normally on their own. When the ovaries are working properly, fertility is restored and the women can get pregnant.

Hormone Replacement Therapy (HRT)

HRT is the most common treatment for women with POI. It gives the body the estrogen and other hormones that the ovaries are not making. HRT improves sexual health and decreases the risks for cardiovascular disease (including heart attacks, stroke, and high blood pressure) and osteoporosis.

Calcium and Vitamin D Supplements

Because women with POI are at higher risk for osteoporosis, they should get at least 1,200 to 1,500 mg of elemental calcium and 1000 IU (international units) of vitamin D, which helps the body absorb calcium, every day. These nutrients are important for bone health. A health care provider may do a bone mineral density test to check for bone loss.

Regular Physical Activity And Healthy Body Weight

Weight-bearing physical activity, such as walking, jogging, and stair climbing, helps build bone strength and prevents osteoporosis. Maintaining a healthy body weight and getting regular physical activity are also important for reducing the risk of heart disease. These factors can affect cholesterol levels, which in turn can change the risk for heart disease.

Treatments For Associated Conditions

POI is associated with other health conditions, including (but not limited to) Addison's disease, Fragile X permutation, thyroid dysfunction, depression, anxierty, and certain other genetic, metabolic, and autoimmune disorders.

Women who have POI as well as one of these associated conditions will require additional treatment for the associated condition. In some cases, treatment involves medication or hormone therapy. Other types of treatments might also be needed.

Emotional Support

For many women who experience infertility, including those with POI, feelings of loss are common. In one study, almost 9 out of 10 women reported feeling moderate to severe emotional distress when they learned of their POI diagnosis. Several organizations offer help finding these types of professionals.

POI In Teens

Receiving a diagnosis of POI can be emotionally difficult for teenagers and their parents. A teen may have a similar emotional experience as an adult who receives the diagnosis, but there are many aspects of the experience that are unique to being a teenager. It is important for parents, the teenager, and health care providers to work closely together to ensure that the teenager gets the right treatment and maintains her emotional and physical health in the long term. There are resources to provide advice and support for parents, teenagers, and health care providers.

Chapter 28

Lichen Sclerosus

What Is Lichen Sclerosus?

Lichen sclerosus is a long-term problem of the skin. It mostly affects the genital and anal areas. Sometimes, lichen sclerosus appears on the upper body, breasts, and upper arms.

Who Gets Lichen Sclerosus?

Lichen sclerosus appears in:

- Women (often after menopause)

- Men (uncommon)

- Children (rare)

What Are The Symptoms?

Early in the disease, small white spots appear on the skin. The spots are usually shiny and smooth. Later, the spots grow into bigger patches. The skin on the patches becomes thin and crinkled. Then the skin tears easily, and bright red or purple bruises are common. Sometimes, the skin becomes scarred. If the disease is a mild case, there may be no symptoms.

Other symptoms are:

- Itching (very common)

- Discomfort or pain

About This Chapter: Information in this chapter is excerpted from "Lichen Sclerosus," National Institute of Arthritis Musculoskeletal and Skin Diseases (NIAMS), November 2014.

- Bleeding
- Blisters

What Causes Lichen Sclerosus?

Doctors don't know the exact cause of lichen sclerosus. Some doctors think a too active immune system and hormone problems may play a role. It is also thought that people inherit the likelihood of getting the disease. Sometimes, lichen sclerosus appears on skin that has been damaged or scarred from some other previous injury.

Lichen sclerosus is not contagious (it can't be caught from another person).

How Is It Diagnosed?

Doctors can look at severe lichen sclerosus and know what it is. But usually, a doctor takes a small piece of the skin patch (biopsy) and looks at it under a microscope. This allows doctors to make sure that it is not a different disease.

How Is It Treated?

If you have patches on the arms or upper body, they usually don't need treatment. The patches go away over time.

Lichen sclerosus of the genital skin should be treated. Even if it isn't painful or itchy, the patches can scar. This can cause problems with urination or sex. There is also a very small chance that skin cancer may develop in the patches.

Surgery is normally a good option for men. Circumcision (removing the foreskin on the penis) is the most widely used therapy for men with lichen sclerosus. The disease usually does not come back. Surgery is normally not a good option for women. When the lichen sclerosus patches are removed from the genitals of women and girls, they usually come back.

Treatment also includes using very strong cortisone cream or ointment on the skin. You put these creams on the patches every day for several weeks. This stops the itching. Then you use the cream or ointment two times a week for a long time to keep the disease from coming back. Treatment does not fix the scarring that may have already occurred.

You need regular followup by a doctor because using these creams and ointments for a long time can cause:

- Thinning and redness of the skin

- Stretch marks where the cream is applied

- Genital yeast infections.

Sometimes, you don't get better when using the cortisone creams. Some things that can keep symptoms from clearing up are:

- Low estrogen levels

- Infection

- Allergy to the medication.

When creams and ointments don't work, your doctor may suggest:

- Retinoids, or vitamin A-like drugs

- Tacrolimus ointment

- Ultraviolet light treatments (not used on skin of the genitals).

If you need medicine, ask your doctor:

- How does the medicine work?

- What are its side effects?

- Why is it the best treatment for my lichen sclerosus?

If a young girl gets lichen sclerosus, she may not require lifelong treatment. Lichen sclerosus sometimes goes away at puberty. Scarring and changes in skin color may remain.

Can People With Lichen Sclerosus Have Sex?

Women with severe lichen sclerosus in the genitals may not be able to have sex. The disease can cause scars that narrow the vagina. Also, sex can hurt and cause the patches to bleed. However, treatment with creams or ointments can help. Women with severe scarring in the vagina may need surgery, but only after lichen sclerosus is controlled with medication.

Is Lichen Sclerosus Related To Cancer?

Lichen sclerosus does not cause skin cancer. However, skin that is scarred by lichen sclerosus is more likely to develop skin cancer. If you have the disease, see the doctor every 6 to 12 months. The doctor can look at and treat any changes in the skin.

What Kind Of Doctor Treats Lichen Sclerosus?

Lichen sclerosus is treated by:

- Dermatologists (doctors who treat the skin)
- Gynecologists (doctors who treat the female reproductive system)
- Urologists (doctors who treat the urinary or urogenital tract)
- Primary health care providers

Chapter 29

Preconception Health And Health Care For Women

All women can benefit from preconception health, whether or not they plan to have a baby one day. This is because part of preconception health is about people getting and staying healthy overall, throughout their lives.

One of the best things a woman can do for herself is to take good care of her health. It's natural to think about eating well and exercising as important parts of being healthy, but there are other things to consider, too. The Centers for Disease Control and Prevention urges all women to make healthy living a priority.

In addition, no one expects an unplanned pregnancy. But it happens often. In fact, about half of all pregnancies in the United States are not planned.

Following are some healthy habits for women:

Make A Plan And Take Action

Whether or not you've written them down, you've probably thought about your goals for having or not having children and how to achieve those goals. It's really important to have a plan and take action, as needed.

About This Chapter: Information in this chapter is excerpted from "About Teen Pregnancy," Centers for Disease Control and Prevention (CDC), June 9, 2014; and information from "NCHS Fact Sheet," Centers for Disease Control and Prevention (CDC), June 4, 2014.

See Your Doctor

At least once each year, see your doctor for a health check-up. Talk with your doctor about preconception health care. If your doctor has not discussed this type of care with you?ask about it! Bring a list of talking points so you don't forget anything.

Be sure to talk with your doctor about:

Medical Conditions

If you currently have any medical conditions, be sure they are in control and being treated. Some of these conditions include: sexually transmitted diseases (STDs), diabetes, thyroid disease,phenylketonuria (PKU), seizure disorders, high blood pressure, arthritis, eating disorders, and chronic diseases.

Lifestyle And Behaviors

Talk with your doctor or other health professional if you smoke, use "street" drugs, or drink excessive amounts of alcohol (binge drinking); live in a stressful or abusive environment; or work with or live around toxic substances. Your doctor can help you with counseling, treatment, and other support services.

Vaccinations (Shots)

Having the right vaccinations at the right time can help keep you healthy.

Take 400 Micrograms Of Folic Acid Every Day

Folic acid is a B vitamin. Every woman needs folic acid every day for the healthy new cells the body makes daily. Think about your skin, hair, and nails. These?and other parts of the body—make new cells each day. Folic acid also is important to help prevent major birth defects of the baby's brain and spine if you do become pregnant.

Stop Smoking, Using "Street" Drugs, And Drinking Excessive Amounts Of Alcohol

Smoking, using "street" drugs, and drinking too much alcohol (binge drinking) are harmful to your health and could lead to serious birth defects for your baby if you have an unintended pregnancy. If you cannot stop drinking, smoking, or using drugs?get help! Contact your health care provider or local treatment center.

Alcohol And Drug Resources

Substance Abuse Treatment Facility Locator

The Substance Abuse and Mental Health Services Administration (SAMHSA) has a treatment facility locator. This locator helps people find drug and alcohol treatment programs in their area.

Alcoholics Anonymous (A.A.)

Alcoholics Anonymous® is a fellowship of men and women who share their experiences, strengths, and hopes with each other so that they can solve their common problem and help others to recover from alcoholism.

Smoking Resource

1-800-QUIT-NOW FREE (784-8669)

Avoid Toxic Substances

Exposure to toxic substances and other harmful materials at work or at home, such as synthetic chemicals, metals, fertilizer, bug spray, and cat or rodent feces, can hurt the reproductive systems of men and women. Learn how to protect yourself from toxic substances at work and at home.

Reach And Maintain A Healthy Weight

People who are overweight or obese have a higher risk for many serious conditions, including heart disease, type 2 diabetes, and certain cancers (endometrial, breast, and colon). People who are underweight also are at risk for serious health problems.

The key to achieving and maintaining a healthy weight isn't about short-term dietary changes. It's about a lifestyle that includes healthy eating and regular physical activity. Staying in control of your weight contributes to good health now and as you age.

If you are underweight, overweight, or obese, talk with your doctor or other health care professional about ways to reach and maintain a healthy weight.

Get Help For Violence

From infants to the elderly, violence affects people in all stages of life. The number of violent deaths tells only part of the story. Many more people survive violence and are left with lifelong physical and emotional scars.

Learn Your Family History

Your family health history can help your doctor provide better care for you. It can help identify whether you have a higher risk for some diseases. It can help your doctor recommend actions for reducing your personal risk for a disease. And, it can help in looking for early warning signs of disease.

Get Mentally Healthy

Mental health is how we think, feel, and act as we cope with life. To be at your best, you need to feel good about your life and value yourself. Everyone feels worried, anxious, sad, or stressed sometimes. However, if these feelings do not go away and they interfere with your daily life, get help. Talk with your doctor or another health care professional about your feelings and treatment options.

When You're Ready? Planning Your Pregnancy

One day, you might decide that you're ready to have a baby. When that time comes, one of the most important things you can do is plan your pregnancy. For some women, getting their body ready for pregnancy takes a few months. For other women, it might take longer. It's never too early to get ready for a healthy pregnancy and baby.

In the meantime, learn how to prevent pregnancy. Several safe and highly effective methods of birth control are available to prevent pregnancy.

Part Four
For Guys Only

Chapter 30

The Male Reproductive System

Like all living things, human beings reproduce. Reproduction is essential for the survival of a species. Most species have males and females for that purpose, with each sex having its own reproductive system.

What Are The Differences Between The Male And Female Reproductive Systems?

There are many differences between male and female reproductive systems. Unlike the human female reproductive system, most of the parts of the male reproductive system are situated outside the body. Where the female reproductive system releases only one egg every month during the menstrual process, the male reproductive system can produces millions of sperm cells in a day. Each system also has a primary function which is unique to the reproduction process. The main function of the male reproductive system is to produce and deliver sperm as well as produce hormones such as testosterone, which is responsible for many of the important physical changes the male goes through during puberty. In addition to being critical for the natural development of a boy, testosterone is essential to the male reproductive system because it stimulates the ongoing production of sperm.

What Is The Male Reproductive System?

The external parts of the male reproductive system consist of the penis, scrotum, and testicles.

"The Male Reproductive System," © 2016 Omnigraphics, Inc. Reviewed November 2015.

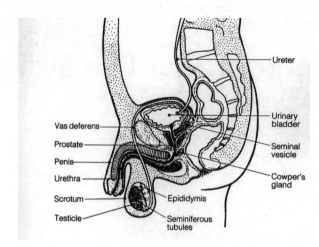

Figure 30.1. The Male Reproductive System

Source: cancer.gov

The internal organs, or accessory glands, include the epididymis, vas deferens, seminal vesicles, urethra, prostate gland, bulbourethral glands, and the ejaculatory duct.

External Organs

Penis

The penis is the male organ used during intercourse. It consists of two main parts, the shaft and the glans. The glans is a cone-shaped structure situated at the end of the penis and is covered by foreskin, which is a thin, loose layer of skin, which is sometimes removed by a medical procedure called circumcision. Circumcision is done for many reasons; for hygiene; social, religious or cultural reasons. The tip of the penis contains the opening of the urethra, a tube that transports urine and semen. Inside, the penis consists of sponge-like tissues which absorb blood and makes the penis become erect for intercourse.

Scrotum

The scrotum is a bag-like structure that can be found behind the penis. It contains the testicles, which produce sperm, the male gamete, and sex hormones. The scrotum protects the testicles and adjusts the body temperature to ensure the survival of sperm. The scrotum contains special muscles in its wall which helps it to contract and relax according to the body temperature necessary for the proper functioning of the sperm.

Testicles

Also called testes, the testicles are two oval organs inside the scrotum. Testicles produce hormones including testosterone, and create sperm. The sperm are produced by seminiferous tubules inside the testes.

Accessory Glands

Urethra

The urethra is a long tube that carries urine from the urinary bladder. In boys, it also brings semen out of the body, during ejaculation. During sexual intercourse, when the penis becomes erect, urine is blocked and only the semen is allowed to come out of the urethra.

Epididymis

One of the accessory organs of the male reproductive system, the epididymis is found inside the body. Before transporting the sperm to vas deferens, epididymis matures the sperm cells.

Vas Deferens

The vas deferens is a long muscular tube connecting the epididymis and the pelvic area. The vas deferens is the duct system that carries semen—the sperm nourishing fluid—to the urethra.

Other accessory glands of the male reproductive system include the **ejaculatory ducts** which empty semen into the urethra; the **seminal vesicles** responsible for producing the majority of the fluid found in semen; the **prostate gland** which produces fluids that nourish and protect the sperm, and the **bulbourethral or Cowper's glands** which produce pre-ejaculate to provide lubrication for semen to pass through the urethra.

What Does The Male Reproductive System Do?

All of the organs that make up the male reproductive system are designed to work in harmony to generate and release sperm into the female's vagina during sexual intercourse. Once released into the vagina if a healthy sperm meets a mature egg conception can begin. In addition, the male reproductive system produces hormones that play a vital role in ensuring that a boy will develop into a sexually mature man who is capable of reproducing.

References:

1. Dr. David T. Derrer, MD. "The Male Reproductive System." WebMD, February 27, 2014.

2. "Male Reproductive System." The Nemours Foundation/KidsHealth, 2015.

3. "Male Reproductive System." PubMed Health Glossary, n.d.

4. "Bulbourethral Glands." Human Anatomy, 2012.

5. "The Male Reproductive System." The Cleveland Clinic Foundation, 2013.

Chapter 31

Puberty And Male Sexual Development

What Is Puberty?

Puberty is a time in your life when your body makes changes that cause you to develop into an adult. These changes affect both how you look like growing taller and developing more muscle. They also affect how you feel — one minute you want to be treated like an adult, at other times you want to be treated like a kid.

What Causes These Changes?

Hormones in your body increase, and these make the changes of puberty happen. For boys it's testosterone. Much of what happens to your body is controlled by your hormones and the "genetic map" that your body is following. Of course, no one can control these two things.

When Does Puberty Happen?

Puberty starts and ends at different times for everyone. Girls develop more and change between the ages of 9 and 13. For boys, puberty typically starts a little later, when they are between 10 and 15 years old. This explains why many girls are taller and more mature than

About This Chapter: Information in this chapter is excerpted from "Questions Answered," Centers for Disease Control and Prevention (CDC), January 22, 2013; information from "Erectile Dysfunction," The National Institute of Diabetes and Digestive and Kidney Diseases (NIDDK), November 2015; information from "NCI Dictionaries," National Cancer Institute (NCI), May 15, 2015; and information from "Menstrual Hygiene Management Toolkit," United States Agency for International Development (USAID), May 2015.

boys for a few years until the boys catch up. Just remember, everyone develops at a different rate.

How Much Will I Grow In Puberty?

During puberty, you may experience a "growth spurt," or period of fast growth. Most girls start their growth spurt between ages 9 and 11, reaching their full height between the ages of 15 and 18. Some girls grow as much as 4 inches per year. Boys typically begin their growth spurt later than girls, between ages 13 and 14. But it lasts longer—until about age 20 or 21. On an average, boys grow about 3 1/2 inches per year during puberty.

There is no way to know for sure how much you will grow. Your body is following a genetic map, which helps determine how you will look as an adult. Things like height, body type, and facial features are determined by your genes. Your special pattern of genes comes to you from members of your family. But, you might ask your parents about what puberty was like for them, and that can help you understand what you should expect.

What Is That Smell?

During puberty, both boys and girls sweat glands are more active. Kids will also sweat more during puberty. A lot of kids notice that they have a new smell under their arms and elsewhere on their bodies when they hit puberty, and believe me, it's not a pretty one. That smell is body odor (you may have heard people call it B.O. for short), and everyone gets it. The hormones become more active, affect the glands in your skin, and the glands make chemicals that smell bad.

So what can you do to feel less stinky? Well, keeping clean can stop you from smelling. You might want to take a shower every day, either in the morning before school or at night before bed. Showering after you've been playing sports or exercising is a really good idea. Another way to cut down on body odor is to use deodorant. If you use a deodorant with antiperspirant, it will cut down on sweat as well.

Does Everyone Get Pimples During Puberty?

About 85–90% of all kids — boys and girls — have acne during puberty, and you can count on a zit attack when you want to look your best. The hormonal changes that are happening inside your body cause the oil glands to become more active. It doesn't mean that you are dirty, it just means that what is happening on the inside has put your oil glands into high gear and can cause acne or pimples. You may notice pimples on your face, your upper back, or your upper chest. Pimples usually start around the beginning of puberty and can hang around for a few years as your body changes.

No One Understands Me. I Am Not In Control. Why Do I Feel This Way?

Just as suddenly as your body starts changing, your mind is also making changes. The same hormones that cause changes in your appearance can also affect your emotions, making you feel like no one understands what you're experiencing. You may feel like your emotions are all over the place. One minute you're happy and bouncing off the walls, the next minute you're losing your temper, or bawling your eyes out.

What's Going On?

Confusion and mixed-up feelings are normal. The different hormones in your body can send your emotions on a roller-coaster ride. Puberty makes almost everyone feel that way. Make no mistake—your body has taken control and you are along for the ride. These changes in emotions are normal and once you've gone through puberty, the emotional roller coaster should slow down. Just keep your cool. It'll gradually become easier as you get used to the new you.

In the meantime, you can control other things that affect how you look, how you feel, and how healthy you are. Taking charge of your health can help you to feel good, and in control during the changes of puberty.

How Does An Erection Occur?

An erection occurs when blood flow increases into the penis, making it expand and become firm. Two long chambers inside the penis, called the corpora cavernosa, contain a spongy tissue that draws the blood into the chambers.

An erection requires a precise sequence of events:

- An erection begins with sensory or mental stimulation, or both. The stimulus may be physical—touch, sound, smell, sight—or a sexual image or thought.

- When the brain senses a sexual urge, it sends impulses to local nerves in the penis that cause the muscles of the corpora cavernosa to relax. As a result, blood flows in through the arteries and fills the spaces in the corpora cavernosa like water filling a sponge.

- The blood creates pressure in the corpora cavernosa, making the penis expand.

- The erection ends after climax or after the sexual arousal has passed. The muscles in the penis contract to stop the inflow of blood. The veins open and the extra blood flows out of the spaces and back into the body.

What Is Ejaculation?

Ejaculation (eh-JAK-yoo-LAY-shun) is the release of semen through the penis during orgasm. This is caused at the peak of sexual excitement. It is not necessary for a boy to ejaculate each and every time he has an erection. During sexual intercourse, ejaculation transports the semen containing the sperm to a woman's reproductive system, thereby impregnating her.

What Is A Wet Dream Or Nocturnal Emission?

This is an ejaculation during sleep. During puberty, this is completely normal and nothing to be embarrassed or concerned about. Wet dreams occur due to the secretion of testosterone and cannot be controlled.

Chapter 32

Peyronie's Disease

What Is Peyronie's Disease?

Peyronie's disease is a disorder in which scar tissue, called a plaque, forms in the penis—the male organ used for urination and sex. The plaque builds up inside the tissues of a thick, elastic membrane called the tunica albuginea. The most common area for the plaque is on the top or bottom of the penis. As the plaque builds up, the penis will curve or bend, which can cause painful erections. Curves in the penis can make sexual intercourse painful, difficult, or impossible. Peyronie's disease begins with inflammation, or swelling, which can become a hard scar.

The plaque that develops in Peyronie's disease is not the same plaque that can develop in a person's arteries. The plaque seen in Peyronie's disease is benign, or noncancerous, and is not a tumor. Peyronie's disease is not contagious or caused by any known transmittable disease.

Early researchers thought Peyronie's disease was a form of impotence, now called erectile dysfunction (ED). ED happens when a man is unable to achieve or keep an erection firm enough for sexual intercourse. Some men with Peyronie's disease may have ED. Usually men with Peyronie's disease are referred to a urologist—a doctor who specializes in sexual and urinary problems.

What Causes Peyronie's Disease?

Medical experts do not know the exact cause of Peyronie's disease. Many believe that Peyronie's disease may be the result of

- acute injury to the penis

About This Chapter: Information in this chapter is excerpted from "Peyronie's Disease," National Institute of Diabetes and Digestive and Kidney Diseases (NIDDK), June 2014.

- chronic, or repeated, injury to the penis
- autoimmune disease—a disorder in which the body's immune system attacks the body's own cells and organs

What Are The Signs And Symptoms Of Peyronie's Disease?

The signs and symptoms of Peyronie's disease may include

- hard lumps on one or more sides of the penis
- pain during sexual intercourse or during an erection
- a curve in the penis either with or without an erection
- narrowing or shortening of the penis
- ED

Symptoms of Peyronie's disease range from mild to severe. Symptoms may develop slowly or appear quickly. In many cases, the pain decreases over time, although the curve in the penis may remain. In milder cases, symptoms may go away without causing a permanent curve.

Cross section of a curved penis during erection

What Are The Complications Of Peyronie's Disease?

Complications of Peyronie's disease may include

- the inability to have sexual intercourse
- ED
- anxiety, or stress, about sexual abilities or the appearance of the penis
- stress on a relationship with a sexual partner
- problems fathering a child because intercourse is difficult

How Is Peyronie's Disease Treated?

A urologist may treat Peyronie's disease with nonsurgical treatments or surgery.

The goal of treatment is to reduce pain and restore and maintain the ability to have intercourse. Men with small plaques, minimal penile curvature, no pain, and satisfactory sexual function may not need treatment until symptoms get worse. Peyronie's disease often resolves on its own without treatment.

A urologist may recommend changes in a man's lifestyle to reduce the risk of ED associated with Peyronie's disease.

Nonsurgical Treatments

Nonsurgical treatments include medications and medical therapies.

Medications. A urologist may prescribe medications aimed at decreasing a man's penile curvature, plaque size, and inflammation. A man may take prescribed medications to treat Peyronie's disease orally—by mouth—or a urologist may inject medications directly into the plaque. Verapamil is one type of topical medication that a man may apply to the skin over the plaque.

- **Oral medications.** Oral medications may include

  - vitamin E

  - potassium para-aminobenzoate (Potaba)

  - tamoxifen

  - colchicine

  - acetyl-L-carnitine

  - pentoxifylline

- **Injections.** Medications injected directly into plaques may include

  - verapamil

  - interferon alpha 2b

  - steroids

  - collagenase (Xiaflex)

To date, collagenase is the first and only medication specifically approved for Peyronie's disease.

Medical therapies. A urologist may use medical therapies to break up scar tissue and decrease plaque size and curvature. Therapies to break up scar tissue may include

- high-intensity, focused ultrasound directed at the plaque

- radiation therapy—high-energy rays, such as X-rays, aimed at the plaque

- shockwave therapy—focused, low-intensity electroshock waves directed at the plaque

A urologist may use iontophoresis—painless, low-level electric current that delivers medications through the skin over the plaque—to decrease plaque size and curvature.

A urologist may use mechanical traction and vacuum devices aimed at stretching or bending the penis to reduce curvature.

Surgery

A urologist may recommend surgery to remove plaque or help straighten the penis during an erection. Medical experts recommend surgery for long-term cases when

- symptoms have not improved

- erections, intercourse, or both are painful

- the curve or bend in the penis does not allow the man to have sexual intercourse

Some men may develop complications after surgery, and sometimes surgery does not correct the effects of Peyronie's disease—such as shortening of the penis. Some surgical methods can cause shortening of the penis. Medical experts suggest waiting 1 year or more from the onset of symptoms before having surgery because the course of Peyronie's disease is different in each man.

A urologist may recommend the following surgeries:

- **grafting.** A urologist will cut or remove the plaque and attach a patch of skin, a vein, or material made from animal organs in its place. This procedure may straighten the penis and restore some lost length from Peyronie's disease. However, some men may experience numbness of the penis and ED after the procedure.

- **plication.** A urologist will remove or pinch a piece of the tunica albuginea from the side of the penis opposite the plaque, which helps to straighten the penis. This procedure is less likely to cause numbness or ED. Plication cannot restore length or girth of the penis and may cause shortening of the penis.

- **device implantation.** A urologist implants a device into the penis that can cause an erection and help straighten it during an erection. Penile implants may be considered if a man has both Peyronie's disease and ED. In some cases, an implant alone will straighten the penis adequately. If the implant alone does not straighten the penis, a urologist may combine implantation with one of the other two surgeries. Once a man has an implant, he must use the device to have an erection.

A urologist performs these surgeries in a hospital.

Lifestyle Changes

A man can make healthy lifestyle changes to reduce the chance of ED associated with Peyronie's disease by

- quitting smoking
- reducing alcohol consumption
- exercising regularly
- avoiding illegal drugs

Chapter 33
Penile Cancer

Overview

The penis is the male sex organ that passes sperm and urine from the body. The glans (head of the penis) is covered with loose skin called the foreskin.

The most common type of penile cancer is squamous cell carcinoma (cancer that begins in flat cells in the top layer of the skin). It usually forms on or under the foreskin. Signs of penile cancer include sores or other skin changes, discharge, and bleeding.

Infection with certain types of human papillomavirus (HPV) causes about one-third of penile cancer cases. Circumcision (removal of the foreskin) may help prevent infection with HPV and decrease the risk of penile cancer. When found early, penile cancer can usually be cured.

General Information About Penile Cancer

Penile Cancer Is A Disease In Which Malignant (Cancer) Cells Form In The Tissues Of The Penis.

The penis is a rod-shaped male reproductive organ that passes sperm and urine from the body. It contains two types of erectile tissue (spongy tissue with blood vessels that fill with blood to make an erection):

- Corpora cavernosa: The two columns of erectile tissue that form most of the penis.

- Corpus spongiosum: The single column of erectile tissue that forms a small portion of the penis. The corpus spongiosum surrounds the urethra (the tube through which urine and sperm pass from the body).

About This Chapter: Information in this chapter is excerpted from "Penile Cancer–For patients," National Cancer Institute (NCI), August 12, 2015.

The erectile tissue is wrapped in connective tissue and covered with skin. The glans (head of the penis) is covered with loose skin called the foreskin.

Human Papillomavirus Infection May Increase The Risk Of Developing Penile Cancer.

Anything that increases your chance of getting a disease is called a risk factor. Having a risk factor does not mean that you will get cancer; not having risk factors doesn't mean that you will not get cancer. Talk with your doctor if you think you may be at risk. Risk factors for penile cancer include the following:

Circumcision may help prevent infection with the human papillomavirus (HPV). A circumcision is an operation in which the doctor removes part or all of the foreskin from the penis. Many boys are circumcised shortly after birth. Men who were not circumcised at birth may have a higher risk of developing penile cancer.

Other risk factors for penile cancer include the following:

- Being age 60 or older.
- Having phimosis (a condition in which the foreskin of the penis cannot be pulled back over the glans).
- Having poor personal hygiene.
- Having many sexual partners.
- Using tobacco products.

Signs Of Penile Cancer Include Sores, Discharge, And Bleeding.

These and other signs may be caused by penile cancer or by other conditions. Check with your doctor if you have any of the following:

- Redness, irritation, or a sore on the penis.
- A lump on the penis.

Tests That Examine The Penis Are Used To Detect (Find) And Diagnose Penile Cancer.

The following tests and procedures may be used:

- **Physical exam and history:** An exam of the body to check general signs of health, including checking the penis for signs of disease, such as lumps or anything else that seems unusual. A history of the patient's health habits and past illnesses and treatments will also be taken.

- **Biopsy:** The removal of cells or tissues so they can be viewed under a microscope by a pathologist to check for signs of cancer. The tissue sample is removed during one of the following procedures:

    - **Fine-needle aspiration (FNA) biopsy:** The removal of tissue or fluid using a thin needle.

    - **Incisional biopsy:** The removal of part of a lump or a sample of tissue that doesn't look normal.

    - **Excisional biopsy:** The removal of an entire lump or area of tissue that doesn't look normal.

What Is Cancer Screening?

Cancer Screening Is Looking For Cancer Before A Person Has Any Symptoms.

Screening tests can help find cancer at an early stage, before symptoms appear. When abnormal tissue or cancer is found early, it may be easier to treat or cure. By the time symptoms appear, the cancer may have grown and spread. This can make the cancer harder to treat or cure.

It is important to remember that when your doctor suggests a screening test, it does not always mean he or she thinks you have cancer. Screening tests are done when you have no cancer symptoms.

There Are Different Kinds Of Screening Tests.

Screening tests include the following:

- Physical exam and history: An exam of the body to check general signs of health, including checking for signs of disease, such as lumps or anything else that seems unusual. A history of the patient's health habits and past illnesses and treatments will also be taken.

- Laboratory tests: Medical procedures that test samples of tissue, blood, urine, or other substances in the body.

- Imaging procedures: Procedures that make pictures of areas inside the body.

- Genetic tests: Tests that look for certain gene mutations (changes) that are linked to some types of cancer.

Screening Tests Have Risks.

Not all screening tests are helpful and most have risks. It is important to know the risks of the test and whether it has been proven to decrease the chance of dying from cancer.

Some Screening Tests Can Cause Serious Problems.

Some screening procedures can cause bleeding or other problems. For example, colon cancer screening with sigmoidoscopy or colonoscopy can cause tears in the lining of the colon.

Finding The Cancer May Not Improve The Person's Health Or Help The Person Live Longer.

Some cancers never cause symptoms or become life-threatening, but if found by a screening test, the cancer may be treated. There is no way to know if treating the cancer would help the person live longer than if no treatment were given. In both teenagers and adults, there is an increased risk of suicide in the first year after being diagnosed with cancer. Also, treatments for cancer have side effects.

For some cancers, finding and treating the cancer early does not improve the chance of a cure or help the person live longer.

Certain factors affect prognosis (chance of recovery) and treatment options.

The prognosis (chance of recovery) and treatment options depend on the following:

- The stage of the cancer.
- The location and size of the tumor.
- Whether the cancer has just been diagnosed or has recurred (come back).

There are three ways that cancer spreads in the body.

Cancer can spread through tissue, the lymph system, and the blood:

- Tissue. The cancer spreads from where it began by growing into nearby areas.
- Lymph system. The cancer spreads from where it began by getting into the lymph system. The cancer travels through the lymph vessels to other parts of the body.
- Blood. The cancer spreads from where it began by getting into the blood. The cancer travels through the blood vessels to other parts of the body.

Recurrent Penile Cancer

Recurrent penile cancer is cancer that has recurred (come back) after it has been treated. The cancer may come back in the penis or in other parts of the body.

Treatment Options

There are different types of treatment for patients with penile cancer. Four main types of standard treatment used are below:

- Surgery

- Radiation therapy

- Chemotherapy

- Biologic therapy

Standard Treatments:

- **Surgery**

  Surgery is the most common treatment for all stages of penile cancer. A doctor may remove the cancer using one of the following operations:

- **Mohs microsurgery**

- **Laser surgery**

- **Cryosurgery**

- **Circumcision**

- **Wide local excision**

- **Amputation of the penis**

Lymph nodes in the groin may be taken out during surgery. Even if the doctor removes all the cancer that can be seen at the time of the surgery, some patients may be given chemotherapy or radiation therapy after surgery to kill any cancer cells that are left. Treatment given after the surgery, to lower the risk that the cancer will come back, is called adjuvant therapy.

- **Radiation therapy** Radiation therapy is a cancer treatment that uses high-energy X-rays or other types of radiation to kill cancer cells or keep them from growing. There are two types of radiation therapy. External radiation therapy uses a machine outside the body to send radiation toward the cancer. Internal radiation therapy uses a radioactive substance sealed in needles, seeds, wires, or catheters that are placed directly into or near the cancer. The way the radiation therapy is given depends on the type and stage of the cancer being treated.

- **Chemotherapy** Chemotherapy is a cancer treatment that uses drugs to stop the growth of cancer cells, either by killing the cells or by stopping them from dividing. When chemotherapy is taken by mouth or injected into a vein or muscle, the drugs enter the bloodstream and can reach cancer cells throughout the body (systemic chemotherapy). When chemotherapy is placed directly onto the skin (topical chemotherapy) or into the cerebrospinal fluid, an organ, or a body cavity such as the abdomen, the drugs mainly affect cancer cells in those areas (regional chemotherapy). The way the chemotherapy is given depends on the type and stage of the cancer being treated.

- **Biologic therapy** Biologic therapy is a treatment that uses the patient's immune system to fight cancer. Substances made by the body or made in a laboratory are used to boost, direct, or restore the body's natural defenses against cancer. This type of cancer treatment is also called biotherapy or immunotherapy.

Follow-up tests may be needed. Some of the tests that were done to diagnose the cancer or to find out the stage of the cancer may be repeated. Some tests will be repeated in order to see how well the treatment is working. Decisions about whether to continue, change, or stop treatment may be based on the results of these tests.

Some of the tests will continue to be done from time to time after treatment has ended. The results of these tests can show if your condition has changed or if the cancer has recurred (come back). These tests are sometimes called follow-up tests or check-ups.

Chapter 34
Epididymitis

Acute epididymitis is a clinical syndrome consisting of pain, swelling, and inflammation of the epididymis that lasts <6 weeks. Sometimes the testis is also involved—a condition referred to as epididymo-orchitis. A high index of suspicion for spermatic cord (testicular) torsion must be maintained in men who present with a sudden onset of symptoms associated with epididymitis, as this condition is a surgical emergency.

Among sexually active men aged <35 years, acute epididymitis is most frequently caused by *C. trachomatis* or *N. gonorrhoeae*. Acute epididymitis caused by sexually transmitted enteric organisms (e.g., *Escherichia coli*) also occurs among men who are the insertive partner during anal intercourse. Sexually transmitted acute epididymitis usually is accompanied by urethritis, which frequently is asymptomatic. Other nonsexually transmitted infectious causes of acute epididymitis (e.g., Fournier's gangrene) are uncommon and should be managed in consultation with a urologist.

Chronic epididymitis is characterized by a ≥6 week history of symptoms of discomfort and/or pain in the scrotum, testicle, or epididymis. Chronic infectious epididymitis is most frequently seen in conditions associated with a granulomatous reaction; Mycobacterium tuberculosis (TB) is the most common granulomatous disease affecting the epididymis and should be suspected, especially in men with a known history of or recent exposure to TB. The differential diagnosis of chronic non-infectious epididymitis, sometimes termed "orchalgia/epididymalgia" is broad (i.e., trauma, cancer, autoimmune, and idiopathic conditions); men with this diagnosis should be referred to a urologist for clinical management.

About This Chapter: Information in this chapter is excerpted from "Epididymitis," Centers for Disease Control and Prevention (CDC), June 4, 2015.

Diagnostic Considerations

Men who have acute epididymitis typically have unilateral testicular pain and tenderness, hydrocele, and palpable swelling of the epididymis. Although inflammation and swelling usually begins in the tail of the epididymis, it can spread to involve the rest of the epididymis and testicle. The spermatic cord is usually tender and swollen. Spermatic cord (testicular) torsion, a surgical emergency, should be considered in all cases, but it occurs more frequently among adolescents and in men without evidence of inflammation or infection. In men with severe, unilateral pain with sudden onset, those whose test results do not support a diagnosis of urethritis or urinary-tract infection, or men in whom diagnosis of acute epididymitis is questionable, immediate referral to a urologist for evaluation of testicular torsion is important because testicular viability might be compromised.

Treatment

To prevent complications and transmission of sexually transmitted infections, presumptive therapy is indicated at the time of the visit before all laboratory test results are available. Selection of presumptive therapy is based on risk for chlamydia and gonorrhea and/or enteric organisms. The goals of treatment of acute epididymitis are 1) microbiologic cure of infection, 2) improvement of signs and symptoms, 3) prevention of transmission of chlamydia and gonorrhea to others, and 4) a decrease in potential chlamydia/gonorrhea epididymitis complications (e.g., infertility and chronic pain). Although most men with acute epididymitis can be treated on an outpatient basis, referral to a specialist and hospitalization should be considered when severe pain or fever suggests other diagnoses (e.g., torsion, testicular infarction, abscess, and necrotizing fasciitis) or when men are unable to comply with an antimicrobial regimen. Because high fever is uncommon and indicates a complicated infection, hospitalization for further evaluation is recommended.

Other Management Considerations

Men who have acute epididymitis confirmed or suspected to be caused by *N. gonorrhoeae* or *C. trachomatis* should be advised to abstain from sexual intercourse until they and their partners have been adequately treated and symptoms have resolved. All men with acute epididymitis should be tested for other STDs, including HIV.

Follow-Up

Men should be instructed to return to their health-care providers if their symptoms fail to improve within 72 hours of the initiation of treatment. Signs and symptoms of epididymitis that do not subside within 3 days require re-evaluation of the diagnosis and therapy. Men who experience swelling and tenderness that persist after completion of antimicrobial therapy should be evaluated for alternative diagnoses, including tumor, abscess, infarction, testicular cancer, tuberculosis, and fungal epididymitis.

Management Of Sex Partners

Men who have acute sexually transmitted epididymitis confirmed or suspected to be caused by *N. gonorrhoeae* or *C. trachomatis* should be instructed to refer for evaluation, testing, and presumptive treatment all sex partners with whom they have had sexual contact within the 60 days preceding onset of symptoms. If the last sexual intercourse was >60 days before onset of symptoms or diagnosis, the most recent sex partner should be treated. Arrangements should be made to link female partners to care. EPT and enhanced referral are effective strategies for treating female sex partners of men who have chlamydia or gonorrhea for whom linkage to care is anticipated to be delayed. Partners should be instructed to abstain from sexual intercourse until they and their sex partners are adequately treated and symptoms have resolved.

Special Considerations

Allergy, Intolerance, And Adverse Reactions

The cross reactivity between penicillins and cephalosporins is <2.5% in persons with a history of penicillin allergy. The risk for penicillin cross-reactivity is highest with first-generation cephalosporins, but is negligible between most second-generation (cefoxitin) and all third-generation (ceftriaxone) cephalosporins. Alternative regimens have not been studied; therefore, clinicians should consult infectious-disease specialists if such regimens are required.

HIV Infection

Men with HIV infection who have uncomplicated acute epididymitis should receive the same treatment regimen as those who are HIV negative. Other etiologic agents have been implicated in acute epididymitis in men with HIV infection, including CMV, salmonella, toxoplasmosis, *Ureaplasma urealyticum*, *Corynebacterium* sp., *Mycoplasma* sp., and *Mima polymorpha*. Fungi and mycobacteria also are more likely to cause acute epididymitis in men with HIV infection than in those who are immunocompetent.

Chapter 35

Testicular Cancer

Overview

The testicles are two glands inside the scrotum (a sac of loose skin below the penis). The testicles make sperm and the hormone testosterone.

Testicular cancer is the most common cancer in men 15–34 years of age. The two main types of testicular tumors are seminoma and nonseminoma. Nonseminomas tend to grow and spread more quickly than seminomas.

The most common sign of testicular cancer is a lump or swelling in the testicle. Most testicular cancers can be cured, even if they are diagnosed at an advanced stage.

Treatment for testicular cancer can cause infertility by decreasing the amount of sperm made by the body. Men who want to have children may want to use sperm banking to store sperm before they begin treatment.

General Information About Testicular Cancer

Testicular Cancer Is A Disease In Which Malignant (Cancer) Cells Form In The Tissues Of One Or Both Testicles.

Almost all testicular cancers start in the germ cells. The two main types of testicular germ cell tumors are seminomas and nonseminomas. These 2 types grow and spread differently and are treated differently. Nonseminomas tend to grow and spread more quickly than seminomas. Seminomas are more sensitive to radiation. A testicular tumor that contains both seminoma and nonseminoma cells is treated as a nonseminoma.

About This Chapter: Information in this chapter is excerpted from "Testicular Cancer–For patients," National Cancer Institute (NCI), December 31, 2014.

Health history can affect the risk of testicular cancer.

Anything that increases the chance of getting a disease is called a risk factor. Having a risk factor does not mean that you will get cancer; not having risk factors doesn't mean that you will not get cancer. Talk with your doctor if you think you may be at risk. Risk factors for testicular cancer include:

- Having had an undescended testicle.

- Having had abnormal development of the testicles.

- Having a personal history of testicular cancer.

- Having a family history of testicular cancer (especially in a father or brother).

- Being white.

Signs And Symptoms Of Testicular Cancer Include Swelling Or Discomfort In The Scrotum.

These and other signs and symptoms may be caused by testicular cancer or by other conditions. Check with your doctor if you have any of the following:

- A painless lump or swelling in either testicle.

- A change in how the testicle feels.

- A dull ache in the lower abdomen or the groin.

- A sudden build-up of fluid in the scrotum.

- Pain or discomfort in a testicle or in the scrotum.

Tests That Examine The Testicles And Blood Are Used To Detect (Find) And Diagnose Testicular Cancer.

The following tests and procedures may be used:

- **Physical exam and history**

- **Ultrasound exam**

- **Serum tumor marker test:** A procedure in which a sample of blood is examined to measure the amounts of certain substances released into the blood by organs, tissues, or tumor cells in the body. Certain substances are linked to specific types of cancer when found in increased levels in the blood. These are called tumor markers.

The following tumor markers are used to detect testicular cancer:

- Alpha-fetoprotein (AFP).

- Beta-human chorionic gonadotropin (β-hCG).

   Tumor marker levels are measured before inguinal orchiectomy and biopsy, to help diagnose testicular cancer.

- **Inguinal orchiectomy:** A procedure to remove the entire testicle through an incision in the groin. A tissue sample from the testicle is then viewed under a microscope to check for cancer cells. (The surgeon does not cut through the scrotum into the testicle to remove a sample of tissue for biopsy, because if cancer is present, this procedure could cause it to spread into the scrotum and lymph nodes. It's important to choose a surgeon who has experience with this kind of surgery.) If cancer is found, the cell type (seminoma or nonseminoma) is determined in order to help plan treatment.

What Is Screening?

Screening is looking for cancer before a person has any symptoms. This can help find cancer at an early stage. When abnormal tissue or cancer is found early, it may be easier to treat. By the time symptoms appear, cancer may have begun to spread.

It is important to remember that your doctor does not necessarily think you have cancer if he or she suggests a screening test. Screening tests are given when you have no cancer symptoms.

If a screening test result is abnormal, you may need to have more tests done to find out if you have cancer. These are called diagnostic tests.

Certain factors affect prognosis (chance of recovery) and treatment options.

The prognosis (chance of recovery) and treatment options depend on the following:

- Stage of the cancer (whether it is in or near the testicle or has spread to other places in the body, and blood levels of AFP, β-hCG, and LDH).

- Type of cancer.

- Size of the tumor.

- Number and size of retroperitoneal lymph nodes.

Testicular cancer can usually be cured in patients who receive adjuvant chemotherapy or radiation therapy after their primary treatment.

Treatment for testicular cancer can cause infertility.

Certain treatments for testicular cancer can cause infertility that may be permanent. Patients who may wish to have children should consider sperm banking before having treatment. Sperm banking is the process of freezing sperm and storing it for later use.

Treatment Options are:

- **Surgery**

- **Radiation therapy**

- **Chemotherapy**

- **Surveillance**

- **High-dose chemotherapy with stem cell transplant**

Chapter 36

Klinefelter Syndrome (KS)

What Is Klinefelter Syndrome (KS)?

The term "Klinefelter syndrome," or KS, describes a set of features that can occur in a male who is born with an extra X chromosome in his cells. It is named after Dr. Henry Klinefelter, who identified the condition in the 1940s.

KS is sometimes called "47,XXY" (47 refers to total chromosomes) or the "XXY condition." Those with KS are sometimes called "XXY males."

In very rare cases, males might have two or more extra X chromosomes in their cells, for instance XXXY or XXXXY, or an extra Y, such as XXYY. This is called poly-X Klinefelter syndrome, and it causes more severe symptoms.

What Causes Klinefelter Syndrome (KS)?

The extra chromosome results from a random error that occurs when a sperm or egg is formed; this error causes an extra X cell to be included each time the cell divides to form new cells. In very rare cases, more than one extra X or an extra Y is included.

How Many People Are Affected By Or At Risk For Klinefelter Syndrome (KS)?

Researchers estimate that 1 male in about 500 newborn males has an extra X chromosome, making KS among the most common chromosomal disorders seen in all newborns. The likelihood of a third or fourth X is much rarer:

About This Chapter: Information in this chapter is excerpted from "Klinefelter Syndrome (KS): Condition Information," National Institute of Child Health and Human Development (NICHD), October 25, 2013.

Table 36.1. Prevalence Of Klinefelter Syndrome Variants

Number of extra X chromosomes	One (XXY)	Two (XXXY)	Three (XXXXY)
Number of newborn males with the condition	1 in 500	1 in 50,000	1 in 85,000 to 100,000

Scientists are not sure what factors increase the risk of KS. The error that produces the extra chromosome occurs at random, meaning the error is not hereditary or passed down from parent to child. Research suggests that older mothers might be slightly more likely to have a son with KS. However, the extra X chromosome in KS comes from the father about one-half of the time.

What Are Common Symptoms Of Klinefelter Syndrome (KS)?

Because XXY males do not really appear different from other males and because they may not have any or have mild symptoms, XXY males often don't know they have KS.

In other cases, males with KS may have mild or severe symptoms. Whether or not a male with KS has visible symptoms depends on many factors, including how much testosterone his body makes, if he is mosaic (with both XY and XXY cells), and his age when the condition is diagnosed and treated.

KS symptoms fall into these main categories:

- Physical Symptoms
- Language and Learning Symptoms
- Social and Behavioral Symptoms
- Symptoms of Poly-X KS

Physical Symptoms

Many physical symptoms of KS result from low testosterone levels in the body. The degree of symptoms differs based on the amount of testosterone needed for a specific age or developmental stage and the amount of testosterone the body makes or has available.

During the first few years of life, when the need for testosterone is low, most XXY males do not show any obvious differences from typical male infants and young boys. Some may have slightly weaker muscles, meaning they might sit up, crawl, and walk slightly later than average. For example, on average, baby boys with KS do not start walking until age 18 months.

After age 5 years, when compared to typically developing boys, boys with KS may be slightly:

- Taller

- Fatter around the belly

- Clumsier

- Slower in developing motor skills, coordination, speed, and muscle strength

Puberty for boys with KS usually starts normally. But because their bodies make less testosterone than non-KS boys, their pubertal development may be disrupted or slow. In addition to being tall, KS boys may have:

- Smaller testes and penis

- Breast growth (about one-third of teens with KS have breast growth)

- Less facial and body hair

- Reduced muscle tone

- Narrower shoulders and wider hips

- Weaker bones, greater risk for bone fractures

- Decreased sexual interest

- Lower energy

- Reduced sperm production

An adult male with KS may have these features:

- Infertility: Nearly all men with KS are unable to father a biologically-related child without help from a fertility specialist

- Small testes, with the possibility of testes shrinking slightly after the teen years

- Lower testosterone levels, which lead to less muscle, hair, and sexual interest and function

- Breasts or breast growth (called gynecomastia, pronounced)

In some cases, breast growth can be permanent, and about 10% of XXY males need breast-reduction surgery.

Language And Learning Symptoms

Most males with KS have normal intelligence quotients (IQs) and successfully complete education at all levels.

KS males may experience some of the following learning and language-related challenges:

- **A delay in learning to talk.**

- **Trouble using language to express their thoughts and needs.**

- **Trouble processing what they hear.**

- **Reading difficulties.**

By adulthood, most males with KS learn to speak and converse normally, although they may have a harder time doing work that involves extensive reading and writing.

Social and Behavioral Symptoms

Many of the social and behavioral symptoms in KS may result from the language and learning difficulties. For instance, boys with KS who have language difficulties might hold back socially and could use help building social relationships.

Boys with KS, compared to typically developing boys, tend to be:

- Quieter

- Less assertive or self-confident

- More anxious or restless

- Less physically active

- More helpful and eager to please

- More obedient or more ready to follow directions

In the teenage years, boys with KS may feel their differences more strongly. As a result, these teen boys are at higher risk of depression, substance abuse, and behavioral disorders. Some teens might withdraw, feel sad, or act out their frustration and anger.

As adults, most men with KS have lives similar to those of men without KS. They successfully complete high school, college, and other levels of education. They have successful and meaningful careers and professions. They have friends and families.

Contrary to research findings published several decades ago, males with KS are no more likely to have serious psychiatric disorders or to get into trouble with the law.

What Are The Treatments For Symptoms In Klinefelter Syndrome (KS)?

It's important to remember that because symptoms can be mild, many males with KS are never diagnosed ore treated.

The earlier in life that KS symptoms are recognized and treated, the more likely it is that the symptoms can be reduced or eliminated. It is especially helpful to begin treatment by early puberty. Puberty is a time of rapid physical and psychological change, and treatment can successfully limit symptoms. However, treatment can bring benefits at any age.

The type of treatment needed depends on the type of symptoms being treated.

- Treating Physical Symptoms

- Treating Language and Learning Symptoms

- Treating Social and Behavioral Symptoms

Treating Physical Symptoms

Treatment for Low Testosterone

About one-half of XXY males' chromosomes have low testosterone levels. These levels can be raised by taking supplemental testosterone. Testosterone treatment can:

- Improve muscle mass

- Deepen the voice

- Promote growth of facial and body hair

- Help the reproductive organs to mature

- Build and maintain bone strength and help prevent osteoporosis in later years

- Produce a more masculine appearance, which can also help relieve anxiety and depression

- Increase focus and attention

- There are various ways to take testosterone:

- Injections or shots, every 2 to 3 weeks

- Pills

- Through the skin, also called transdermal; current methods include wearing a testosterone patch or rubbing testosterone gel on the skin

177

Males taking testosterone treatment should work closely with an endocrinologist, a doctor who specializes in hormones and their functions, to ensure the best outcome from testosterone therapy.

Is testosterone therapy right for every XXY male?

Not all males with XXY condition benefit from testosterone therapy.

For males whose testosterone level is low to normal, the benefits of taking testosterone are less clear than for when testosterone is very low. Side effects, although generally mild, can include acne, skin rashes from patches or gels, breathing problems (especially during sleep), and higher risk of an enlarged prostate gland or prostate cancer in older age. In addition, testosterone supplementation will not increase testicular size, decrease breast growth, or correct infertility.

Although the majority of boys with KS grow up to live as males, some develop atypical gender identities. For these males, supplemental testosterone may not be suitable. Gender identity should be discussed with health care specialists before starting treatment.

Treatment for Enlarged Breasts

No approved drug treatment exists for this condition of over-developed breast tissue, termed gynecomastia. Some health care providers recommend surgery—called mastectomy—to remove or reduce the breasts of XXY males.

When adult men have breasts, they are at higher risk for breast cancer than other men and need to be checked for this condition regularly. The mastectomy lowers the risk of cancer and can reduce the social stress associated with XXY males having enlarged breasts.

Because it is a surgical procedure, mastectomy carries a variety of risks. XXY males who are thinking about mastectomy should discuss all the risks and benefits with their health care provider.

Treatment for Infertility

Between 95% and 99% of XXY men are infertile because they do not produce enough sperm to fertilize an egg naturally. But, sperm are found in more than 50% of men with KS.

Advances in assistive reproductive technology (ART) have made it possible for some men with KS to conceive. One type of ART, called testicular sperm extraction with intracytoplasmic sperm injection (TESE-ICSI), has shown success for XXY males. For this procedure, a surgeon removes sperm from the testes and places one sperm into an egg.

Like all ART, TESE-ICSI carries both risks and benefits. For instance, it is possible that the resulting child might have the XXY condition. In addition, the procedure is expensive and is often is not covered by health insurance plans. Importantly, there is no guarantee the procedure will work.

Recent studies suggest that collecting sperm from adolescent XXY males and freezing the sperm until later might result in more pregnancies during subsequent fertility treatments. This is because although XXY males may make some healthy sperm during puberty, this becomes more difficult as they leave adolescence and enter adulthood.

Treating Language And Learning Symptoms

Some, but not all, children with KS have language development and learning delays. They might be slow to learn to talk, read, and write, and they might have difficulty processing what they hear. But various interventions, such as speech therapy and educational assistance, can help to reduce and even eliminate these difficulties. The earlier treatment begins, the better the outcomes.

Parents might need to bring these types of problems to the teacher's attention. Because these boys can be quiet and cooperative in the classroom, teachers may not notice the need for help.

Boys and men with KS can benefit by visiting therapists who are experts in areas such as coordination, social skills, and coping. XXY males might benefit from any or all of the following:

Physical therapists design activities and exercises to build motor skills and strength and to improve muscle control, posture, and balance.

Occupational therapists help build skills needed for daily functioning, such as social and play skills, interaction and conversation skills, and job or career skills that match interests and abilities.

Behavioral therapists help with specific social skills, such as asking other kids to play and starting conversations. They can also teach productive ways of handling frustration, shyness, anger, and other emotions that can arise from feeling "different."

Mental health therapists or counselors help males with KS find ways to cope with feelings of sadness, depression, self-doubt, and low self-esteem. They can also help with substance abuse problems. These professionals can also help families deal with the emotions of having a son with KS.

Family therapists provide counseling to a man with KS, his spouse, partner, or family. They can help identify relationship problems and help patients develop communication skills and understand other people's needs.

Parents of XXY males have also mentioned that taking part in **physical activities at low-key levels,** such as karate, swimming, tennis, and golf, were helpful in improving motor skills, coordination, and confidence.

With regard to education, some boys with KS will qualify to receive state-sponsored special needs services to address their developmental and learning symptoms. But, because these symptoms may be mild, many XXY males will not be eligible for these services. Families can contact a local school district official or special education coordinator to learn more about whether XXY males can receive the following free services:

- The Early Intervention Program for Infants and Toddlers with Disabilities is required by two national laws, the Individuals with Disabilities and Education Improvement Act (IDEIA) and the Individuals with Disabilities Education Act (IDEA). Every state operates special programs for children from birth to age, helping them develop in areas such as behavior, development, communication, and social play.

- An Individualized Education Plan (IEP) for school is created and administered by a team of people, starting with parents and including teachers and school psychologists. The team works together to design an IEP with specific academic, communication, motor, learning, functional, and socialization goals, based on the child's educational needs and specific symptoms.

Treating Social And Behavioral Symptoms

Many of the professionals and methods for treating learning and language symptoms of the XXY condition are similar to or the same as the ones used to address social and behavioral symptoms.

For instance, boys with KS may need help with social skills and interacting in groups. Occupational or behavioral therapists might be able to assist with these skills. Some school districts and health centers might also offer these types of skill-building programs or classes.

In adolescence, symptoms such as lack of body hair could make XXY males uncomfortable in school or other social settings, and this discomfort can lead to depression, substance abuse, and behavioral problems or "acting out." They might also have questions about their masculinity or gender identity. In these instances, consulting a psychologist, counselor, or psychiatrist may be helpful.

Contrary to research results released decades ago, current research shows that XXY males are no more likely than other males to have serious psychiatric disorders or to get into trouble with the law.

Is There A Cure For Klinefelter Syndrome (KS)?

Currently, there is no way to remove chromosomes from cells to "cure" the XXY condition.

But many symptoms can be successfully treated, minimizing the impact the condition has on length and quality of life. Most adult XXY men have full independence and have friends, families, and normal social relationships. They live about as long as other men, on average.

If someone you know is diagnosed with KS:

- **Recognize your feelings.**
- **Educate yourself about the disorder.**
- **Be actively involved in your son's, family member's, or partner's/spouse's care.**
- **Encourage your son, family member, partner/spouse to do activities.**
- **Work with your teachers/educators and supervisors/co-workers.**
- Contact these people regularly to compare how he is doing at home and at school/work.
- When appropriate, encourage him to talk with his teachers, educators, supervisor, and co-workers. Suggest using brief notes, telephone calls, and meetings to identify problems and propose solutions.
- **Encourage your son's, family member's, partner's/spouse's independence.** Although it is important to be supportive, realize that watching over too much can send the message that you think he is not able to do things on his own.
- **Share the following information with health care providers about XXY problems:**

XXY males may have	Consider recommending
Delayed early expressive language and speech milestones	Early speech therapy and language evaluation
Difficulty during transition from elementary school to middle school or high school	Re-testing to identify learning areas that require extra attention at or before entrance to middle/high school
Difficulty with math at all ages	Testing to identify problem areas and remediation for math disabilities
Difficulty with complex language processing, specifically with understanding and creating spoken language	Language evaluation, increased opportunities to communicate through written language, possibly getting written notes from lectures/discussions
Decreased running speed, agility, and overall strength in childhood	Physical therapy, occupational therapy, activities that build strength

Frequently Asked Questions

Can KS Lead To Cancer?

Compared with the general male population, men with KS may have a higher chance over time of getting breast cancer, non-Hodgkin lymphoma, and lung cancer. There are ways to reduce this risk, such as removing the breasts and avoiding use of tobacco products. In general, XXY males are also at lower risk for prostate cancer.

If I Have KS, Will I Be Able To Get A Woman Pregnant?

It is possible that an XXY male could get a woman pregnant naturally. Although sperm are found in more than 50% of men with KS, low sperm production could make conception very difficult.

A few men with KS have recently been able to father a biologically related child by undergoing assisted fertility services, specifically, a procedure called testicular sperm extraction with intracytoplasmic sperm injection (TESE-ICSI). TESE-ICSI, this carries a slightly higher risk of chromosomal disorders in the child, including having an extra X.

What Is The Best Way To Teach Or Communicate With Males Who Have KS?

Research has identified some ways in which educators and parents can improve learning and communication among XXY males, including:

- Using images and visual clues
- Teaching them new words
- Encouraging conversation
- Using examples in language
- Minimizing distractions
- Breaking tasks into small steps
- Creating opportunities for social interaction and understanding
- Reminding them to stay focused

Chapter 37

Preconception Health And Health Care For Men

When most people hear the term preconception health, they think about women. However, preconception health is important for men, too. There are things men can do for their own health, as well as for the women and children in their lives.

1. Make A Plan And Take Action

Whether or not you've written them down, you've probably thought about your goals for having or not having children and how to achieve those goals. This is called a reproductive life plan. It's really important to have a plan and take action. Every woman, man, and couple can benefit from having a reproductive life plan based on her, his, or their own personal values, goals, and resources.

Questions To Get Started

When making a reproductive life plan, the following questions might be helpful. These are probably not all of the questions that you will want to ask yourself, but they will help you to get started.

Text in this chapter is excerpted from "Information For Men," Centers for Disease Control and Prevention (CDC), January 9, 2015; and text from "My Reproductive Life Plan," Centers for Disease Control and Prevention (CDC), August 27, 2014.

If you DO NOT want to have children, you might ask yourself:

- How do I plan to prevent pregnancy? Am I sure that I or my partner will be able to use the method chosen without any problems?
- What will I do if my partner becomes pregnant by accident?
- What steps can I take to be as healthy as possible?
- What medical conditions (such as diabetes, obesity, and high blood pressure) or other concerns (such as smoking, drinking alcohol, and using drugs) do I need to talk about with my doctor?
- Is it possible I could ever change my mind and want to have children one day?

If you DO want to have children one day:

- How old do I want to be when I start and when I stop having children?
- How many children do I want to have?
- How many years do I want between my children?
- What method do I plan to use to prevent pregnancy until I'm ready to have children? Am I sure that I or my partner will be able to use this method without any problems?
- What, if anything, do I want to change about my health, relationships, home, school, work, finances, or other parts of my life to get ready to have children?
- What steps can I take to be as healthy as possible, even if I'm not ready to have children yet?
- What medical conditions (such as diabetes, obesity, and high blood pressure) or other concerns (such as smoking, drinking alcohol, and using drugs) do I need to talk about with my doctor?

2. Prevent And Treat Sexually Transmitted Diseases (STDs)

Get screened and treated for any sexually transmitted diseases (STDs). Continue to protect yourself and your partner from STDs during pregnancy. Pregnancy does not provide a woman or the baby she is carrying any protection against STDs. The consequences of an STD can be significantly more serious, even life threatening, for a woman and her unborn baby if the woman becomes infected with an STD while pregnant. In addition, some STDs can cause infertility (not being able to get pregnant) in a woman.

3. Stop Smoking, Using "Street" Drugs, And Drinking Excessive Amounts Of Alcohol

Smoking, using "street" drugs, and drinking too much alcohol (binge drinking) is harmful to your health.

Secondhand smoke can cause early death and disease among children and adults who do not smoke. A pregnant woman who is exposed to secondhand smoke has 20% higher chance of giving birth to a baby with low birthweight than women who are not exposed to second-hand smoke during pregnancy.

In addition, drinking too much alcohol and using "street" drugs can cause infertility among men.

If you cannot stop drinking, smoking, or using drugs, get help! Contact your doctor or local treatment center.

4. Be Careful About Toxic Substances

Exposure to toxic substances and other harmful materials at work or at home, such as synthetic chemicals, metals, fertilizer, bug spray, and cat or rodent feces, can hurt the reproductive systems of men and women. They can make it more difficult for a couple to get pregnant. Exposure to even small amounts during pregnancy, infancy, childhood, or puberty can lead to certain diseases. Learn how to protect yourself and your loved ones from toxic substances and other harmful materials at work and at home.

5. Prevent Infertility

Sometimes a man is born with problems that affect his sperm. Other times, problems start later in life due to illness or injury. A man's sperm can be changed by his overall health and lifestyle. Some things that can reduce the health or number of sperm include:

- Type 1 diabetes
- Heavy alcohol use
- Some "street" drugs, such as marijuana, cocaine, and anabolic steroids
- Smoking cigarettes
- Age
- Obesity
- Hazardous substances, including bug spray and metals, such as lead
- Diseases such as mumps, serious conditions like kidney disease, or hormone problems
- Medicines (prescription, nonprescription, and herbal products)
- Radiation treatment and chemotherapy for cancer

If you are concerned about fertility, talk with your doctor or another health professional.

6. Reach And Maintain A Healthy Weight

People who are overweight or obese have a higher risk for many serious conditions, including heart disease, type 2 diabetes, and certain cancers. In addition, obesity among men is associated directly with increasing male infertility. People who are underweight also are at risk for serious health problems.

The key to achieving and maintaining a healthy weight isn't about short-term dietary changes. It's about a lifestyle that includes healthy eating and regular physical activity. Staying in control of your weight contributes to good health now and as you age.

If you are underweight, overweight, or obese, talk with your doctor or another health professional about ways to reach and maintain a healthy weight.

7. Learn Your Family History

Collecting your family's health history can be important for your child's health. You might not realize that your sister's heart defect or your cousin's sickle cell disease could affect your child, but sharing this family history information with your doctor can be important.

Based on your family history, your doctor might refer you for genetic counseling. Other reasons people go for genetic counseling include having had several miscarriages, infant deaths, or trouble getting pregnant (infertility) or a genetic condition or birth defect that occurred during a previous pregnancy.

8. Get Help For Violence

From infants to the elderly, violence affects people in all stages of life. The number of violent deaths tells only part of the story. Many more people survive violence and are left with lifelong physical and emotional scars.

If someone is violent toward you or you are violent toward your loved ones?get help. Violence destroys relationships and families. If you are violent, you can choose to stop.

9. Get Mentally Healthy

Mental health is how we think, feel, and act as we cope with life. To be at your best, you need to feel good about your life and value yourself. Everyone feels worried, anxious, sad, or stressed sometimes. However, if these feelings do not go away and they interfere with your daily life, get help. Talk with your doctor or another health care professional about your feelings and treatment options.

10. Support Your Partner

As partners, men can encourage and support the health of women. For example, if your partner is trying to eat healthier to get ready for pregnancy you can join her and eat healthier, too. Or if your partner has a medical condition, you can encourage her to see her doctor and remind her to follow her treatment plan.

Part Five
Pregnancy Prevention

Chapter 38

Teen Pregnancy Facts

Teen Pregnancy In The United States

In 2013, a total of 273,105 babies were born to women aged 15–19 years, for a live birth rate of 26.5 per 1,000 women in this age group. This is a record low for U.S. teens in this age group, and a drop of 10% from 2012. Birth rates fell 13% for women aged 15–17 years, and 8% for women aged 18–19 years. Still, the U.S. teen pregnancy rate is substantially higher than in other western industrialized nations.

While reasons for the declines are not clear, teens seem to be less sexually active, and sexually active teens seem to be using birth control than in previous years.

Disparities In Teen Birth Rates

Teen birth rates declined for all races and for Hispanics in 2013 from 2012. Among 15–19 year olds, from 2012–2013 teen birth rates decreased 9% for non-Hispanic whites, 11% for non-Hispanic blacks and American Indian/Alaska Natives (AI/AN), and 10% for Asian/ Pacific Islanders and Hispanics. Despite these declines, substantial disparities persist in teen birth rates, and teen pregnancy and childbearing continue to carry significant social and economic costs. In 2013, non-Hispanic black and Hispanic teen birth rates were still more than two times higher than the rate for non-Hispanic white teens, and American Indian/Alaska Native teen birth rates remained more than one and a half times higher than the white teen birth rate.

About This Chapter: Information in this chapter is excerpted from "About Teen Pregnancy," Centers for Disease Control and Prevention (CDC), June 9, 2014; and information from "NCHS Fact Sheet," Centers for Disease Control and Prevention (CDC), June 4, 2014.

Non-Hispanic black youth, Hispanic/Latino youth, American Indian/Alaska Native youth, and socioeconomically disadvantaged youth of any race or ethnicity experience the highest rates of teen pregnancy and childbirth. Together, black and Hispanic teens comprised 57% of U.S. teen births in 2013. CDC is focusing on these priority populations because of the need for greater public health efforts to improve the life opportunities of adolescents facing significant health disparities, as well as to have the greatest impact on overall U.S. teen birth rates. Other priority populations for CDC's teen pregnancy prevention efforts include young people in foster care and the juvenile justice system, and those otherwise living in conditions of risk.

The Importance Of Prevention

Teen pregnancy and childbearing bring substantial social and economic costs through immediate and long-term impacts on teen parents and their children.

- In 2010, teen pregnancy and childbirth accounted for at least $9.4 billion in costs to U.S. taxpayers for increased health care and foster care, increased incarceration rates among children of teen parents, and lost tax revenue because of lower educational attainment and income among teen mothers.

- Pregnancy and birth are significant contributors to high school drop out rates among girls. Only about 50% of teen mothers receive a high school diploma by 22 years of age, versus approximately 90% of women who had not given birth during adolescence.

- The children of teenage mothers are more likely to have lower school achievement and drop out of high school, have more health problems, be incarcerated at some time during adolescence, give birth as a teenager, and face unemployment as a young adult.

These effects remain for the teen mother and her child even after adjusting for those factors that increased the teenager's risk for pregnancy, such as growing up in poverty, having parents with low levels of education, growing up in a single-parent family, and having poor performance in school.

Overview

Teenage pregnancy rates dropped 44 percent overall from 1990 to 2009. The rate fell from its historic peak in 1990, 116.8 per 1,000 teenagers aged 15-19 years, to 65.3 in 2009. The 2009 pregnancy rate for teenagers was the lowest ever reported since the national series of estimates began in 1976.

Trends In Teen Pregnancy By Age

The declines in teenage pregnancy have been much steeper for younger than for older teenagers.

- The rate for teenagers 15-17 years of age dropped more than half, from 77.1 per 1,000 in 1990 to 36.4 in 2009.

- The rate for older teenagers 18-19 years of age fell as well, by 38 percent from its 1991 peak (172.1 per 1,000) to 106.3 in 2009.

- The rates in 2009 for these age groups were also lower than for any year during the 1976-2009 period.

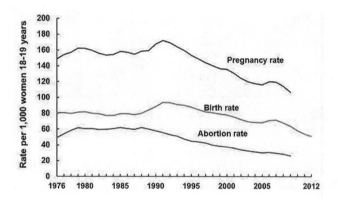

Figure 38.1. Pregnancy, Birth, And Abortion Rates

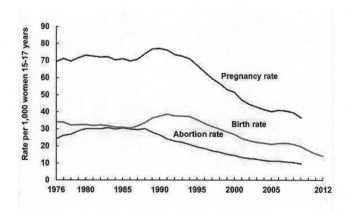

Figure 38.2. Pregnancy, birth, And Abortion Rates

Rates By Race And Hispanic Origin

Pregnancy rates dropped for teenagers in all race/Hispanic groups between 1990 and 2009. Overall, in 2009 pregnancy rates for non-Hispanic white and black teenagers aged 15-19 declined 51 percent each, with much larger declines for younger than for older teenagers in each group. The rates for Hispanic teenagers began to decline after 1992 (the peak year); the overall teen pregnancy rate for this group fell 42 percent from 1992 to 2009.

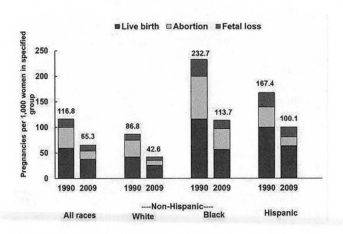

Figure 38.3. Pregnancy, Birth, Abortion And Fetal Loss Rates For Teenagers 15-19 Years By Race And Hispanic Origin

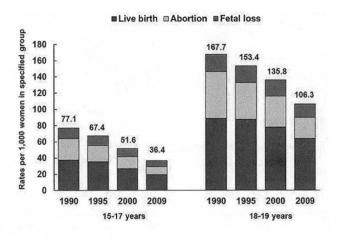

Figure 38.4. Pregnancy, Birth, Abortion And Fetal Loss Rates For Teenagers 15-17 And 18-19 Years

Changes In Pregnancy Rates By Outcome

All components of the pregnancy rates for teenagers aged 15-19 (births, abortions, and fetal losses) declined from 1990 through 2009. The teenage birth rate fell 39 percent from its 1991 peak (61.8 per 1,000) to 37.9 in 2009. As shown in the charts on the preceding page, the birth rates have continued to fall to record lows through 2012. Abortion rates for teenagers dropped more rapidly than birth rates, by 60 percent from 1990 (40.3 per 1,000) to 2009 (16.3 per 1,000).

Birth and abortion rates fell for Hispanic, non-Hispanic white and black teenagers 15-19 through 2009. Birth rates for each group fell about 40 percent or more during 1991-2009 and just-published data show that each rate has continued to drop through 2012. Abortion rates fell 49-70 percent for each group during 1991-2009.

Factors Accounting For The Recent Decline In Teen Pregnancy

The recent declines in teen pregnancy and childbearing are sustained, widespread, and broad-based. The declines have been attributed to a number of factors, including strong teen pregnancy prevention messages. The latest data from the 2006-2010 National Survey of Family Growth (NSFG) show a continuation of a long-term downward trend in the percent of teens who are sexually experienced and of a long-term upward trend in the use of contraception at first sex. Additionally, the NSFG has documented increased use of dual methods of contraception (that is, condoms and hormonal methods) among sexually active female and male teenagers. It has been suggested that the declining economy beginning in 2007 has likely played a role in the decreased rates for teenagers as well as for adult women under 40. Findings from the next release of the NSFG, based on interviews conducted September 2011-September 2013 (available in the Fall of 2014) are expected to help explain the most recent trends and variations in pregnancy and birth rates and the behavioral, social, and economic factors that account for them. Data from CDC's 2013 Youth Risk Behavior Surveillance System forthcoming in 2014 may also help to explain geographic patterns in these behaviors affecting teen pregnancy and birth rates.

Chapter 39

Birth Control: An Overview

What Is The Best Method Of Birth Control (Or Contraception)?

There is no "best" method of birth control. Each method has its pros and cons.

All women and men can have control over when, and if, they become parents. Making choices about birth control, or contraception, isn't easy. There are many things to think about. To get started, learn about birth control methods you or your partner can use to prevent pregnancy. You can also talk with your doctor about the choices.

Before choosing a birth control method, think about:

- Your overall health
- How often you have sex
- The number of sex partners you have
- If you want to have children someday
- How well each method works to prevent pregnancy
- Possible side effects
- Your comfort level with using the method

Keep in mind, even the most effective birth control methods can fail. But your chances of getting pregnant are lowest if the method you choose always is used correctly and every time you have sex.

About This Chapter: Information in this chapter is excerpted from "Birth control methods fact sheet," Office on Women's Health (OWH), July 16, 2012.

What Are The Different Types Of Birth Control?

You can choose from many methods of birth control. They are grouped by how they work:

Types Of Birth Control
- **Continuous abstinence**
- **Natural family planning/rhythm method**
- **Barrier methods**
  - Contraceptive sponge
  - Diaphragm, cervical cap, and cervical shield
  - Female condom
  - Male condom
- **Hormonal methods**
  - Oral contraceptives — combined pill ("The pill")
  - Oral contraceptives — progestin-only pill ("Mini-pill")
  - The patch
  - Shot/injection
  - Vaginal ring
- **Implantable devices**
  - Implantable rods
  - Intrauterine devices
- **Permanent birth control methods**
  - Sterilization implant
  - Surgical sterilization
- **Emergency contraception**

Detailed information on each type is provided in the following charts. Talk with your doctor if you have questions about any of the choices.

Continuous Abstinence

This means not having sex (vaginal, anal, or oral) at any time. It is the only sure way to prevent pregnancy and protect against sexually transmitted infections (STIs), including HIV.

Natural Family Planning/Rhythm Method

This method is when you do not have sex or use a barrier method on the days you are most fertile (most likely to become pregnant). You can read about barrier methods in the following chart.

A woman who has a regular menstrual cycle has about 9 or more days each month when she is able to get pregnant. These fertile days are about 5 days before and 3 days after ovulation, as well as the day of ovulation.

To have success with this method, you need to learn about your menstrual cycle. Then you can learn to predict which days you are fertile or "unsafe." To learn about your cycle, keep a written record of:

- When you get your period

- What it is like (heavy or light blood flow)

- How you feel (sore breasts, cramps)

This method also involves checking your cervical mucus and recording your body temperature each day. Cervical mucus is the discharge from your vagina. You are most fertile when it is clear and slippery like raw egg whites. Use a basal thermometer to take your temperature and record it in a chart. Your temperature will rise 0.4 to 0.8° F on the first day of ovulation. You can talk with your doctor or a natural family planning instructor to learn how to record and understand this information.

Hormonal Methods — Prevent Pregnancy By Interfering With Ovulation, Fertilization, And/Or Implantation Of The Fertilized Egg

Oral contraceptives — combined pill ("The pill")

The pill contains the hormones estrogen and progestin. It is taken daily to keep the ovaries from releasing an egg. The pill also causes changes in the lining of the uterus and the cervical mucus to keep the sperm from joining the egg.

Many types of oral contraceptives are available. Talk with your doctor about which is best for you.

Implantable devices — Devices that are inserted into the body and left in place for a few years.

Implantable rod

This is a matchstick-size, flexible rod that is put under the skin of the upper arm. It is often called by its brand name, Implanon. The rod releases a progestin, which causes changes in the lining of the uterus and the cervical mucus to keep the sperm from joining an egg. Less often, it stops the ovaries from releasing eggs. It is effective for up to 3 years.

Intrauterine devices or IUDs

An IUD is a small device shaped like a "T" that goes in your uterus.

Permanent Birth Control Methods — For People Who Are Sure They Never Want To Have A Child Or They Do Not Want More Children

Sterilization implant (essure)

Essure is the first non-surgical method of sterilizing women. A thin tube is used to thread a tiny spring-like device through the vagina and uterus into each fallopian tube. The device works by causing scar tissue to form around the coil. This blocks the fallopian tubes and stops the egg and sperm from joining.

It can take about 3 months for the scar tissue to grow, so it's important to use another form of birth control during this time. Then you will have to return to your doctor for a test to see if scar tissue has fully blocked your tubes.

Surgical sterilization

For women, surgical sterilization closes the fallopian tubes by being cut, tied, or sealed. This stops the eggs from going down to the uterus where they can be fertilized. The surgery can be done a number of ways. Sometimes, a woman having cesarean birth has the procedure done at the same time, so as to avoid having additional surgery later.

For men, having a vasectomy keeps sperm from going to his penis, so his ejaculate never has any sperm in it. Sperm stays in the system after surgery for about 3 months. During that time, use a backup form of birth control to prevent pregnancy. A simple test can be done to check if all the sperm is gone; it is called a semen analysis.

Emergency Contraception — Used If A Woman's Primary Method Of Birth Control Fails. It Should Not Be Used As A Regular Method Of Birth Control.

Emergency contraception (Plan B One-Step or Next Choice. It is also called the "morning after pill.")

Emergency contraception keeps a woman from getting pregnant when she has had unprotected vaginal intercourse. "Unprotected" can mean that no method of birth control was used. It can also mean that a birth control method was used but it was used incorrectly, or did not work (like a condom breaking). Or, a woman may have forgotten to take her birth control pills. She also may have been abused or forced to have sex. These are just some of the reasons women may need emergency contraception.

A single-pill dose or two-pill dose of emergency contraception is available over-the-counter (OTC) for women ages 17 and older.

Can All Types Of Birth Control Prevent Sexually Transmitted Infections (STIs)?

No. The male latex condom is the only birth control method proven to help protect you from STIs, including HIV. Research is being done to find out how effective the female condom is at preventing STIs and HIV.

How Well Do Different Kinds Of Birth Control Work? Do They Have Side Effects?

All birth control methods work the best if used correctly and every time you have sex. Be sure you know the right way to use them. Sometimes doctors don't explain how to use a method because they assume you already know. Talk with your doctor if you have questions. They are used to talking about birth control. So don't feel embarrassed about talking to him or her.

Some birth control methods can take time and practice to learn. For example, some people don't know you can put on a male condom "inside out." Also, not everyone knows you need to leave a little space at the tip of the condom for the sperm and fluid when a man ejaculates, or has an orgasm.

Here is a list of some birth control methods with their failure rates and possible side effects.

Table 39.1. Birth Control Methods, Failure Rates, And Side Effects

Method	Failure rate (the number of pregnancies expected per 100 women)	Some side effects and risks
Sterilization surgery for women	Less than 1 pregnancy	• Pain • Bleeding • Complications from surgery • Ectopic (tubal) pregnancy

Table 39.1. Continued

Method	Failure rate (the number of pregnancies expected per 100 women)	Some side effects and risks
Sterilization implant for women (Essure)	Less than 1 pregnancy	• Pain • Ectopic (tubal) pregnancy
Sterilization surgery for men	Less than 1 pregnancy	• Pain • Bleeding • Complications from surgery
Implantable rod (Implanon)	Less than 1 pregnancy Might not work as well for women who are overweight or obese.	• Acne • Weight gain • Ovarian cysts • Mood changes • Depression • Hair loss • Headache • Upset stomach • Dizziness • Sore breasts • Changes in period • Lower interest in sex
Intrauterine device (ParaGard, Mirena)	Less than 1 pregnancy	• Cramps • Bleeding between periods • Pelvic inflammatory disease • Infertility • Tear or hole in the uterus
Shot/injection (Depo-Provera)	Less than 1 pregnancy	• Bleeding between periods • Weight gain • Sore breasts • Headaches • Bone loss with long-term use
Oral contraceptives (combination pill, or "the pill")	5 pregnancies Being overweight may increase the chance of getting pregnant while using the pill.	• Dizziness • Upset stomach • Changes in your period • Changes in mood • Weight gain • High blood pressure • Blood clots • Heart attack • Stroke • New vision problems

Table 39.1. Continued

Method	Failure rate (the number of pregnancies expected per 100 women)	Some side effects and risks
Oral contraceptives (continuous/extended use, or "no-period pill")	5 pregnancies Being overweight may increase the chance of getting pregnant while using the pill.	• Same as combination pill • Spotting or bleeding between periods • Hard to know if pregnant
Oral contraceptives (progestin-only pill, or "mini-pill")	5 pregnancies Being overweight may increase the chance of getting pregnant while using the pill.	• Spotting or bleeding between periods • Weight gain • Sore breasts
Skin patch (Ortho Evra)	5 pregnancies May not work as well in women weighing more than 198 pounds.	• Similar to side effects for the combination pill • Greater exposure to estrogen than with other methods
Vaginal ring (NuvaRing)	5 pregnancies	• Similar to side effects for the combination pill • Swelling of the vagina • Irritation • Vaginal discharge
Male condom	11-16 pregnancies	• Allergic reactions
Diaphragm with spermicide	15 pregnancies	• Irritation • Allergic reactions • Urinary tract infection • Toxic shock if left in too long
Sponge with spermicide (Today Sponge)	16-32 pregnancies	• Irritation • Allergic reactions • Hard time taking it out • Toxic shock if left in too long
Cervical cap with spermicide	17-23 pregnancies	• Irritation • Allergic reactions • Abnormal Pap smear • Toxic shock if left in too long
Female condom	20 pregnancies	• Irritation • Allergic reactions
Natural family planning (rhythm method)	25 pregnancies	None

Table 39.1. Continued

Method	Failure rate (the number of pregnancies expected per 100 women)	Some side effects and risks
Spermicide alone	30 pregnancies It works best if used along with a barrier method, such as a condom.	• Irritation • Allergic reactions • Urinary tract infection
Emergency contraception ("morning-after pill," "Plan B One-Step," "Next Choice")	1 pregnancy It must be used within 72 hours of having unprotected sex. Should not be used as regular birth control; only in emergencies.	• Upset stomach • Vomiting • Lower stomach pain • Fatigue • Headache and dizziness • Irregular bleeding • Breast tenderness

Where Can I Get Birth Control? Do I Need To See A Doctor?

Where you get birth control depends on what method you choose.

You can buy these forms over the counter:

- Male condoms

- Female condoms

- Sponges

- Spermicides

- Emergency contraception pills (girls younger than 17 need a prescription)

You need a prescription for these forms:

- Oral contraceptives: the pill, the mini-pill

- Skin patch

- Vaginal ring

- Diaphragm (your doctor needs to fit one to your shape)

- Cervical cap

- Cervical shield

- Shot/injection (you get the shot at your doctor's office)

- IUD (inserted by a doctor)

- Implantable rod (inserted by a doctor)

You will need surgery or a medical procedure for:

- Sterilization, female and male

Are There Any Foams Or Gels I Can Use To Keep From Getting Pregnant?

You can buy spermicides over the counter. They work by killing sperm. They come in many forms:

- Foam
- Gel
- Cream
- Film
- Suppository
- Tablet

Spermicides are put in the vagina no more than 1 hour before having sex. If you use a film, suppository, or tablet, wait at least 15 minutes before having sex so the spermicide can dissolve. Do not douche or rinse out your vagina for at least 6 to 8 hours after having sex. You will need to use more spermicide each time you have sex.

Spermicides work best if used along with a barrier method, such as a condom, diaphragm, or cervical cap. Some spermicides are made just for use with the diaphragm and cervical cap. Check the package to make sure you are buying what you need.

All spermicides contain sperm-killing chemicals. Some contain nonoxynol-9, which may raise your risk of HIV if you use it a lot. It irritates the tissue in the vagina and anus, so it can cause the HIV virus to enter the body more freely. Some women are sensitive to nonoxynol-9 and need to use spermicides without it. Medications for vaginal yeast infections may lower the effectiveness of spermicides. Also, spermicides do not protect against sexually transmitted infections.

How Effective Is Withdrawal As A Birth Control Method?

Not very! Withdrawal is when a man takes his penis out of a woman's vagina (or "pulls out") before he ejaculates, or has an orgasm. This stops the sperm from going to the egg. "Pulling out" can be hard for a man to do. It takes a lot of self-control.

Even if you use withdrawal, sperm can be released before the man pulls out. When a man's penis first becomes erect, pre-ejaculate fluid may be on the tip of the penis. This fluid has sperm in it. So you could still get pregnant.

Withdrawal does not protect you from STIs or HIV.

Everyone I Know Is On The Pill. Is It Safe?

Today's pills have lower doses of hormones than ever before. This has greatly lowered the risk of side effects. But there are still pros and cons with taking birth control pills. Pros include having:

- More regular and lighter periods

- Fewer menstrual cramps

- A lower risk of ovarian and endometrial cancers, pelvic inflammatory disease (PID), noncancerous ovarian cysts, and iron deficiency anemia

Cons include a higher chance, for some women, of:

- Heart disease, high blood pressure, and blood clots

- Nausea, headaches, sore breasts, and weight gain

- Irregular bleeding

- Depression

Many of these side effects go away after taking the pill for a few months. Women who smoke, are older than 35, or have a history of blood clots or breast or endometrial cancer are more at risk of bad side effects and may not be able to take the pill. Talk with your doctor about whether the pill is right for you.

Will Birth Control Pills Protect Me From Sexually Transmitted Infections (STIs), Including HIV/AIDS?

No, they won't protect you. Birth control pills and most other birth control methods will not protect you from STIs, including HIV (the virus that causes AIDS). They only protect against pregnancy.

The male latex condom is the best birth control method that also can protect you from STIs, including HIV. If you are allergic to latex, polyurethane condoms are a good alternative. If your partner can't or won't use a male condom, female condoms also create a barrier that can help protect you from STIs.

It is important to only use latex or polyurethane condoms to protect you from STIs. "Natural" or "lambskin" condoms have tiny pores that may allow for the passage of viruses like HIV, hepatitis B, and herpes. If you use non-lubricated male condoms for vaginal or anal sex, you can add lubrication with water-based lubricants (like K-Y jelly) that you can buy at a drug store. Never use oil-based products, such as massage oils, baby oil, lotions, or petroleum jelly, to lubricate a male condom. These will weaken the condom, causing it to tear or break. Use a new condom with each sex act.

I've Heard My Girlfriends Talking About Dental Dams — What Are They?

The dental dam is a square piece of rubber that is used by dentists during oral surgery and other procedures. It is not a method of birth control. But it can be used to help protect people from STIs, including HIV, during oral-vaginal or oral-anal sex. It is placed over the opening to the vagina or the anus before having oral sex. You can buy dental dams at surgical supply stores.

Chapter 40

Barrier Birth Control Methods

Barrier Methods: Block Sperm From Reaching The Egg

Male Condom

Figure 40.1. Male Condom

What Is It?

- A thin film sheath placed over the erect penis.

About This Chapter: Information in this chapter is excerpted from "Birth Control: Medicines To Help You," U.S. Food and Drug Administration (FDA), January 8, 2015.

How Do I Use It?

- Put it on the erect penis right before sex.

- Pull out before the penis softens.

- Hold the condom against the base of the penis before pulling out.

- Use it only once and then throw it away.

How Do I Get It?

- You do not need a prescription.

- You can buy it over-the-counter or online.

Chance Of Getting Pregnant With Typical Use (Number Of Pregnancies Expected Per 100 Women Who Use This Method For One Year)

- Out of 100 women who use this method, 18 may get pregnant.

- The most important thing is that you use a condom every time you have sex.

Some Risks

- Irritation

- Allergic reactions (If you are allergic to latex, you can try condoms made of polyurethane).

Does It Protect Me From Sexually Transmitted Infections (STIs)?

- Yes. Except for abstinence, latex condoms are the best protection against HIV/AIDS and other STIs when used correctly and consistently.

Female Condom

Figure 40.2. Female Condom

What Is It?

- A thin, lubricated pouch that is put into the vagina. It consists of a nitrile (non-latex) sheath, a flexible outer ring, and a polyurethane inner ring to place in the vagina. Nitrile is also commonly used to make surgical gloves.

How Do I Use It?

- Put the female condom into the vagina before sex.

- Follow the directions on the package to be sure the penis stays within the condom during sex and does not move alongside the condom.

- Use it only once and then throw it away.

How Do I Get It?

- You do not need a prescription.

- You can buy it over-the-counter or online.

Chance Of Getting Pregnant With Typical Use (Number Of Pregnancies Expected Per 100 Women Who Use This Method For One Year)

- Out of 100 women who use this method, about 21 may get pregnant.

- The most important thing is that you use a condom every time you have sex.

Some Risks

- Discomfort or pain during insertion or sex.

- Burning sensation, rash or itching.

Does It Protect Me From Sexually Transmitted Infections (STIs)?

- Yes.

- Female condoms offer highly effective protection against both HIV and other STIs when used correctly and consistently.

Diaphragm With Spermicide

Spermicides containing N9 can irritate the vagina and rectum. It may increase the risk of getting the AIDS virus (HIV) from an infected partner.

Figure 40.3. Diaphragm With Spermicide

What Is It?

- A dome-shaped flexible disk with a flexible rim.

- Made from latex rubber or silicone.

- It covers the cervix.

How Do I Use It?

- You need to put spermicidal jelly on the inside of the diaphragm before putting it into the vagina.

- You must put the diaphragm into the vagina before having sex.

- You must leave the diaphragm in place at least 6 hours after having sex.

- It can be left in place for up to 24 hours. You need to use more spermicide every time you have sex.

How Do I Get It?

- You need a prescription.

- A doctor or nurse will need to do an exam to find the right size diaphragm for you.

- You should have the diaphragm checked after childbirth or if you lose more than 15 pounds. You might need a different size.

Chance Of Getting Pregnant With Typical Use (Number Of Pregnancies Expected Per 100 Women Who Use This Method For One Year)

- Out of 100 women who use this method, about 12 may get pregnant.

Some Risks

- Irritation, allergic reactions, and urinary tract infection.

- If you keep it in place longer than 24 hours, there is a risk of toxic shock syndrome. Toxic shock is a rare but serious infection.

Does It Protect Me From Sexually Transmitted Infections (STIs)?

No.

Sponge With spermide

Figure 40.4. Sponge With Spermide

Spermicides Containing N9 Can Irritate The Vagina And Rectum. It May Increase The Risk Of Getting The Aids Virus (HIV) From An Infected Partner.

What Is It?

- A disk-shaped polyurethane device with the spermicide nonoxynol-9.

How Do I Use It?

- Put it into the vagina before you have sex.

- Protects for up to 24 hours.

- You do not need to use more spermicide each time you have sex.

- You must leave the sponge in place for at least 6 hours after having sex.

- You must take the sponge out within 30 hours after you put it in. Throw it away after you use it.

How Do I Get It?

- You do not need a prescription.

- You can buy it over-the-counter.

Chance Of Getting Pregnant With Typical Use (Number Of Pregnancies Expected Per 100 Women Who Use This Method For One Year)

- Out of 100 women who use this method, 12 to 24 may get pregnant.

- It may not work as well for women who have given birth. Childbirth stretches the vagina and cervix and the sponge may not fit as well.

Some Risks

- Irritation

- Allergic reactions

- Some women may have a hard time taking the sponge out.

- If you keep it in place longer than 24-30 hours, there is a risk of toxic shock syndrome. Toxic shock is a rare but serious infection.

Does It Protect Me From Sexually Transmitted Infections (STIs)?

No.

Cervical Cap With Spermicide

Figure 40.5. Cervical Cap With Spermicide

Spermicides containing N9 can irritate the vagina and rectum. It may increase the risk of getting the AIDS virus (HIV) from an infected partner.

What Is It?

- A soft latex or silicone cup with a round rim, which fits snugly around the cervix.

How Do I Use It?

- You need to put spermicidal jelly inside the cap before you use it.
- You must put the cap in the vagina before you have sex.
- You must leave the cap in place for at least 6 hours after having sex.
- You may leave the cap in for up to 48 hours.
- You do NOT need to use more spermicide each time you have sex.

How Do I Get It?

- You need a prescription.

Chance Of Getting Pregnant With Typical Use (Number Of Pregnancies Expected Per 100 Women Who Use This Method For One Year)

- Out of 100 women who use this method, about 17 to 23 may get pregnant.
- It may not work as well for women who have given birth. Childbirth stretches the vagina and cervix and the cap may not fit as well.

Some Risks

- Irritation, allergic reactions, and abnormal Pap test.
- You may find it hard to put in.
- If you keep it in place longer than 48 hours, there is a risk of toxic shock syndrome. Toxic shock is a rare but serious infection.

Does It Protect Me From Sexually Transmitted Infections (STIs)?

No.

Spermicide Alone

Spermicides containing N9 can irritate the vagina and rectum. It may increase the risk of getting the AIDS virus (HIV) from an infected partner.

Figure 40.6. Spermicide Alone

What Is It?

•   A foam, cream, jelly, film, or tablet that you put into the vagina.

How Do I Use It?

• You need to put spermicide into the vagina 5 to 90 minutes before you have sex.

• You usually need to leave it in place at least 6 to 8 hours after sex; do not douche or rinse the vagina for at least 6 hours after sex.

• Instructions can be different for each type of spermicide. Read the label before you use it.

How Do I Get It?

• You do not need a prescription.

• You can buy it over-the-counter.

Chance Of Getting Pregnant With Typical Use (Number Of Pregnancies Expected Per 100 Women Who Use This Method For One Year)

• Out of 100 women who use this method, about 28 may get pregnant.

• Different studies show different rates of effectiveness.

Some Risks

• Irritation

• Allergic reactions

- Urinary tract infection
- If you are also using a medicine for a vaginal yeast infection, the spermicide might not work as well.

Does It Protect Me From Sexually Transmitted Infections (STIs)?

No.

Chapter 41

Using Condoms (Male And Female)

How Well Do Condoms Prevent HIV?

Condoms are an important tool in preventing the spread of HIV.

When used consistently and correctly, condoms are highly effective in preventing HIV. They are also effective at preventing sexually transmitted diseases (STDs) that are transmitted through bodily fluids, such as gonorrhea and chlamydia. However, they provide less protection against STDs spread through skin-to-skin contact like human papillomavirus (genital warts), genital herpes, and syphilis.

Although highly effective when used consistently and correctly, there is still a chance of getting HIV if you only use condoms, so adding other prevention methods can further reduce your risk.

Two Types Of Condoms

There are two types of condoms: male and female.

Male Condoms

- A male condom is a thin sheath worn over a man's erect penis to keep seminal fluid (cum) or pre-seminal fluid (pre-cum) from entering his partner's body during oral, anal, or vaginal sex.

About This Chapter: Information in this chapter is excerpted from "Using Condoms," U.S. Department of Health and Human Services (HHS), September 29, 2014.

- Male condoms are made of different substances. Latex condoms provide the best protection against HIV. Polyurethane (plastic) or polyisoprene (synthetic rubber) condoms are good options for people with latex allergies. Natural membrane condoms (such as those made out of lambskin) do not protect as well against HIV and certain other STDs because they are porous, meaning that infections can pass through them.

- Lubricants can help prevent condoms from breaking. Water-based and silicon-based lubricants are safe to use with latex condoms. However, oil-based lubricants (e.g., petroleum jelly, shortening, mineral oil, massage oils, body lotions, and cooking oil) should not be used with latex condoms because they can weaken latex and cause breakage.

Female Condoms

- A female condom is a thin pouch worn inside the woman's vagina to keep her partner's seminal fluid (cum) or pre-seminal fluid (pre-cum) from entering her body during intercourse. The female condom has a ring on each end. The inside ring holds the condom in place inside the vagina. The outer ring stays outside the vagina so it covers the labia.

- Female condoms are made of a rubber-like substance called nitrile. (They are not latex.)

- When worn in the vagina, female condoms are just as effective as male condoms at preventing STDs, HIV and pregnancy. Some people use female condoms for anal sex. However, we do not know how well female condoms prevent HIV and other STDs when used for anal sex. But we do know that HIV cannot travel through the nitrile barrier.

- It is safe to use either water-based or oil-based lubricants with nitrile female condoms.

How To Use A Condom Consistently And Correctly

Male and female condoms can be used to protect you from HIV or other STDs. But don't use them both at the same time. If used together, they won't stay in place, and they can tear or become damaged. Read the instructions on the condom package and practice before using them for the first time. Also, follow these guidelines:

Male Condom

- Keep male condoms in a cool, dry place. Don't keep them in your wallet or in your car. This can cause them to break or tear.

- Check the wrapper for tears and for the expiration date, to make sure the condom is not too old to use. Carefully open the wrapper. Don't use your teeth or fingernails. Make sure the condom looks okay to use. Don't use a condom that is gummy, brittle, discolored, or has even a tiny hole.

- Put on the condom as soon as the penis is erect, but before it touches the vagina, mouth, or anus.

- If the condom does not have a reservoir tip, pinch the tip enough to leave a half-inch space for semen to collect. Holding the tip, unroll the condom all the way to the base of the erect penis.

- Be sure to use adequate lubrication during vaginal and anal sex. Only use water-based or silicone-based lubricants. Don't use oil-based lubricants (e.g., petroleum jelly, shortening, mineral oil, massage oils, body lotions, and cooking oil) with latex condoms because they can weaken latex and cause breakage. Put the lubricant on the outside of the condom.

- After ejaculation and before the penis gets soft, grip the rim of the condom and carefully withdraw. Then gently pull the condom off the penis, making sure that semen doesn't spill out.

- Wrap the condom in a tissue and throw it in the trash where others won't handle it.

- If you feel the condom break at any point during sexual activity, stop immediately, withdraw, remove the broken condom, and put on a new condom.

- Use a new condom if you want to have sex again or in a different way.

Female Condom

- Store the female condom at normal room temperature.

- Check the wrapper for tears and for the expiration date, to make sure the condom is not too old to use. Carefully open the wrapper. Don't use your teeth or fingernails. Make sure the condom looks OK to use. The condom will be moist and may be slippery.

- Put the condom into the vagina up to eight hours before having sex, but before the penis touches the vagina. The condom cannot disappear inside your body.

- To insert the condom, squeeze the inner ring with your thumb and middle finger and insert it into the vagina like a tampon. Then, use your index finger to push the inner ring as far up as it will go, without twisting the condom. There should be about an inch of condom outside your vagina to allow for the condom to expand during sex.

- The condom comes pre-lubricated. But it is okay to use either water- or oil-based lubricants. Put the lubricant on the inside and outside of the condom.

- During sex, make sure the outer ring of the condom isn't pushed into your vagina.

- After sex, hold the condom in place while your partner withdraws his penis. Remove the condom before standing up. Grasp the outside ring and twist the condom to trap in fluid and gently remove. Or, you can hold the condom tight around your partner's penis and he can pull out his penis and the condom at the same time, being careful not to spill any fluid out of the condom.

- Wrap the condom in a tissue and throw it in the trash where others won't handle it.

- Use a new condom if you want to have sex again or in a different way.

Chapter 42

Other Birth Control Methods

Birth Control: Medicines To Help You

If you do not want to get pregnant, there are many birth control options to choose from. No one product is best for everyone. The only sure way to avoid pregnancy and sexually transmitted infections (STIs or STDs) is not to have any sexual contact (abstinence). This page lists FDA-approved products for birth control. Talk to your doctor, nurse, or pharmacist about the best method for you.

There Are Different Kinds Of Medicines And Devices For Birth Control:

- Barrier Methods

- Hormonal Methods

- Emergency Contraception

- Implanted Devices

- Permanent Methods

Some Things To Think About When You Choose Birth Control:

- Your health.

- How often you have sex.

- How many sexual partners you have.

About This Chapter: Information in this chapter is excerpted from "Birth Control: Medicines To Help You," U.S. Food and Drug Administration (FDA), January 8, 2015.

- If you want to have children in the future.

- If you will need a prescription or if you can buy the method over-the-counter.

- The number of pregnancies expected per 100 women who use a method for one year. For comparison, about 85 out of 100 sexually active women who do not use any birth control can expect to become pregnant in a year.

- This page lists pregnancy rates of typical use. Typical use shows how effective the different methods are during actual use (including sometimes using a method in a way that is not correct or not consistent).

Tell Your Doctor, Nurse, Or Pharmacist If You:

- Smoke.

- Have liver disease.

- Have blood clots.

- Have family members who have had blood clots.

- Are taking any other medicines, like antibiotics.

- Are taking any herbal products, like St. John's Wort.

To Avoid Pregnancy:

- No matter which method you choose, it is important to follow all of the directions carefully. If you don't, you raise your chance of getting pregnant.

- The best way to avoid pregnancy and sexually transmitted infections (STIs) is to practice total abstinence (do not have any sexual contact).

Hormonal Methods: Prevent Pregnancy By Interfering With Ovulation And Possibly Fertilization Of The Egg

Oral Contraceptives (Combined Pill)

"The Pill"

What is it?

- A pill that has two hormones (estrogen and progestin) to stop the ovaries from releasing eggs

- It also thickens the cervical mucus, which keeps sperm from getting to the egg.

Figure 42.1. Oral Contraceptives (Combined Pill)

How do I use it?

- You should swallow the pill at the same time every day, whether or not you have sex.

- If you miss one or more pills, or start a pill pack too late, you may need to use another method of birth control, like a condom

How do I get it?

- You need a prescription.

Chance of getting pregnant with typical use (Number of pregnancies expected per 100 women who use this method for one year)

- Out of 100 women who use this method, about 9 may get pregnant.

Some Side Effects

- Changes in your cycle (period)

- Nausea

- Breast tenderness

- Headache

Less Common Serious Side Effects

- It is not common, but some women who take the pill develop high blood pressure.

- It is rare, but some women will have blood clots, heart attacks, or strokes.

Does it protect me from sexually transmitted infections (STIs)?

No.

Oral Contraceptives (Progestin-only)

"The Mini Pill"

Figure 42.2. Oral Contraceptives (Progestin-Only)

What is it?
- A pill that has only one hormone, a progestin.
- It thickens the cervical mucus, which keeps sperm from getting to the egg.
- Less often, it stops the ovaries from releasing eggs.

How do I use it?
- You should swallow the pill at the same time every day, whether or not you have sex.
- If you miss one or more pills, or start a pill pack too late, you may need to use another method of birth control, like a condom.

How do I get it?
- You need a prescription.

Chance of getting pregnant with typical use (Number of pregnancies expected per 100 women who use this method for one year
- Out of 100 women who use this method, about 9 may get pregnant.

Some Side Effects
- Irregular bleeding
- Headache
- Breast tenderness

- Nausea

- Dizziness

Does it protect me from sexually transmitted infections (STIs)?

No.

Oral Contraceptives (Extended/Continuous Use)
"Pill"

Figure 42.3. Oral Contraceptives (Extended/Continuous Use) "Pill"

What is it?

- A pill that has two hormones (estrogen and progestin) to stop the ovaries from releasing eggs.

- It also thickens the cervical mucus, which keeps sperm from getting to the egg.

- These pills are designed so women have fewer or no periods.

How do I use it?

- You should swallow the pill at the same time every day, whether or not you have sex.

- If you miss one or more pills, or start a pill pack too late, you may need to use another method of birth control, like a condom.

How do I get it?

- You need a prescription.

Chance of getting pregnant with typical use (Number of pregnancies expected per 100 women who use this method for one year)

- Out of 100 women who use this method, about 9 may get pregnant.

Some Side Effects and Risks

- Risks are similar to other oral contraceptives with estrogen and progestin.

- You may have more light bleeding and spotting between periods than with 21 or 24 day oral contraceptives.

- It may be harder to know if you become pregnant, since you will likely have fewer periods or no periods.

Does it protect me from sexually transmitted infections (STIs)?

No.

Patch

Figure 42.4. Patch

What is it?

- This is a skin patch you can wear on the lower abdomen, buttocks, or upper arm or back.

- It has two hormones (estrogen and progestin) that stop the ovaries from releasing eggs

- It also thickens the cervical mucus, which keeps sperm from getting to the egg.

How do I use it?

- You put on a new patch and take off the old patch once a week for 3 weeks (21 total days).

- Don't put on a patch during the fourth week. Your menstrual period should start during this patch-free week.

- If the patch comes loose or falls off, you may need to use another method of birth control, like a condom.

How do I get it?

- You need a prescription.

Chance of getting pregnant with typical use (Number of pregnancies expected per 100 women who use this method for one year)

- Out of 100 women who use this method, about 9 may get pregnant.

Some Risks

- It will expose you to higher levels of estrogen compared to most combined oral contraceptives.

- It is not known if serious risks, such as blood clots and strokes, are greater with the patch because of the greater exposure to estrogen.

Does it protect me from sexually transmitted infections (STIs)?

No.

Vaginal Contraceptive Ring

Figure 42.5. Vaginal Contraceptive Ring

What is it?

- It is a flexible ring that is about 2 inches around.

- It releases two hormones (progestin and estrogen) to stop the ovaries from releasing eggs.

- It also thickens the cervical mucus, which keeps sperm from getting to the egg.

How do I use it?

- You put the ring into your vagina.

- Keep the ring in your vagina for 3 weeks and then take it out for 1 week. Your menstrual period should start during this ring-free week.

- If the ring falls out and stays out for more than 3 hours, replace it but use another method of birth control, like a condom, until the ring has been in place for 7 days in a row.

- Read the directions and talk to your doctor, nurse or pharmacist about what to do.

How do I get it?

- You need a prescription.

Chance of getting pregnant with typical use (Number of pregnancies expected per 100 women who use this method for one year)

- Out of 100 women who use this method, about 9 may get pregnant.

Some Side Effects and Risks

- Vaginal discharge, discomfort in the vagina, and mild irritation.

- Other risks are similar to oral contraceptives (combined pill).

Does it protect me from sexually transmitted infections (STIs)?

No.

Shot/Injection

Figure 42.6. Shot/Injection

What is it?

- A shot of the hormone progestin, either in the muscle or under the skin.

How does it work?

- The shot stops the ovaries from releasing eggs

- It also thickens the cervical mucus, which keeps the sperm from getting to the egg.

How do I get it?

- You need one shot every 3 months from a healthcare provider.

Chance of getting pregnant with typical use (Number of pregnancies expected per 100 women who use this method for one year)

- Out of 100 women who use this method, including women who don't get the shot on time, 6 may get pregnant.

Some Risks

- You may lose bone density if you get the shot for more than 2 years in a row.

- Bleeding between periods

- Headaches

- Weight gain

- Nervousness

- Abdominal discomfort

Does it protect me from sexually transmitted infections (STIs)?

No.

Emergency Contraception: May be used if you did not use birth control or if your regular birth control fails. It should not be used as a regular form of birth control

Plan B, Plan B One-Step, And Next Choice (Levonorgestrel)

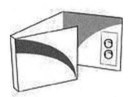

Figure 42.7. Plan B, Plan B One-Step, And Next Choice (Levonorgestrel)

What is it?

- These are pills with the hormone progestin.

- They help prevent pregnancy after birth control failure or unprotected sex.

How does it work?

- It works mainly by stopping the release of an egg from the ovary. It may also work by preventing fertilization of an egg (the uniting of sperm with the egg) or by preventing attachment (implantation) to the womb (uterus).

- For the best chance for it to work, you should start taking the pill(s) as soon as possible after unprotected sex.

231

- You should take emergency contraception within three days after having unprotected sex.

How do I get it?

- You can buy Plan B One-Step over-the-counter. You do not need a prescription.

- You can buy Plan B and Next Choice over-the-counter if you are age 17 years or older. If you are younger than age 17, you need a prescription.

Chance of getting pregnant

- Seven out of every 8 women who would have gotten pregnant will not become pregnant after taking Plan B, Plan B One-Step, or Next Choice.

Some Risks

- Nausea, vomiting, abdominal pain, fatigue and headache

Does it protect me from sexually transmitted infections (STIs)?

No.

Ella (Ulipristal Acetate)

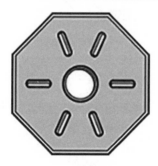

Figure 42.8. Ella (Ulipristal Acetate)

What is it?

- A pill that blocks the hormone progesterone.

- It helps prevent pregnancy after birth control failure or unprotected sex.

- It works mainly by stopping or delaying the ovaries from releasing an egg. It may also work by changing the lining of the womb (uterus) that may prevent attachment (implantation).

How do I use it?

- For the best chance for it to work, you should take the pill as soon as possible after unprotected sex.

- You should take Ella within five days after unprotected sex.

How do I get it?

- You need a prescription.

Chance of getting pregnant

- Six or 7 out of every 10 women who would have gotten pregnant will not become pregnant after taking ella.

Some Risks

- Headache
- Nausea
- Abdominal pain

- Menstrual pain
- Tiredness
- Dizziness

Does it protect me from sexually transmitted infections (STIs)?

No.

Implanted Devices: Inserted/Implanted Into The Body And Can Be Kept In Place For Several Years

Copper IUD

Figure 42.9. Copper IUD

What is it?

- A T-shaped device containing copper that is put into the uterus by a healthcare provider.

How does it work?

- The IUD prevents sperm from reaching the egg, from fertilizing the egg, and may prevent the egg from attaching (implanting) in the womb (uterus).

- It does not stop the ovaries from making an egg each month.

- The Copper IUD can be used for up to 10 years.

- After the IUD is taken out, it is possible to get pregnant.

How do I get it?

- A doctor or other healthcare provider needs to put in the IUD.

Chance of getting pregnant with typical use (Number of pregnancies expected per 100 women who use this method for one year)

- Out of 100 women who use this method, less than 1 may get pregnant.

Some Side Effects

- Cramps

- Irregular bleeding

Uncommon Risks

- Pelvic inflammatory disease

- Infertility

Rare Risk

- IUD is stuck in the uterus or found outside the uterus.

- Life-threatening infection.

Does it protect me from sexually transmitted infections (STIs)?

No.

IUD With Progestin

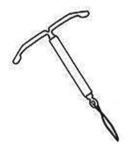

Figure 42.10. IUD With Progestin

What is it?

- A T-shaped device containing a progestin that is put into the uterus by a healthcare provider.

How does it work?

- It may thicken the mucus of your cervix, which makes it harder for sperm to get to the egg, and also thins the lining of your uterus.

- After a doctor or other healthcare provider puts in the IUD, it can be used for up to 3 to 5 years, depending on the type.

- After the IUD is taken out, it is possible to get pregnant.

How do I get it?

- A doctor or other healthcare provider needs to put in the IUD.

Chance of getting pregnant with typical use(Number of pregnancies expected per 100 women who use this method for one year

- Out of 100 women who use this method, less than 1 may get pregnant.

Some Side Effects

- Irregular bleeding

- No periods

- Abdominal/pelvic pain

- Ovarian cysts

Uncommon Risks

- Pelvic inflammatory disease

- Infertility

Rare Risk

- IUD is stuck in the uterus or found outside the uterus

- Life-threatening infection.

Does it protect me from sexually transmitted infections (STIs)?

No.

Implantable Rod

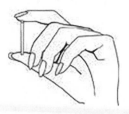

Figure 42.11. Implantable Rod

What is it?

- A thin, matchstick-sized rod that contains the hormone progestin.

- It is put under the skin on the inside of your upper arm.

How does it work?

- It stops the ovaries from releasing eggs.

- It thickens the cervical mucus, which keeps sperm from getting to the egg.

- It can be used for up to 3 years.

How do I get it?

- After giving you local anesthesia, a doctor or nurse will put it under the skin of your arm with a special needle.

Chance of getting pregnant with typical use (Number of pregnancies expected per 100 women who use this method for one year)

- Out of 100 women who use this method, less than 1 may get pregnant.

Some Side Effects

- changes in bleeding patterns

- weight gain

- breast and abdominal pain

Does it protect me from sexually transmitted infections (STIs)?

No.

Permanent Methods: For People Who Are Sure They Never Want To Have A Child Or Do Not Want Any More Children.

Sterilization Surgery For Men (Vasectomy)

This method is for men who are sure they never want to have a child or do not want any more children. If you are thinking about reversal, vasectomy may not be right for you. Sometimes it is possible to reverse the operation, but there are no guarantees. Reversal involves complicated surgery that might not work.

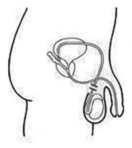

Figure 42.12. Sterilization Surgery For Men (Vasectomy)

What is it?

- This is a surgery a man has only once.

- It is permanent

How does it work?

- A surgery blocks a man's vas deferens (the tubes that carry sperm from the testes to other glands).

- Semen (the fluid that comes out of a man's penis) never has any sperm in it.

- It takes about three months to clear sperm out of a man's system. You need to use another form of birth control until a test shows there are no longer any sperm in the seminal fluid.

How do I get it?

- A man needs to have surgery.

- Local anesthesia is used.

Chance of getting pregnant with typical use (Number of pregnancies expected per 100 women who use this method for one year)

- Out of 100 women whose partner has had a vasectomy, less than 1 may get pregnant.

Some Risks

- Pain

- Bleeding

- Infection

Does it protect me from sexually transmitted infections (STIs)?

No.

The success of reversal surgery depends on:

- The length of time since the vasectomy was performed.

- Whether or not antibodies to sperm have developed.

- The method used for vasectomy

- Length and location of the segments of vas deferens that were removed or blocked.

Sterilization Surgery For Women

Surgical Implant (Also Called Trans-Abdominal Surgical Sterilization)

What is it?

- A device is placed on the outside of each fallopian tube.

How does it work?

- One way is by tying and cutting the tubes — this is called tubal ligation. The fallopian tubes also can be sealed using an instrument with an electrical current. They also can be closed with clips, clamps, or rings. Sometimes, a small piece of the tube is removed.

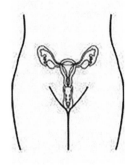

Figure 42.13. Surgical Implant

- The woman's fallopian tubes are blocked so the egg and sperm can't meet in the fallopian tube. This stops you from getting pregnant.
- This is a surgery a woman has only once.
- It is permanent.

How do I get it?
- This is a surgery you ask for.
- You will need general anesthesia.

Chance of getting pregnant with typical use (Number of pregnancies expected per 100 women who use this method for one year)
- Out of 100 women who use this method, less than 1 may get pregnant.

Some Risks
- Pain
- Bleeding
- Infection or other complications after surgery
- Ectopic (tubal) pregnancy

Does it protect me from sexually transmitted infections (STIs)?
No.

Sterilization Implant for Women (Transcervical Surgical Sterilization Implant)

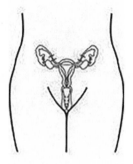

Figure 42.14. Sterilization Implant For Women

What is it?

- Small flexible, metal coil that is put into the fallopian tubes through the vagina.

- The device works by causing scar tissue to form around the coil. This blocks the fallopian tubes and stops you from getting pregnant.

How does it work?

- The device is put inside the fallopian tube with a special catheter.

- You need to use another birth control method during the first 3 months. You will need an X-ray to make sure the device is in the right place.

- It is permanent.

How do I get it?

- The devices are placed into the tubes using a camera placed in the uterus.

- Once the tubes are found, the devices are inserted. No skin cutting (incision) is needed.

- You may need local anesthesia.

- Since it is inserted through the vagina, you do not need an incision (cutting).

Chance of getting pregnant with typical use (Number of pregnancies expected per 100 women who use this method for one year)

- Out of 100 women who use this method, less than 1 may get pregnant.

Some Risks

- Mild to moderate pain after insertion

- Ectopic (tubal) pregnancy

Does it protect me from sexually transmitted infections (STIs)?

No.

Chapter 43

Fertility Awareness

About This Chapter: Information in this chapter is excerpted from "Fertility Awareness (Natural Family Planning)," Office of Population Affairs (OPA), a component of the U.S. Department of Health and Human Services (HHS), August 2014.

What Is Fertility Awareness?

Fertility awareness-based methods help women and couples understand how to avoid pregnancy or how to become pregnant. A woman learns to recognize signs of her fertile days. She is most likely to become pregnant (conceive) during her fertile days.

A woman with a 28-day menstrual cycle has about 6 days a month when she can get pregnant. These include the five days before she ovulates (when an egg is released) and the day she ovulates. As most women have variable menstrual cycles, fertility awareness methods teach women and couples how to monitor the fertile phase. Predicting the fertile phase can be more difficult in women with variable length cycles.

Fertility awareness involves paying close attention to the menstrual cycle by using methods that include:

- Basal Body Temperature Method (BBT)
- Cervical Mucus Method
- Computation of Standard Days

When the BBT and cervical mucus methods are used together, it is known as the *symptothermal method.*

Basal Body Temperature Method

Basal body temperature is the "baseline" temperature when you first wake up in the morning. During ovulation—when the ovaries release an egg and you can get pregnant—the basal temperature goes up a little. You can predict the days you are likely to be fertile if you track and record your basal temperature each day for a few months.

How it Works

Your basal temperature is typically between 96 and 98 degrees before you ovulate. After you ovulate, your temperature will rise just a bit, usually less than one degree. Such a small change is hard to detect and is best done with a basal body thermometer which is available at drug stores. Write down and keep track of your temperature each day.

Knowing when your temperature increases will not tell you for sure when you are fertile, but it can give a pretty good idea. You are most likely to get pregnant two to three days before your temperature peaks and the day after that. After your temperature has been higher for three days, the chances of getting pregnant drop.

Keep in mind that sperm can survive in a woman's body for up to a week after she has sex. And the best chance of pregnancy is if there are sperm present in a woman's tubes when an egg is released. If you have sex without birth control up to a week before and for a day or two after you ovulate, you have the greatest chance of getting pregnant.

Cervical Mucus Method

With this method, you pay attention to the changes that happen with your cervical mucus (such as color and thickness) over the month.

How it Works

Just after your period ends, there a few "dry days" when no mucus is present. These are days when you aren't likely to conceive (get pregnant).

As an egg gets ready to be released (known as ovulation), more mucus is produced and it's often cloudy or whitish with a sticky feel. These are fertile days and couples wishing to avoid pregnancy should not have unprotected sex on those days.

The most mucus is produced just before ovulation. Here, it's clear and slippery, like raw egg whites. It can be thick enough so it spreads apart on your fingers. **This is the time a woman is most likely to get pregnant.**

After three or four "slippery" days, less mucus is produced and anything you see is probably sticky and a darker "cloudy" color. This is usually followed by a few "dry" days before your period starts again. The time between the "slippery days' and when your period starts are when pregnancy isn't likely to happen.

Use a tissue or your fingers to check your mucus several times each day. Note whether it's cloudy and tacky or clear and slippery. Chart the changes on a calendar. You can label days as Dry, Sticky/Cloudy, and Slippery/Clear.

Standard Days Method

With the standard days method, you predict fertile days by charting and recording how long your menstrual cycles last.

How It Works

Track how many days each of your menstrual cycles last. Use a calendar and write down when each cycle starts, beginning with the first day of your period. Keep a record of how many days your cycle lasts each month.

To get the best information, you'll need to track and record how long your cycles last for at least six months to get a highly accurate charting of your menstrual cycle. If you can do this as long as 12 months, it's even better. To predict the first day you're likely to be fertile—the most likely time for you to get pregnant if you have sex without birth control—in your new cycle:

- You will need your menstrual cycle information from at least the past six months, a calendar and a pen.

- Subtract 18 days from the total days of your shortest cycle. Take that number and count ahead from the very first day of your next period (count the day your period begins).

- Example: your shortest cycle lasted 27 days. 27-18= 9 days. On your calendar circle the date your next period starts, and beginning with that day count ahead 9 days. So if you period starts on the 2nd day of the month, you'd count ahead to the 10th day of the month. Put an "X" on the calendar for that day.

To predict the last day you're likely to be fertile in the cycle:

- Subtract 11 days from the total days of your longest cycle. Take that number and count ahead from the very first day of your next period (count the day your period begins).

- Example: your longest cycle lasted 29 days. 29-11=18 days. On your calendar circle the date your next period begins, and starting with that day count ahead 18 days. If your period starts on the 2nd day of the month, you'd count ahead to the 19th day of the month. Put an "X" on the calendar for that day.

The days between the two "X's" are when you're most likely to get pregnant. If you don't want to get pregnant, then don't have sex on those days, or use birth control (like a condom, diaphragm, or cervical cap).

Keep this in mind: the standard days method can predict the days you are most likely to be fertile, but isn't always 100% accurate, especially if your cycles don't always last the same number of days. It's best to use other fertility awareness methods, too.

Certain devices such as Cycle Beads can also help you track your cycle.

How Effective Is Fertility Awareness?

Of 100 couples who use natural family planning methods each year, up to 25 may become pregnant. Couples using more than one method correctly will increase the ability to accurately identify the fertile period.

Advantages Of Fertility Awareness Methods

- Fertility awareness methods are safe and reasonably effective in preventing pregnancy.

- These methods can help you avoid pregnancy. They can also work if you want to become pregnant by helping to predict which days you are most fertile.

- These methods are relatively inexpensive and do not require an office visit, although it's an excellent idea to discuss your plan with a healthcare provider. To find a family planning center near you, use the family planning clinic locator found at www.hhs.gov/opa/

- Natural family planning has no side effects other than pregnancy and does not cause problems with using medication.

- Fertility awareness methods are good to use if preventing pregnancy is not your highest priority.

Drawbacks Of Fertility Awareness Methods

- Your partner must agree and cooperate.

- Fertility awareness methods provide no protection against sexually transmitted infections (STIs) including HIV.

- Most women don't have totally regular menstrual cycles or periods, so you cannot definitely know the exact days you can get pregnant.

- Fertility awareness takes time and effort each day to track days of menstrual cycle, chart temperature and/or cervical mucus.

- Viral infections that cause low-grade fevers can affect basal body temperature.

- Some medications such as antibiotics or antihistamines may change cervical mucus.

- If preventing pregnancy is a high priority, more effective methods of birth control should be chosen.

Chapter 44

Withdrawal

What Is Withdrawal All About?

Withdrawal, or the pull-out method, has been practiced for centuries, to avoid the risk of unwanted pregnancy during sexual intercourse. Scientifically known as *Coitus interruptus* (Latin for interrupted intercourse), withdrawal happens when a man removes his penis from the vagina before ejaculating (the moment when semen spurts out of the penis).

What Is The Logic Behind Withdrawal?

Withdrawal prevents sperm from entering the woman's vagina, thereby preventing contact between the sperm and the egg.

Why Use Withdrawal?

Withdrawal continues to be a popular birth control method among younger couples. There are a number of factors that make this an attractive option including:

- it can be used when no other method is available

- is free

- has none of the side effects that can be associated with other birth control methods.

Is Withdrawal Fail Proof?

No. For a number of reasons withdrawal is an unreliable form of birth control.

"Withdrawal," © 2016 Omnigraphics, Inc. Reviewed November 2015.

The practice of withdrawal requires a lot of trust, self-control and experience. It requires the male partner to know the sexual responses of his own body so as to know when to pull out. It is generally not recommended for teens and sexually inexperienced men. If done incorrectly and a man is unable to predict, and unable to control the exact moment of his ejaculation this method could be very ineffective.

What Are The Risks?

Even if the guy pulls out in time, there is still a risk of pregnancy from pre-ejaculate, or pre-cum sperm that is still in the urinary tract from a previous ejaculation. It is advisable for a guy to urinate, to get rid of all the pre-cum from the urethra before intercourse and clean properly to get rid of any fluid, before having intercourse again.

While withdrawal may prevent unwanted pregnancy if practiced correctly, it does not protect the couple engaged in intercourse from the risk of sexually transmitted diseases (STDs) and human immunodeficiency virus (HIV). It is always wiser to protect yourself from the risk of pregnancy, STDs and the transmission of HIV by correctly and consistently using male latex condoms and/or other contraceptive methods.

For women who do not want to risk pregnancy due to medical or personal reasons, it is always better to rely on other forms of birth control such as diaphragms, caps, or a female condom.

References:

1. "Withdrawal method (*coitus interruptus*)." Mayo Clinic Staff, March 5, 2015.

2. Dr. David Delvin. "*Coitus interruptus* (Withdrawal method)." NetDoctor, December, 22 2014.

Part Six
Sexually Transmitted Diseases (STDs)

Chapter 45

Sexually Transmitted Diseases (STDs) – An Overview

What Are STDs And STIs?

What's the difference between STDs (sexually transmitted diseases) and STIs (sexually transmitted infections)? They are really the same thing. So why do some doctors use the word "infections" instead of "diseases"? Because the word "diseases" can make people think of having an obvious problem — but many STDs often have no signs or symptoms.

It can be hard to think about illness when you're feeling attracted to someone. But STDs are serious stuff, and you owe it to yourself to know the facts.

STDs spread very easily, and young people have been hit hard by them. In fact, 1 out of 4 teenage girls has an STD.

Untreated STDs can cause some scary health problems. These include problems with your reproductive system, like not being able to have children when you want to. And they include pain, cancer, and permanent damage to your body.

What Are STDs (STIs)?

Sexually transmitted diseases or STDs (also called sexually transmitted infections or STIs) are caused by many different bacteria and viruses — and even tiny insects. You can get an STD by having sexual contact with someone who already has one. That means you can get an STD

About This Chapter: Information in this chapter is excerpted from "What Are STDs And STIs?" Office on Women's Health (OWH), April 15, 2014.

through sexual intercourse, or by putting your mouth, hands, or genitals on the genitals or on the sores of someone who is infected.

Keep in mind that women who have sex with women also are at risk for some STDs.

Can STDs Be Cured For Good?

Some STDs can be treated and cured and will go away completely. Even if you get treated, though, you can get the STD again if you continue to have sex — especially if you have unprotected sex.

Ask your doctor or nurse about treatment for your partner. Otherwise, you might just keep giving the infection back and forth to each other.

Some STDs can't be cured, but you can get help with the symptoms. A few STDs can put your life in danger if they are not treated.

How Can I Keep From Getting STDs?

The surest way to avoid getting an STD is not to have sexual intercourse or other kinds of intimate sexual contact. Even waiting to have sex until you are older lowers your chances of getting an STD. It's also a good idea to stay away from drugs and alcohol, which can lead to having unsafe sex.

If you do have sex, you'll be safer if:

- Both you and your partner get tested for STDs (and treated if necessary)

- The two of you have sex only with each other

- You always use a latex condom (and use it correctly)

Lots of myths about STDs get passed around. Have you heard that you can prevent STDs by douching, urinating, or washing after sex? Well, unfortunately, none of these methods work.

There is no vaccine to prevent most STDs. But there are vaccines that can help prevent two STDs:

- The hepatitis B vaccine can help protect against this dangerous STD, which can damage your liver. Most people get the hepatitis B vaccine as babies, but it's a good idea to ask whether you've already gotten yours.

- The HPV vaccine guards against some forms of human papillomavirus . HPV can cause genital warts and cervical cancer.

254

How Do You Know If You Have An STD?

The only way to know if you have an STD is to be tested. You may have symptoms from an STD. But lots of infections have no symptoms, especially in the early stages. By the time symptoms do show up, the infection may already have done damage.

If you have symptoms that could be coming from an STD, like stomach pain, see a doctor right away. Also see a doctor if fluid comes out of your vagina that is yellow, gray, or green, or has a strong smell. A clear or whitish fluid could be normal discharge, but if it's new and you have been sexually active, ask your doctor about it.

If you are having sex — or have had sex even once — see your doctor to find out which STD tests you may need.

Do Condoms Protect Against STDs?

Latex condoms can lower your chances of getting HIV and some other STDs a lot. They don't totally remove the risk, though. And they work better at preventing some STDs than others.

Remember that you have to use condoms right and every time.

Who Can Get An STD?

Here are some key points about who can get an STD:

- Anyone who has sexual contact — including oral sex, anal sex, and contact between genital areas — can get an STD.

- STDs affect women and men of all ages and racial and ethnic backgrounds.

- Teenage girls and young women get STDs more easily than older women do.

- Young women who have sex with women are still at risk for STDs.

- Becoming sexually active at an earlier age and having more partners increase the chances of getting an STD.

- If you have sex with someone who has an STD you can catch it even if that person has no symptoms.

How Can I Get Tested For STDs?

Sometimes people are too scared or embarrassed to ask for STD information or testing. But keep in mind that many STDs are easy to treat — and dangerous if they're not detected and treated.

When you visit your doctor, he or she probably will examine your skin, throat, and genital area for sores, growths, and rashes. He or she also may look inside your vagina and at your cervix.

Your doctor may take a sample to test from:

- Fluid or tissue from your genital, vaginal, or anal areas

- Your blood

- Your urine (pee)

Of course, you may be nervous during these tests, but they usually are painless and quick.

When the doctor gets the results, he or she will let you know if you have an STD and what to do to take care of your health. Sometimes, your doctor may want to treat you even before you get your test results. If so, you should still follow up to get the results and any other care you need.

Can I Ask The Doctor Personal Questions About Sex And STDs?

Doctors and nurses are there to talk to you about anything you need to protect your health!

If you are worried about your doctor telling your parents or guardians you are having sex, ask about his or her privacy policy before you begin. It's possible your doctor may encourage you to talk to your parents. But in most states, doctors can't share information about your reproductive health (especially about STDs) with anyone else without your permission. They can share the information without your permission only in special situations, such as if they think you have been sexually abused.

If you're having sex, it's very important to see your doctor regularly. You also might suggest that your partner see a doctor, too. That way, your partner can get any necessary tests and helpful information to stay well, too.

What Should I Do If I Have An STD Or Think I May Have An STD?

If you think you have an STD, follow these important steps:

- **Try to talk to your parents/guardians.** If you don't feel like you can do this, talk to someone else you trust, like a nurse or a teacher.

- **Make an appointment right away to see a health care provider,** such as a pediatrician, an adolescent medicine specialist, or a gynecologist. Read more about people who can take care of your health. If you are worried about anyone knowing, keep in mind that you can get confidential care at a family planning clinic.

- **Be sure to tell your sexual partner if you think you have an STD.** Both of you should be tested and treated if necessary, or you can pass it back and forth. Remember that your partner can have the STD and not have any symptoms.

- **If you have an STD, follow your doctor's instructions carefully.**

- **Avoid all sexual activity while you are being treated for an STD.**

- **Some STDs like HPV (human papillomavirus) and HIV cannot be cured** and can be passed to someone else, even if you don't have symptoms. Talk with your doctor about ways to help protect your partner.

- For STDs that can be cured, get a follow-up test to make sure that the infection is gone.

- **If you think you might be pregnant, be sure to tell your doctor.** Some medicines aren't safe to take if you are pregnant, so you may need to take a different drug to treat the STD.

What Is PID?

PID stands for pelvic inflammatory disease. It is a serious infection in your reproductive system that you can get from having some STDs. PID can lead to problems like ongoing pain in your pelvic area and not being able to have a baby when you are ready.

Teen girls (and young women) who have sex are most at risk for PID. This is partly because having a cervix that is still developing increases the chances of getting STDs that can lead to PID. And the more sex partners you have, the greater your chances of getting PID.

If you want to avoid getting STDs, your best bet is not to have sex. Latex condoms can reduce the chance of getting STDs that can lead to PID, but you have to use condoms the right way and every time.

If you are having sex, make sure to see your doctor and get tested for STDs. Treating STDs early can help prevent PID.

Chapter 46
STD Prevention

Take Control

Protect yourself and your sexual partners. Effective strategies for reducing STD risk include:

Abstinence

The most reliable way to avoid infection is to not have sex (i.e., anal, vaginal or oral).

Vaccination

Vaccines are safe, effective, and recommended ways to prevent hepatitis B and HPV. HPV vaccines for males and females can protect against some of the most common types of HPV. It is best to get all three doses (shots) *before becoming sexually active.* However, HPV vaccines are recommended for all teen girls and women through age 26 and all teen boys and men through age 21, who did not get all three doses of the vaccine when they were younger. You should also get vaccinated for hepatitis B if you were not vaccinated when you were younger.

Mutual Monogamy

Mutual monogamy means that you agree to be sexually active with only one person, who has agreed to be sexually active only with you. Being in a long-term mutually monogamous relationship with an uninfected partner is one of the most reliable ways to avoid STDs. But

About This Chapter: Information in this chapter is excerpted from "Sexually Transmitted Diseases (STDs) – Prevention," Centers for Disease Control and Prevention (CDC), November 5, 2013; and information from "Condom Fact Sheet In Brief," Centers for Disease Control and Prevention (CDC), March 5, 2013.

you must both be certain you are not infected with STDs. It is important to have an open and honest conversation with your partner.

Reduced number of sex partners:

Reducing your number of sex partners can decrease your risk for STDs. It is still important that you and your partner get tested, and that you share your test results with one another.

Condoms

Correct and consistent use of the male latex condom is highly effective in reducing STD transmission. Use a condom every time you have anal, vaginal, or oral sex.

If you have latex allergies, synthetic non-latex condoms can be used. But it is important to note that these condoms have higher breakage rates than latex condoms. Natural membrane condoms are not recommended for STD prevention.

STDs, Including HIV

HIV Infection

- Consistent and correct use of latex condoms is highly effective in preventing sexual transmission of HIV, the virus that causes AIDS.

Other STDs and Associated Conditions

- Consistent and correct use of latex condoms reduces the risk for many STDs that are transmitted by genital fluids (STDs such as chlamydia, gonorrhea, and trichomoniasis).

- Consistent and correct use of latex condoms reduces the risk for genital ulcer diseases, such as genital herpes, syphilis, and chancroid, only when the infected area or site of potential exposure is protected.

- Consistent and correct use of latex condoms may reduce the risk for genital human papillomavirus (HPV) infection and HPV-associated diseases (e.g., genital warts and cervical cancer).

How to Use a Condom Consistently and Correctly

- Use a new condom for every act of vaginal, anal and oral sex throughout the entire sex act (from start to finish). Before any genital contact, put the condom on the tip of the erect penis with the rolled side out.

- If the condom does not have a reservoir tip, pinch the tip enough to leave a half-inch space for semen to collect. Holding the tip, unroll the condom all the way to the base of the erect penis.

- After ejaculation and before the penis gets soft, grip the rim of the condom and carefully withdraw. Then gently pull the condom off the penis, making sure that semen doesn't spill out.

- Wrap the condom in a tissue and throw it in the trash where others won't handle it.

- If you feel the condom break at any point during sexual activity, stop immediately, withdraw, remove the broken condom, and put on a new condom.

- Ensure that adequate lubrication is used during vaginal and anal sex, which might require water-based lubricants. Oil-based lubricants (e.g., petroleum jelly, shortening, mineral oil, massage oils, body lotions, and cooking oil) should not be used because they can weaken latex, causing breakage.

Put Yourself To The Test

Knowing your STD status is a critical step to stopping STD transmission. If you know you are infected you can take steps to protect yourself and your partners.

Be sure to ask your healthcare provider to test you for STDs—asking is the only way to know whether you are receiving the right tests. And don't forget to tell your partner to ask a healthcare provider about STD testing as well.

Many STDs can be easily diagnosed and treated. If either you or your partner is infected, both of you need to receive treatment at the same time to avoid getting re-infected.

Chapter 47

Chlamydia

What Is Chlamydia?

Chlamydia is a common STD that can infect both men and women. It can cause serious, permanent damage to a woman's reproductive system, making it difficult or impossible for her to get pregnant later on. Chlamydia can also cause a potentially fatal ectopic pregnancy (pregnancy that occurs outside the womb).

How Is Chlamydia Spread?

You can get chlamydia by having vaginal, anal, or oral sex with someone who has chlamydia.

Chlamydia can be spread:

- If your sex partner is male you can still get chlamydia even if he does not ejaculate (cum).

- If you've had chlamydia and were treated in the past, you can still get infected again if you have unprotected sex with someone who has chlamydia.

- If you are pregnant, you can give chlamydia to your baby during childbirth.

How Can I Reduce My Risk Of Getting Chlamydia?

The only way to avoid STDs is to not have vaginal, anal, or oral sex.

If you are sexually active, you can do the following things to lower your chances of getting chlamydia:

About This Chapter: Information in this chapter is excerpted from "Chlamydia - CDC Fact Sheet," Centers for Disease Control and Prevention (CDC), January 23, 2014.

- Being in a long-term mutually monogamous relationship with a partner who has been tested and has negative STD test results;

- Using latex condoms the right way every time you have sex.

Am I At Risk For Chlamydia?

Anyone who has sex can get chlamydia through unprotected vaginal, anal, or oral sex. However, sexually active young people are at a higher risk of getting chlamydia. This is due to behaviors and biological factors common among young people. Gay, bisexual, and other men who have sex with men are also at risk since chlamydia can be spread through oral and anal sex.

Have an honest and open talk with your health care provider and ask whether you should be tested for chlamydia or other STDs. If you are a sexually active woman younger than 25 years, or an older woman with risk factors such as new or multiple sex partners, or a sex partner who has a sexually transmitted infection, you should get a test for chlamydia every year. Gay, bisexual, and men who have sex with men; as well as pregnant women should also be tested for chlamydia.

I'm pregnant. How Does Chlamydia Affect My Baby?

If you are pregnant and have chlamydia, you can pass the infection to your baby during delivery. This could cause an eye infection or pneumonia in your newborn. Having chlamydia may also make it more likely to deliver your baby too early.

If you are pregnant, you should be tested for chlamydia at your first prenatal visit. Testing and treatment are the best ways to prevent health problems.

How Do I know If I Have chlamydia?

Most people who have chlamydia have no symptoms. If you do have symptoms, they may not appear until several weeks after you have sex with an infected partner. Even when chlamydia causes no symptoms, it can damage your reproductive system.

Women with symptoms may notice

- An abnormal vaginal discharge;

- A burning sensation when urinating.

Symptoms in men can include

- A discharge from their penis;

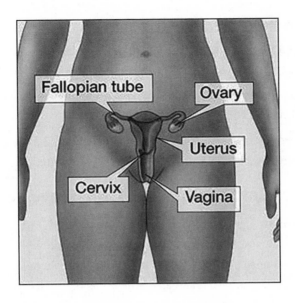

Figure 47.1. Female Anatomy Showing Fallopian Tubes, Ovary, Cervix, Uterus, And Vagina

- A burning sensation when urinating;

- Pain and swelling in one or both testicles (although this is less common).

Men and women can also get infected with chlamydia in their rectum, either by having receptive anal sex, or by spread from another infected site (such as the vagina). While these infections often cause no symptoms, they can cause

- Rectal pain;

- Discharge;

- Bleeding.

You should be examined by your doctor if you notice any of these symptoms or if your partner has an STD or symptoms of an STD, such as an unusual sore, a smelly discharge, burning when urinating, or bleeding between periods.

How Will My Doctor Know If I Have Chlamydia?

There are laboratory tests to diagnose chlamydia. Your health care provider may ask you to provide a urine sample or may use (or ask you to use) a cotton swab to get a sample from your vagina to test for chlamydia.

Can Chlamydia Be Cured?

Yes, chlamydia can be cured with the right treatment. It is important that you take all of the medication your doctor prescribes to cure your infection. When taken properly it will stop the infection and could decrease your chances of having complications later on. Medication for chlamydia should not be shared with anyone.

Repeat infection with chlamydia is common. You should be tested again about three months after you are treated, even if your sex partner(s) was treated.

I Was Treated For Chlamydia. When Can I Have Sex Again?

You should not have sex again until you and your sex partner(s) have completed treatment. If your doctor prescribes a single dose of medication, you should wait seven days after taking the medicine before having sex. If your doctor prescribes a medicine for you to take for seven days, you should wait until you have taken all of the doses before having sex.

What Happens If I Don't Get Treated?

The initial damage that chlamydia causes often goes unnoticed. However, chlamydia can lead to serious health problems.

If you are a woman, untreated chlamydia can spread to your uterus and fallopian tubes (tubes that carry fertilized eggs from the ovaries to the uterus), causing pelvic inflammatory disease (PID). PID often has no symptoms, however some women may have abdominal and pelvic pain. Even if it doesn't cause symptoms initially, PID can cause permanent damage to your reproductive system and lead to long-term pelvic pain, inability to get pregnant, and potentially deadly ectopic pregnancy (pregnancy outside the uterus).

Men rarely have health problems linked to chlamydia. Infection sometimes spreads to the tube that carries sperm from the testicles, causing pain and fever. Rarely, chlamydia can prevent a man from being able to have children.

Untreated chlamydia may also increase your chances of getting or giving HIV – the virus that causes AIDS.

Chapter 48

Gonorrhea

Anyone who is sexually active can get gonorrhea. Gonorrhea can cause very serious complications when not treated, but can be cured with the right medication.

What Is gonorrhea?

Gonorrhea is a sexually transmitted disease (STD) that can infect both men and women. It can cause infections in the genitals, rectum, and throat. It is a very common infection, especially among young people ages 15-24 years.

How Is Gonorrhea Spread?

You can get gonorrhea by having vaginal, anal, or oral sex with someone who has gonorrhea. A pregnant woman with gonorrhea can give the infection to her baby during childbirth.

How Can I Reduce My Risk Of Getting Gonorrhea?

The only way to avoid STDs is to not have vaginal, anal, or oral sex.

If you are sexually active, you can do the following things to lower your chances of getting gonorrhea:

- Being in a long-term mutually monogamous relationship with a partner who has been tested and has negative STD test results;

- Using latex condoms the right way every time you have sex.

About This Chapter: Information in this chapter is excerpted from "Gonorrhea - CDC Fact Sheet," Centers for Disease Control and Prevention (CDC), January 29, 2014.

Am I At Risk For Gonorrhea?

Any sexually active person can get gonorrhea through unprotected vaginal, anal, or oral sex.

If you are sexually active, have an honest and open talk with your health care provider and ask whether you should be tested for gonorrhea or other STDs. If you are a sexually active man who is gay, bisexual, or who has sex with men, you should be tested for gonorrhea every year. If you are a sexually active women younger than 25 years or an older women with risk factors such as new or multiple sex partners, or a sex partner who has a sexually transmitted infection, you should be tested for gonorrhea every year.

I'm Pregnant. How Does Gonorrhea Affect My Baby?

If you are pregnant and have gonorrhea, you can give the infection to your baby during delivery. This can cause serious health problems for your baby. If you are pregnant, it is important that you talk to your health care provider so that you get the correct examination, testing, and treatment, as necessary. Treating gonorrhea as soon as possible will make health complications for your baby less likely.

How Do I Know If I Have Gonorrhea?

Some men with gonorrhea may have no symptoms at all. However, men who do have symptoms, may have:

- A burning sensation when urinating;
- A white, yellow, or green discharge from the penis;
- Painful or swollen testicles (although this is less common).

Most women with gonorrhea do not have any symptoms. Even when a woman has symptoms, they are often mild and can be mistaken for a bladder or vaginal infection. Women with gonorrhea are at risk of developing serious complications from the infection, even if they don't have any symptoms.

Symptoms in women can include:

- Painful or burning sensation when urinating;
- Increased vaginal discharge;
- Vaginal bleeding between periods.

Rectal infections may either cause no symptoms or cause symptoms in both men and women that may include:

- Discharge
- Anal itching
- Soreness
- Bleeding
- Painful bowel movements

You should be examined by your doctor if you notice any of these symptoms or if your partner has an STD or symptoms of an STD, such as an unusual sore, a smelly discharge, burning when urinating, or bleeding between periods.

How Will My Doctor Know If I Have Gonorrhea?

Most of the time, urine can be used to test for gonorrhea. However, if you have had oral and/or anal sex, swabs may be used to collect samples from your throat and/or rectum. In some cases, a swab may be used to collect a sample from a man's urethra (urine canal) or a woman's cervix (opening to the womb).

Can Gonorrhea Be Cured?

Yes, gonorrhea can be cured with the right treatment. It is important that you take all of the medication your doctor prescribes to cure your infection. Medication for gonorrhea should not be shared with anyone. Although medication will stop the infection, it will not undo any permanent damage caused by the disease.

It is becoming harder to treat some gonorrhea, as drug-resistant strains of gonorrhea are increasing. If your symptoms continue for more than a few days after receiving treatment, you should return to a health care provider to be checked again.

I Was Treated For Gonorrhea. When Can I Have Sex Again?

You should wait seven days after finishing all medications before having sex. To avoid getting infected with gonorrhea again or spreading gonorrhea to your partner(s), you and your sex partner(s) should avoid having sex until you have each completed treatment. If you've had gonorrhea and took medicine in the past, you can still get infected again if you have unprotected sex with a person who has gonorrhea.

What Happens If I Don't Get Treated?

Untreated gonorrhea can cause serious and permanent health problems in both women and men.

In women, untreated gonorrhea can cause pelvic inflammatory disease (PID). Some of the complications of PID are

- Formation of scar tissue that blocks fallopian tubes;

- Ectopic pregnancy (pregnancy outside the womb);

- Infertility (inability to get pregnant);

- Long-term pelvic/abdominal pain.

In men, gonorrhea can cause a painful condition in the tubes attached to the testicles. In rare cases, this may cause a man to be sterile, or prevent him from being able to father a child.

Rarely, untreated gonorrhea can also spread to your blood or joints. This condition can be life-threatening.

Untreated gonorrhea may also increase your chances of getting or giving HIV – the virus that causes AIDS.

Chapter 49

Syphilis

What Is Syphilis?

Syphilis is an STD that can cause long-term complications if not treated correctly. Symptoms in adults are divided into stages. These stages are primary, secondary, latent, and late syphilis.

How Is Syphilis Spread?

You can get syphilis by direct contact with a syphilis sore during vaginal, anal, or oral sex. Sores can be found on the penis, vagina, anus, in the rectum, or on the lips and in the mouth. Syphilis can also be spread from an infected mother to her unborn baby.

What Does Syphilis Look Like?

Syphilis has been called 'the great imitator' because it has so many possible symptoms, many of which look like symptoms from other diseases. The painless syphilis sore that you would get after you are first infected can be confused for an ingrown hair, zipper cut, or other seemingly harmless bump. The non-itchy body rash that develops during the second stage of syphilis can show up on the palms of your hands and soles of your feet, all over your body, or in just a few places. Syphilis can also affect the eye and can lead to permanent blindness. This is called ocular syphilis. You could also be infected with syphilis and have very mild symptoms or none at all.

About This Chapter: Information in this chapter is excerpted from "Syphilis - CDC Fact Sheet," Centers for Disease Control and Prevention (CDC), January 29, 2014.

How Can I Reduce My Risk Of Getting Syphilis?

The only way to avoid STDs is to not have vaginal, anal, or oral sex.

If you are sexually active, you can do the following things to lower your chances of getting syphilis:

- Being in a long-term mutually monogamous relationship with a partner who has been tested and has negative STD test results;

- Using latex condoms the right way every time you have sex. Condoms prevent transmission of syphilis by preventing contact with a sore. Sometimes sores occur in areas not covered by a condom. Contact with these sores can still transmit syphilis.

Am I At Risk For Syphilis?

Any sexually active person can get syphilis through unprotected vaginal, anal, or oral sex. Have an honest and open talk with your health care provider and ask whether you should be tested for syphilis or other STDs. You should get tested regularly for syphilis if you are pregnant, are a man who has sex with men, have HIV infection, and/or have partner(s) who have tested positive for syphilis.

I'm Pregnant. How Does Syphilis Affect My Baby?

If you are pregnant and have syphilis, you can give the infection to your unborn baby. Having syphilis can lead to a low birth weight baby. It can also make it more likely you will deliver your baby too early or stillborn (a baby born dead). To protect your baby, **you should be tested for syphilis during your pregnancy and at delivery and receive immediate treatment if you test positive.**

An infected baby may be born without signs or symptoms of disease. However, if not treated immediately, the baby may develop serious problems within a few weeks. Untreated babies can have health problems such as cataracts, deafness, or seizures, and can die.

How Do I Know If I Have Syphilis?

Symptoms of syphilis in adults can be divided into stages:

Primary Stage

During the first (primary) stage of syphilis, you may notice a single sore, but there may be multiple sores. The sore is the location where syphilis entered your body. The sore is usually firm, round, and painless. Because the sore is painless, it can easily go unnoticed. The sore lasts 3 to 6 weeks and heals regardless of whether or not you receive treatment. Even though the sore goes away, you must still receive treatment so your infection does not move to the secondary stage.

Secondary Stage

During the secondary stage, you may have skin rashes and/or sores in your mouth, vagina, or anus (also called mucous membrane lesions). This stage usually starts with a rash on one or more areas of your body. The rash can show up when your primary sore is healing or several weeks after the sore has healed. The rash can look like rough, red, or reddish brown spots on the palms of your hands and/or the bottoms of your feet. The rash usually won't itch and it is sometimes so faint that you won't notice it. Other symptoms you may have can include fever, swollen lymph glands, sore throat, patchy hair loss, headaches, weight loss, muscle aches, and fatigue (feeling very tired). The symptoms from this stage will go away whether or not you receive treatment. Without the right treatment, your infection will move to the latent and possibly late stages of syphilis.

Latent and Late Stages

The latent stage of syphilis begins when all of the symptoms you had earlier disappear. If you do not receive treatment, you can continue to have syphilis in your body for years without any signs or symptoms. Most people with untreated syphilis do not develop late stage syphilis. However, when it does happen it is very serious and would occur 10–30 years after your infection began. Symptoms of the late stage of syphilis include difficulty coordinating your muscle movements, paralysis (not able to move certain parts of your body), numbness, blindness, and dementia (mental disorder). In the late stages of syphilis, the disease damages your internal organs and can result in death.

A syphilis infection is called an 'early' case if a patient has been infected for a year or less, such as during the primary or secondary stages of syphilis. People who have 'early' syphilis infections can more easily spread the infection to their sex partners. The majority of early syphilis cases are currently found among men who have sex with men, but women and unborn children are also at risk of infection.

How Will My Doctor Know If I Have Syphilis?

Most of the time, a blood test can be used to test for syphilis. Some health care providers will diagnose syphilis by testing fluid from a syphilis sore.

Can Syphilis Be Cured?

Yes, syphilis can be cured with the right antibiotics from your health care provider. However, treatment will not undo any damage that the infection has already done.

I've Been Treated. Can I Get Syphilis Again?

Having syphilis once does not protect you from getting it again. Even after you've been successfully treated, you can still be re-infected. Only laboratory tests can confirm whether you have syphilis. Follow-up testing by your health care provider is recommended to make sure that your treatment was successful.

Because syphilis sores can be hidden in the vagina, anus, under the foreskin of the penis, or in the mouth, it may not be obvious that a sex partner has syphilis. Unless you know that your sex partner(s) has been tested and treated, you may be at risk of getting syphilis again from an untreated sex partner.

Chapter 50
Chancroid

Chancroid is caused by infection with the bacterium Haemophilus ducreyi. Clinical manifestations include genital ulcers and inguinal lymphadenopathy or buboes. Reported cases of chancroid declined steadily between 1987 and 2001. Since then, the number of reported cases has fluctuated somewhat, while still appearing to decline overall. In 2014, a total of 6 cases of chancroid were reported in the United States. Only 3 states reported one or more cases of chancroid in 2014.

Although the overall decline in reported chancroid cases most likely reflects a decline in the incidence of this disease, these data should be interpreted with caution because Haemophilus ducreyi, the causative organism of chancroid, is difficult to culture; as a result, this condition may be underdiagnosed.

When infection does occur, it is usually associated with sporadic outbreaks. Worldwide, chancroid appears to have declined as well, although infection might still occur in some regions of Africa and the Caribbean. Like genital herpes and syphilis, chancroid is a risk factor in the transmission and acquisition of HIV infection

Treatment

Successful treatment for chancroid cures the infection, resolves the clinical symptoms, and prevents transmission to others. In advanced cases, scarring can result despite successful therapy.

About This Chapter: Information in this chapter is excerpted from "Other Sexually Transmitted Diseases," Centers for Disease Control and Prevention (CDC), November 17, 2015; and information from "Chancroid," Centers for Disease Control and Prevention (CDC), June 4, 2015.

Recommended Regimens

Azithromycin 1 g orally in a single dose

or

Ceftriaxone 250 mg IM in a single dose

or

Ciprofloxacin 500 mg orally twice a day for 3 days

or

Erythromycin base 500 mg orally three times a day for 7 days

Azithromycin and ceftriaxone offer the advantage of single-dose therapy. Worldwide, several isolates with intermediate resistance to either ciprofloxacin or erythromycin have been reported. However, because cultures are not routinely performed, data are limited regarding the current prevalence of antimicrobial resistance.

Other Management Considerations

Men who are uncircumcised and patients with HIV infection do not respond as well to treatment as persons who are circumcised or HIV-negative. Patients should be tested for HIV infection at the time chancroid is diagnosed. If the initial test results were negative, a serologic test for syphilis and HIV infection should be performed 3 months after the diagnosis of chancroid.

Follow-Up

Patients should be re-examined 3–7 days after initiation of therapy. If treatment is successful, ulcers usually improve symptomatically within 3 days and objectively within 7 days after therapy. If no clinical improvement is evident, the clinician must consider whether 1) the diagnosis is correct, 2) the patient is coinfected with another STD, 3) the patient is infected with HIV, 4) the treatment was not used as instructed, or 5) the H. ducreyi strain causing the infection is resistant to the prescribed antimicrobial. The time required for complete healing depends on the size of the ulcer; large ulcers might require >2 weeks. In addition, healing is slower for some uncircumcised men who have ulcers under the foreskin. Clinical resolution of fluctuant lymphadenopathy is slower than that of ulcers and might require needle aspiration or incision and drainage, despite otherwise successful therapy. Although needle aspiration of buboes is a simpler procedure, incision and drainage might be preferred because of reduced need for subsequent drainage procedures.

Management Of Sex Partners

Regardless of whether symptoms of the disease are present, sex partners of patients who have chancroid should be examined and treated if they had sexual contact with the patient during the 10 days preceding the patient's onset of symptoms.

Special Considerations

Pregnancy

Data suggest ciprofloxacin presents a low risk to the fetus during pregnancy, with a potential for toxicity during breastfeeding. Alternate drugs should be used during pregnancy and lactation. No adverse effects of chancroid on pregnancy outcome have been reported.

HIV Infection

Persons with HIV infection who have chancroid should be monitored closely because they are more likely to experience treatment failure and to have ulcers that heal slowly. Persons with HIV infection might require repeated or longer courses of therapy, and treatment failures can occur with any regimen. Data are limited concerning the therapeutic efficacy of the recommended single-dose azithromycin and ceftriaxone regimens in persons with HIV infection.

Chapter 51

Lymphogranuloma Venereum (LGV)

Lymphogranuloma venereum (LGV) is caused by *C. trachomatis* serovars L1, L2, or L3. The most common clinical manifestation of LGV among heterosexuals is tender inguinal and/or femoral lymphadenopathy that is typically unilateral. A self-limited genital ulcer or papule sometimes occurs at the site of inoculation. However, by the time patients seek care, the lesions have often disappeared. Rectal exposure in women or MSM can result in proctocolitis mimicking inflammatory bowel disease, and clinical findings may include mucoid and/ or hemorrhagic rectal discharge, anal pain, constipation, fever, and/or tenesmus. Outbreaks of LGV protocolitis have been reported among MSM. LGV can be an invasive, systemic infection, and if it is not treated early, LGV proctocolitis can lead to chronic colorectal fistulas and strictures; reactive arthropathy has also been reported. However, reports indicate that rectal LGV can be asymptomatic. Persons with genital and colorectal LGV lesions can also develop secondary bacterial infection or can be coinfected with other sexually and nonsexually transmitted pathogens.

Treatment

At the time of the initial visit (before diagnostic tests for chlamydia are available), persons with a clinical syndrome consistent with LGV, including proctocolitis or genital ulcer disease with lymphadenopathy, should be presumptively treated for LGV. As required by state law, these cases should be reported to the health department.

About This Chapter: Information in this chapter is excerpted from "Lymphogranuloma Venereum (LGV)," Centers for Disease Control and Prevention (CDC), June 4, 2015.

Treatment cures infection and prevents ongoing tissue damage, although tissue reaction to the infection can result in scarring. Buboes might require aspiration through intact skin or incision and drainage to prevent the formation of inguinal/femoral ulcerations.

Recommended Regimen
Doxycycline 100 mg orally twice a day for 21 days

Alternative Regimen
Erythromycin base 500 mg orally four times a day for 21 days

Although clinical data are lacking, azithromycin 1 g orally once weekly for 3 weeks is probably effective based on its chlamydial antimicrobial activity. Fluoroquinolone-based treatments also might be effective, but the optimal duration of treatment has not been evaluated.

Other Management Considerations

Patients should be followed clinically until signs and symptoms have resolved. Persons who receive an LGV diagnosis should be tested for other STDs, especially HIV, gonorrhea, and syphilis. Those who test positive for another infection should be referred for or provided with appropriate care and treatment.

Follow-Up

Patients should be followed clinically until signs and symptoms resolve.

Management Of Sex Partners

Persons who have had sexual contact with a patient who has LGV within the 60 days before onset of the patient's symptoms should be examined and tested for urethral, cervical, or rectal chlamydial infection depending on anatomic site of exposure. They should be presumptively treated with a chlamydia regimen (azithromycin 1 g orally single dose or doxycycline 100 mg orally twice a day for 7 days).

Special Considerations

Pregnancy

Pregnant and lactating women should be treated with erythromycin. Doxycycline should be avoided in the second and third trimester of pregnancy because of risk for discoloration of teeth and bones, but is compatible with breastfeeding. Azithromycin might prove useful for treatment of LGV in pregnancy, but no published data are available regarding an effective dose and duration of treatment.

HIV Infection

Persons with both LGV and HIV infection should receive the same regimens as those who are HIV negative. Prolonged therapy might be required, and delay in resolution of symptoms might occur.

Chapter 52

Genital Herpes

What Is Genital Herpes?

Genital herpes is an STD caused by two types of viruses. The viruses are called herpes simplex type 1 and herpes simplex type 2.

How Common Is Genital Herpes?

Genital herpes is common in the United States. In the United States, about one out of every six people aged 14 to 49 years have genital herpes.

How Is Genital Herpes Spread?

You can get herpes by having vaginal, anal, or oral sex with someone who has the disease.

Fluids found in a herpes sore carry the virus, and contact with those fluids can cause infection. You can also get herpes from an infected sex partner who does not have a visible sore or who may not know he or she is infected because the virus can be released through your skin and spread the infection to your sex partner(s).

How Can I Reduce My Risk Of Getting Herpes?

The only way to avoid STDs is to not have vaginal, anal, or oral sex.

If you are sexually active, you can do the following things to lower your chances of getting herpes:

About This Chapter: Information in this chapter is excerpted from "Genital Herpes - CDC Fact Sheet," Centers for Disease Control and Prevention (CDC), January 23, 2014.

- Being in a long-term mutually monogamous relationship with a partner who has been tested and has negative STD test results;

- Using latex condoms the right way every time you have sex.

Herpes symptoms can occur in both male and female genital areas that are covered by a latex condom. However, outbreaks can also occur in areas that are not covered by a condom so condoms may not fully protect you from getting herpes.

I'm Pregnant. How Could Genital Herpes Affect My Baby?

If you are pregnant and have genital herpes, it is even more important for you to go to pre-natal care visits. You need to tell your doctor if you have ever had symptoms of, been exposed to, or been diagnosed with genital herpes. Sometimes genital herpes infection can lead to mis-carriage. It can also make it more likely for you to deliver your baby too early. Herpes infection can be passed from you to your unborn child and cause a potentially deadly infection (neonatal herpes). It is important that you avoid getting herpes during pregnancy.

If you are pregnant and have genital herpes, you may be offered herpes medicine towards the end of your pregnancy to reduce the risk of having any symptoms and passing the disease to your baby. At the time of delivery your doctor should carefully examine you for symptoms. If you have herpes symptoms at delivery, a 'C-section' is usually performed.

How Do I Know If I Have Genital Herpes?

Most people who have herpes have no, or very mild symptoms. You may not notice mild symptoms or you may mistake them for another skin condition, such as a pimple or ingrown hair. Because of this, most people who have herpes do not know it.

Genital herpes sores usually appear as one or more blisters on or around the genitals, rectum or mouth. The blisters break and leave painful sores that may take weeks to heal. These symptoms are sometimes called "having an outbreak." The first time someone has an outbreak they may also have flu-like symptoms such as fever, body aches, or swollen glands.

Repeat outbreaks of genital herpes are common, especially during the first year after infection. Repeat outbreaks are usually shorter and less severe than the first outbreak. Although the infection can stay in the body for the rest of your life, the number of outbreaks tends to decrease over a period of years.

You should be examined by your doctor if you notice any of these symptoms or if your partner has an STD or symptoms of an STD, such as an unusual sore, a smelly discharge, burning when urinating, or, for women specifically, bleeding between periods.

How Will My Doctor Know If I Have Herpes?

Often times, your healthcare provider can diagnose genital herpes by simply looking at your symptoms. Providers can also take a sample from the sore(s) and test it. Have an honest and open talk with your health care provider and ask whether you should be tested for herpes or other STDs.

Can Herpes Be Cured?

There is no cure for herpes. However, there are medicines that can prevent or shorten outbreaks. One of these herpes medicines can be taken daily, and makes it less likely that you will pass the infection on to your sex partner(s).

What Happens If I Don't Get Treated?

Genital herpes can cause painful genital sores and can be severe in people with suppressed immune systems. If you touch your sores or the fluids from the sores, you may transfer herpes to another part of your body, such as your eyes. Do not touch the sores or fluids to avoid spreading herpes to another part of your body. If you touch the sores or fluids, immediately wash your hands thoroughly to help avoid spreading your infection.

Some people who get genital herpes have concerns about how it will impact their overall health, sex life, and relationships. It is best for you to talk to a health care provider about those concerns, but it also is important to recognize that while herpes is not curable, it can be managed. Since a genital herpes diagnosis may affect how you will feel about current or future sexual relationships, it is important to understand how to talk to sexual partners about STDs.

Can I Still Have Sex If I Have Herpes?

If you have herpes, you should tell your sex partner(s) and let him or her know that you do and the risk involved. Using condoms may help lower this risk but it will not get rid of the risk completely. Having sores or other symptoms of herpes can increase your risk of spreading the disease. Even if you do not have any symptoms, you can still infect your sex partners.

What Is The Link Between Genital Herpes And HIV?

Genital herpes can cause sores or breaks in the skin or lining of the mouth, vagina, and rectum. The genital sores caused by herpes can bleed easily. When the sores come into contact with the mouth, vagina, or rectum during sex, they increase the risk of giving or getting HIV if you or your partner has HIV.

Chapter 53

Human Papillomavirus (HPV)

What Is Human Papillomavirus (HPV)?

HPV is the most common sexually transmitted infection (STI). HPV is a different virus than HIV and HSV (herpes). HPV is so common that nearly all sexually active men and women get it at some point in their lives. There are many different types of HPV. Some types can cause health problems including genital warts and cancers. But there are vaccines that can stop these health problems from happening.

How Is HPV spread?

You can get HPV by having vaginal, anal, or oral sex with someone who has the virus. It is most commonly spread during vaginal or anal sex. HPV can be passed even when an infected person has no signs or symptoms.

Anyone who is sexually active can get HPV, even if you have had sex with only one person. You also can develop symptoms years after you have sex with someone who is infected making it hard to know when you first became infected.

Does HPV Cause Health Problems?

In most cases, HPV goes away on its own and does not cause any health problems. But when HPV does not go away, it can cause health problems like genital warts and cancer.

Genital warts usually appear as a small bump or group of bumps in the genital area. They can be small or large, raised or flat, or shaped like a cauliflower. A healthcare provider can usually diagnose warts by looking at the genital area.

About This Chapter: Information in this chapter is excerpted from "Genital HPV Infection - Fact Sheet," Centers for Disease Control and Prevention (CDC), January 23, 2014.

Does HPV Cause Cancer?

HPV can cause cervical and other cancers including cancer of the vulva, vagina, penis, or anus. It can also cause cancer in the back of the throat, including the base of the tongue and tonsils (called oropharyngeal cancer).

Cancer often takes years, even decades, to develop after a person gets HPV. The types of HPV that can cause genital warts are not the same as the types of HPV that can cause cancers.

There is no way to know which people who have HPV will develop cancer or other health problems. People with weak immune systems (including individuals with HIV/AIDS) may be less able to fight off HPV and more likely to develop health problems from it.

How Can I Avoid HPV And The Health Problems It Can Cause?

You can do several things to lower your chances of getting HPV.

Get vaccinated. HPV vaccines are safe and effective. They can protect males and females against diseases (including cancers) caused by HPV when given in the recommended age groups (see "Who should get vaccinated?" below). HPV vaccines are given in three shots over six months; it is important to get all three doses.

Get screened for cervical cancer. Routine screening for women aged 21 to 65 years old can prevent cervical cancer.

If you are sexually active

- Use latex condoms the right way every time you have sex. This can lower your chances of getting HPV. But HPV can infect areas that are not covered by a condom - so condoms may not give full protection against getting HPV;

- Be in a mutually monogamous relationship – or have sex only with someone who only has sex with you.

Who Should Get Vaccinated?

All boys and girls ages 11 or 12 years should get vaccinated.

Catch-up vaccines are recommended for males through age 21 and for females through age 26, if they did not get vaccinated when they were younger.

The vaccine is also recommended for gay and bisexual men (or any man who has sex with a man) through age 26. It is also recommended for men and women with compromised immune systems (including people living with HIV/AIDS) through age 26, if they did not get fully vaccinated when they were younger.

How Do I Know If I Have HPV?

There is no test to find out a person's "HPV status." Also, there is no approved HPV test to find HPV in the mouth or throat.

There are HPV tests that can be used to screen for cervical cancer. These tests are recommended for screening only in women aged 30 years and older. They are not recommended to screen men, adolescents, or women under the age of 30 years.

Most people with HPV do not know they are infected and never develop symptoms or health problems from it. Some people find out they have HPV when they get genital warts. Women may find out they have HPV when they get an abnormal Pap test result (during cervical cancer screening). Others may only find out once they've developed more serious problems from HPV, such as cancers.

How Common Is HPV And The Health Problems Caused By HPV?

HPV (the virus): About 79 million Americans are currently infected with HPV. About 14 million people become newly infected each year. HPV is so common that most sexually-active men and women will get at least one type of HPV at some point in their lives.

Health problems related to HPV include genital warts and cervical cancer.

Genital warts: About 360,000 people in the United States get genital warts each year.

Cervical cancer: More than 11,000 women in the United States get cervical cancer each year.

There are other conditions and cancers caused by HPV that occur in persons living in the United States.

I'm Pregnant. Will Having HPV Affect My Pregnancy?

If you are pregnant and have HPV, you can get genital warts or develop abnormal cell changes on your cervix. Abnormal cell changes can be found with routine cervical cancer screening. You should get routine cervical cancer screening even when you are pregnant.

Can I Be Treated For HPV Or Health Problems Caused By HPV?

There is no treatment for the virus itself. However, there are treatments for the health problems that HPV can cause:

- **Genital warts** can be treated by you or your physician. If left untreated, genital warts may go away, stay the same, or grow in size or number.

- **Cervical precancer** can be treated. Women who get routine Pap tests and follow up as needed can identify problems before cancer develops. Prevention is always better than treatment.

- **Other HPV-related cancers** are also more treatable when diagnosed and treated early.

Chapter 54

Hepatitis

Overview

What Is Hepatitis?

"Hepatitis" means inflammation of the liver. Toxins, certain drugs, some diseases, heavy alcohol use, and bacterial and viral infections can all cause hepatitis. Hepatitis is also the name of a family of viral infections that affect the liver; the most common types are Hepatitis A, Hepatitis B, and Hepatitis C.

What Is The Difference Between Hepatitis A, Hepatitis B, And Hepatitis C?

Hepatitis A, Hepatitis B, and Hepatitis C are diseases caused by three different viruses. Although each can cause similar symptoms, they have different modes of transmission and can affect the liver differently. Hepatitis A appears only as an acute or newly occurring infection and does not become chronic. People with Hepatitis A usually improve without treatment. Hepatitis B and Hepatitis C can also begin as acute infections, but in some people, the virus remains in the body, resulting in chronic disease and long-term liver problems. There are vaccines to prevent Hepatitis A and B; however, there is not one for Hepatitis C. If a person has had one type of viral hepatitis in the past, it is still possible to get the other types.

What Is Hepatitis B?

Hepatitis B is a contagious liver disease that ranges in severity from a mild illness lasting a few weeks to a serious, lifelong illness. It results from infection with the Hepatitis B virus. Hepatitis B can be either "acute" or "chronic."

About This Chapter: Information in this chapter is excerpted from "Hepatitis B FAQs for the Public," National Institute of Allergy and Infectious Diseases (NIAID), July 21, 2015.

Acute Hepatitis B virus infection is a short-term illness that occurs within the first 6 months after someone is exposed to the Hepatitis B virus. Acute infection can — but does not always — lead to chronic infection.

Chronic Hepatitis B virus infection is a long-term illness that occurs when the Hepatitis B virus remains in a person's body.

Transmission/Exposure

How Likely Is It That Acute Hepatitis B Will Become Chronic?

The likelihood depends upon the age at which someone becomes infected. The younger a person is when infected with Hepatitis B virus, the greater his or her chance of developing chronic Hepatitis B. Approximately 90% of infected infants will develop chronic infection. The risk goes down as a child gets older. Approximately 25%–50% of children infected between the ages of 1 and 5 years will develop chronic hepatitis. The risk drops to 6%–10% when a person is infected over 5 years of age. Worldwide, most people with chronic Hepatitis B were infected at birth or during early childhood.

How Is Hepatitis B Spread?

Hepatitis B is spread when blood, semen, or other body fluid infected with the Hepatitis B virus enters the body of a person who is not infected. People can become infected with the virus during activities such as:

- Birth (spread from an infected mother to her baby during birth)
- Sex with an infected partner
- Sharing needles, syringes, or other drug-injection equipment
- Sharing items such as razors or toothbrushes with an infected person
- Direct contact with the blood or open sores of an infected person
- Exposure to blood from needlesticks or other sharp instruments

Can A Person Spread Hepatitis B And Not Know It?

Yes. Many people with chronic Hepatitis B virus infection do not know they are infected since they do not feel or look sick. However, they still can spread the virus to others and are at risk of serious health problems themselves.

Can Hepatitis B Be Spread Through Sex?

Yes. Among adults in the United States, Hepatitis B is most commonly spread through sexual contact and accounts for nearly two-thirds of acute Hepatitis B cases. In fact, Hepatitis B is 50–100 times more infectious than HIV and can be passed through the exchange of body fluids, such as semen, vaginal fluids, and blood.

Can Hepatitis B Be Spread Through Food?

Unlike Hepatitis A, it is not spread routinely through food or water. However, there have been instances in which Hepatitis B has been spread to babies when they have received food pre-chewed by an infected person.

What Are Ways Hepatitis B Is Not Spread?

Hepatitis B virus is not spread by sharing eating utensils, breastfeeding, hugging, kissing, holding hands, coughing, or sneezing.

Who Is At Risk For Hepatitis B?

Although anyone can get Hepatitis B, some people are at greater risk, such as those who:

- Have sex with an infected person
- Have multiple sex partners
- Have a sexually transmitted disease
- Are men who have sexual contact with other men
- Inject drugs or share needles, syringes, or other drug equipment
- Live with a person who has chronic Hepatitis B
- Are infants born to infected mothers
- Are exposed to blood on the job
- Are hemodialysis patients
- Travel to countries with moderate to high rates of Hepatitis B

If I Think I Have Been Exposed To The Hepatitis B Virus, What Should I Do?

If you are concerned that you might have been exposed to the Hepatitis B virus, call your health professional or your health department. If a person who has been exposed to Hepatitis

B virus gets the Hepatitis B vaccine and/or a shot called "HBIG" (Hepatitis B immune globulin) within 24 hours, Hepatitis B infection may be prevented.

Symptoms

Does Acute Hepatitis B Cause Symptoms?

Sometimes. Although a majority of adults develop symptoms from acute Hepatitis B virus infection, many young children do not. Adults and children over the age of 5 years are more likely to have symptoms. Seventy percent of adults will develop symptoms from the infection.

What Are The Symptoms Of Acute Hepatitis B?

Symptoms of acute Hepatitis B, if they appear, can include:

- Fever
- Fatigue
- Loss of appetite
- Nausea
- Vomiting

- Abdominal pain
- Dark urine
- Clay-colored bowel movements
- Joint pain
- Jaundice (yellow color in the skin or the eyes)

What Are The Symptoms Of Chronic Hepatitis B?

Some people have ongoing symptoms similar to acute Hepatitis B, but most individuals with chronic Hepatitis B remain symptom free for as long as 20 or 30 years. About 15%–25% of people with chronic Hepatitis B develop serious liver conditions, such as cirrhosis (scarring of the liver) or liver cancer. Even as the liver becomes diseased, some people still do not have symptoms, although certain blood tests for liver function might begin to show some abnormalities.

How Will I Know If I Have Hepatitis B?

Talk to your health professional. Since many people with Hepatitis B do not have symptoms, doctors diagnose the disease by one or more blood tests. These tests look for the presence of antibodies or antigens and can help determine whether you:

- have acute or chronic infection
- have recovered from infection

- are immune to Hepatitis B
- could benefit from vaccination

How Serious Is Chronic Hepatitis B?

Chronic Hepatitis B is a serious disease that can result in long-term health problems, including liver damage, liver failure, liver cancer, or even death. Approximately 2,000–4,000 people die every year from Hepatitis B-related liver disease.

Treatment

How Is Acute Hepatitis B Treated?

There is no medication available to treat acute Hepatitis B. During this short-term infection, doctors usually recommend rest, adequate nutrition, and fluids, although some people may need to be hospitalized.

How Is Chronic Hepatitis B Treated?

It depends. People with chronic Hepatitis B virus infection should seek the care or consultation of a doctor with experience treating Hepatitis B. This can include some internists or family medicine practitioners, as well as specialists such as infectious disease physicians, gastroenterologists, or hepatologists (liver specialists). People with chronic Hepatitis B should be monitored regularly for signs of liver disease and evaluated for possible treatment. Several medications have been approved for Hepatitis B treatment, and new drugs are in development. However, not every person with chronic Hepatitis B needs to be on medication, and the drugs may cause side effects in some patients.

Prevention/Vaccination

Can Hepatitis B Be Prevented?

Yes. The best way to prevent Hepatitis B is by getting the Hepatitis B vaccine. The Hepatitis B vaccine is safe and effective and is usually given as 3-4 shots over a 6-month period.

What Is The Hepatitis B Vaccine Series?

The Hepatitis B vaccine series is a sequence of shots that stimulate a person's natural immune system to protect against HBV. After the vaccine is given, the body makes antibodies that protect a person against the virus. An antibody is a substance found in the blood that is produced in response to a virus invading the body. These antibodies are then stored in the body and will fight off the infection if a person is exposed to the Hepatitis B virus in the future.

Who Should Get Vaccinated Against Hepatitis B?

Hepatitis B vaccination is recommended for:

- All infants, starting with the first dose of Hepatitis B vaccine at birth
- All children and adolescents younger than 19 years of age who have not been vaccinated
- People whose sex partners have Hepatitis B
- Sexually active persons who are not in a long-term, mutually monogamous relationship.
- Persons seeking evaluation or treatment for a sexually transmitted disease
- Men who have sexual contact with other men
- People who share needles, syringes, or other drug-injection equipment
- People who have close household contact with someone infected with the Hepatitis B virus
- Health care and public safety workers at risk for exposure to blood or blood-contaminated body fluids on the job
- People with end-stage renal disease, including predialysis, hemodialysis, peritoneal dialysis, and home dialysis patients
- Residents and staff of facilities for developmentally disabled persons
- Travelers to regions with moderate or high rates of Hepatitis B
- People with chronic liver disease
- People with HIV infection
- Anyone who wishes to be protected from Hepatitis B virus infection

When Should A Person Get The Hepatitis B Vaccine Series?

Children and Adolescents

- All children should get their first dose of Hepatitis B vaccine at birth and complete the vaccine series by 6–18 months of age.
- All children and adolescents younger than 19 years of age who have not yet gotten the vaccine should also be vaccinated. "Catch-up" vaccination is recommended for children and adolescents who were never vaccinated or who did not get the entire vaccine series.

Adults:

- Any adult who is at risk for Hepatitis B virus infection or who wants to be vaccinated should talk to a health professional about getting the vaccine series.

Is The Hepatitis B Vaccine Series Effective?

Yes, the Hepatitis B vaccine is very effective at preventing Hepatitis B virus infection. After receiving all three doses, Hepatitis B vaccine provides greater than 90% protection to infants, children, and adults immunized before being exposed to the virus.

Who Should Not Receive The Hepatitis B Vaccine?

The Hepatitis B vaccine is not recommended for people who have had serious allergic reactions to a prior dose of Hepatitis B vaccine or to any part of the vaccine. Also, it not recommended for anyone who is allergic to yeast because yeast is used when making the vaccine. Tell your doctor if you have any severe allergies.

Is There A Vaccine That Will Protect Me From Both Hepatitis A And Hepatitis B?

Yes, there is a combination vaccine that protects people from both Hepatitis A and Hepatitis B. The combined Hepatitis A and B vaccine is usually given as three separate doses over a 6-month period.

Can I Get The Hepatitis B Vaccine At The Same Time As Other Vaccines?

Yes. Getting two different vaccines at the same time has not been shown to be harmful.

Where Can I Get The Hepatitis B Vaccine?

Talk to your doctor or health professional or call your health department. Some clinics offer free or low-cost vaccines.

Chapter 55

Molluscum Contagiosum

Molluscum contagiosum is an infection caused by a poxvirus (molluscum contagiosum virus). The result of the infection is usually a benign, mild skin disease characterized by lesions (growths) that may appear anywhere on the body. Within 6–12 months, Molluscum contagiosum typically resolves without scarring but may take as long as 4 years.

The lesions, known as Mollusca, are small, raised, and usually white, pink, or flesh-colored with a dimple or pit in the center. They often have a pearly appearance. They're usually smooth and firm. In most people, the lesions range from about the size of a pinhead to as large as a pencil eraser (2 to 5 millimeters in diameter). They may become itchy, sore, red, and/or swollen.

Mollusca may occur anywhere on the body including the face, neck, arms, legs, abdomen, and genital area, alone or in groups. The lesions are rarely found on the palms of the hands or the soles of the feet.

Transmission

The virus that causes molluscum spreads from direct person-to-person physical contact and through contaminated fomites. Fomites are inanimate objects that can become contaminated with virus; in the instance of molluscum contagiosum this can include linens such as clothing and towels, bathing sponges, pool equipment, and toys. Although the virus might be spread by sharing swimming pools, baths, saunas, or other wet and warm environments, this has not

About This Chapter: Information in this chapter is excerpted from "Molluscum Contagiosum," Centers for Disease Control and Prevention (CDC), May 11, 2015.

been proven. Researchers who have investigated this idea think it is more likely the virus is spread by sharing towels and other items around a pool or sauna than through water.

Someone with molluscum can spread it to other parts of their body by touching or scratching a lesion and then touching their body somewhere else. This is called autoinoculation. Shaving and electrolysis can also spread mollusca to other parts of the body.

Molluscum can spread from one person to another by sexual contact. Many, but not all, cases of molluscum in adults are caused by sexual contact.

Conflicting reports make it unclear whether the disease may be spread by simple contact with seemingly intact lesions or if the breaking of a lesion and the subsequent transferring of core material is necessary to spread the virus.

The molluscum contagiosum virus remains in the top layer of skin (epidermis) and does not circulate throughout the body; therefore, it cannot spread through coughing or sneezing.

Since the virus lives only in the top layer of skin, once the lesions are gone the virus is gone and you cannot spread it to others. Molluscum contagiosum is not like herpes viruses, which can remain dormant ("sleeping") in your body for long periods and then reappear.

Risk Factors

Who Is At Risk For Infection?

Molluscum contagiosum is common enough that you should not be surprised if you see someone with it or if someone in your family becomes infected. Although not limited to children, it is most common in children 1 to 10 years of age.

People at increased risk for getting the disease include:

- People with weakened immune systems (i.e., HIV-infected persons or persons being treated for cancer) are at higher risk for getting molluscum contagiosum. Their growths may look different, be larger, and be more difficult to treat.

- Atopic dermatitis may also be a risk factor for getting molluscum contagiosum due to frequent breaks in the skin. People with this condition also may be more likely to spread molluscum contagiousm to other parts of their body for the same reason.

- People who live in warm, humid climates where living conditions are crowded.

In addition, there is evidence that molluscum infections have been on the rise in the United States since 1966, but these infections are not routinely monitored because they are seldom serious and routinely disappear without treatment.

Treatment Options

What Are The Treatment Options?

Because molluscum contagiosum is self-limited in healthy individuals, treatment may be unnecessary. Nonetheless, issues such as lesion visibility, underlying atopic disease, and the desire to prevent transmission may prompt therapy.

Treatment for molluscum is usually recommended if lesions are in the genital area (on or near the penis, vulva, vagina, or anus). If lesions are found in this area it is a good idea to visit your health-care provider as there is a possibility that you may have another disease spread by sexual contact.

Be aware that some treatments available through the internet may not be effective and may even be harmful.

Physical Removal

Physical removal of lesions may include cryotherapy (freezing the lesion with liquid nitrogen), curettage (the piercing of the core and scraping of caseous or cheesy material), and laser therapy. These options are rapid and require a trained health care provider, may require local anesthesia, and can result in post-procedural pain, irritation, and scarring.

It is not a good idea to try and remove lesions or the fluid inside of lesions yourself. By removing lesions or lesion fluid by yourself you may unintentionally autoinoculate other parts of the body or risk spreading it to others. By scratching or scraping the skin you could cause a bacterial infection.

Oral Therapy

Gradual removal of lesions may be achieved by oral therapy. This technique is often desirable for pediatric patients because it is generally less painful and may be performed by parents at home in a less threatening environment. Oral cimetidine has been used as an alternative treatment for small children who are either afraid of the pain associated with cryotherapy, curettage, and laser therapy or because the possibility of scarring is to be avoided. While cimetidine is safe, painless, and well tolerated, facial mollusca do not respond as well as lesions elsewhere on the body.

Topical Therapy

Podophyllotoxin cream (0.5%) is reliable as a home therapy for men but is not recommended for pregnant women because of presumed toxicity to the fetus. Each lesion must be treated individually as the therapeutic effect is localized. Other options for topical therapy include iodine and salicylic acid, potassium hydroxide, tretinoin, cantharidin (a blistering agent usually applied in an office setting), and imiquimod (T cell modifier). These treatments must be prescribed by a health care professional.

Therapy For Immunocompromised Persons

Most therapies are effective in immunocompetent patients; however, patients with HIV/AIDS or other immunosuppressing conditions often do not respond to traditional treatments. In addition, these treatments are largely ineffective in achieving long-term control in HIV patients.

Low CD4 cell counts have been linked to widespread facial mollusca and therefore have become a marker for severe HIV disease. Thus far, therapies targeted at boosting the immune system have proven the most effective therapy for molluscum contagiosum in immunocompromised persons. In extreme cases, intralesional interferon has been used to treat facial lesions in these patients. However, the severe and unpleasant side effects of interferon, such as influenza-like symptoms, site tenderness, depression, and lethargy, make it a less-than-desirable treatment. Furthermore, interferon therapy proved most effective in otherwise healthy persons. Radiation therapy is also of little benefit.

Prevention

How Can I Keep It From Spreading?

The best way to avoid getting molluscum is by following good hygiene habits. Remember that the virus lives only in the skin and once the lesions are gone, the virus is gone and you cannot spread the virus to others.

Wash your hands

There are ways to prevent the spread of molluscum contagiosum. The best way is to follow good hygiene (cleanliness) habits. Keeping your hands clean is the best way to avoid molluscum infection, as well as many other infections. Hand washing removes germs that may have been picked up from other people or from surfaces that have germs on them.

Don't scratch or pick at molluscum lesions

It is important not to touch, pick, or scratch skin that has lesions, that includes not only your own skin but anyone else's. Picking and scratching can spread the virus to other parts of the body and makes it easier to spread the disease to other people too.

Keep molluscum lesions covered

It is important to keep the area with molluscum lesions clean and covered with clothing or a bandage so that others do not touch the lesions and become infected. Do remember to keep the affected skin clean and dry.

Any time there is no risk of others coming into contact with your skin, such as at night when you sleep, uncover the lesions to help keep your skin healthy.

Be careful during sports activities

Do not share towels, clothing, or other personal items.

People with molluscum should not take part in contact sports like wrestling, basketball, and football unless all lesions can be covered by clothing or bandages.

Activities that use shared gear like helmets, baseball gloves and balls should also be avoided unless all lesions can be covered.

Swimming should also be avoided unless all lesions can be covered by watertight bandages. Personal items such as towels, goggles, and swim suits should not be shared. Other items and equipment such as kick boards and water toys should be used only when all lesions are covered by clothing or watertight bandages.

Other ways to avoid sharing your infection

Do not shave or have electrolysis on areas with lesions.

Don't share personal items such as unwashed clothes, hair brushes, wrist watches, and bar soap with others.

If you have lesions on or near the penis, vulva, vagina, or anus, avoid sexual activities until you see a health care provider.

Long-Term Effects

What Are The Long-Term Effects?

Recovery from one molluscum infection does not prevent future infections. Molluscum contagiosum is not like herpes viruses which can remain dormant ("sleeping") in your body for long periods of time and then reappear. If you get new molluscum contagiosum lesions after you are cured, it means you have come in contact with an infected person or object again.

303

Complications

The lesions caused by molluscum are usually benign and resolve without scarring. However scratching at the lesion, or using scraping and scooping to remove the lesion, can cause scarring. For this reason, physically removing the lesion is not often recommended in otherwise healthy individuals.

The most common complication is a secondary infection caused by bacteria. Secondary infections may be a significant problem in immunocompromised patients, such as those with HIV/AIDS or those taking immunosuppressing drug therapies. In these cases, treatment to prevent further spread of the infection is recommended.

Chapter 56

Human Immunodeficiency Virus (HIV) And Acquired Immune Deficiency Syndrome (AIDS)

Human Immunodeficiency Virus (HIV)

HIV stands for human immunodeficiency virus. If left untreated, HIV can lead to the disease AIDS (acquired immunodeficiency syndrome).

Figure 56.1. What Is HIV/AIDS

Unlike some other viruses, the human body cannot get rid of HIV. That means that once you have HIV, you have it for life. No safe and effective cure for HIV currently exists, but scientists are working hard to find one, and remain hopeful.

About This Chapter: Information in this chapter is excerpted from "What Is HIV/AIDS?" U.S. Department of Health and Human Services (HHS), August 27, 2015.

HIV affects specific cells of the immune system, called CD4 cells, or T cells. Over time, if left untreated, HIV can destroy so many of these cells that the body can't fight off infections and disease. However, with proper medical care, HIV can be controlled. Treatment for HIV is called antiretroviral therapy or ART. It involves taking a combination of HIV medicines (called an HIV regimen) every day. Today, a person who diagnosed with HIV before the disease is far advanced and who gets and stays on ART can live a nearly normal life span.

The only way to know for sure if you have HIV is to get tested. Testing is relatively simple. You can ask your health care provider for an HIV test. Many medical clinics, substance abuse programs, community health centers, and hospitals offer them, too. You can also get an FDA-approved home HIV testing kit (the Home Access HIV-1 Test System or the OraQuick In-Home HIV Test) from a drugstore.

Acquired Immunodeficiency Syndrome (AIDS)

AIDS stands for acquired immunodeficiency syndrome. AIDS is the final stage of HIV infection, and not everyone who has HIV advances to this stage.

AIDS is the stage of infection that occurs when your immune system is badly damaged and you become vulnerable to opportunistic infections. When the number of your CD4 cells falls below 200 cells per cubic millimeter of blood (200 cells/mm3), you are considered to have progressed to AIDS. (Normal CD4 counts are between 500 and 1,600 cells/mm3.) You can also be diagnosed with AIDS if you develop one or more opportunistic infections, regardless of your CD4 count.

Without treatment, people who are diagnosed with AIDS typically survive about 3 years. Once someone has a dangerous opportunistic illness, life expectancy without treatment falls to about 1 year. People with AIDS need medical treatment to prevent death.

Where Did HIV Come From?

Scientists identified a type of chimpanzee in West Africa as the source of HIV infection in humans. They believe that the chimpanzee version of the immunodeficiency virus (called simian immunodeficiency virus, or SIV) most likely was transmitted to humans and mutated into HIV when humans hunted these chimpanzees for meat and came into contact with their infected blood. Studies show that HIV may have jumped from apes to humans as far back as the late 1800s. Over decades, the virus slowly spread across Africa and later into other parts of the world. We know that the virus has existed in the United States since at least the mid- to late 1970s.

Chapter 57

Young People And HIV

> - 1 in 4 new HIV infections occurs in youth ages 13 to 24 years
> - About 12,000 youth in 2010, or about 1,000 per month, were infected with HIV.
> - About 60% of all youth, with HIV do not know they are infected, are not getting treated, and can unknowingly pass the virus on to others.

About 50,000 people are infected with HIV each year, and 1 in 4 is 13 to 24 years old. Youth make up 7% of the more than 1 million people in the US living with HIV. About 12,000 youth were infected with HIV in 2010. The greatest number of infections occurred among gay and bisexual youth. Nearly half of all new infections among youth occur in African American males.

The risk for HIV for most youth begins when they start having sex or start injecting drugs. HIV causes a serious infection that, without treatment, leads to AIDS and early death. All youth should know how HIV is transmitted and prevented, understand what puts them at risk for HIV, and be tested if they are at risk.

Problem

Many people get infected with HIV as a teen or young adult

About This Chapter: Information in this chapter is excerpted from "HIV Among Youth in the US," Centers for Disease Control and Prevention (CDC), November 27, 2012.

New HIV infections In Youth In 2010

- About 1 in 4 (26%) of all new HIV infections is among youth ages 13 to 24 years. About 4 in 5 of these infections occur in males.

- Nearly 60% of new infections in youth occur in African Americans, about 20% in Hispanics/Latinos, and about 20% in whites.

- Over half (54%) of new infections among young gay and bisexual males are in African Americans.

- About 87% of young males got HIV from male to- male sex, 6% from heterosexual sex, 2% from injection drug use and about 5% from a combination of male-to-male sex and injection drug use.

- About 86% of young females got HIV through heterosexual sex and 13% from injection drug use.

- More new infections occurred among young African American males than in any other group of youth by race/ethnicity and sex.

Most Youth Are Not Getting Tested For HIV

- About 60% of youth with HIV do not know they are infected and so don't receive treatment, putting them at risk for sickness and early death. These youth can also unknowingly pass HIV to others.

- Young men are far more likely than young women to have HIV and are also less likely to get tested.

- African American youth are more likely to get tested for HIV than youth of other races or ethnicities.

- Youth who report being at risk for HIV are also more likely to get tested, but still many youth at risk have never been tested.

Many Factors Put Youth At Risk

- The risk for HIV for most youth begins when they start having sex or injecting drugs. (A small number of children are born with HIV.)

- For both males and females, having sex under the influence of drugs or alcohol can increase risky behaviors that could lead to becoming infected with HIV.

- The risk for getting HIV is higher in communities where a higher percentage of people already have HIV because partners are more likely to be infected.

  - African Americans have a greater burden of HIV than other racial or ethnic groups in the United States so they are at higher risk.

  - Gay and bisexual men are 40 times more likely to have HIV than other men. Research has shown that young gay and bisexual males who have sex with older partners are at a greater risk for HIV infection. This is because an older partner is more likely to have had more sexual partners or other risks, and is more likely to be infected with HIV.

- Less than half (44%) of gay and bisexual males in high school used condoms the last time they had sex.

Preventing Risky Behaviors In Youth

- Many effective programs reduce risky behaviors for youth. Prevention education for youth can be provided in the home, in schools, and in community and web-based programs.

- Youth, particularly those at high risk, should be taught early about HIV prevention with information they can understand and use. This includes education about risks and skills to help delay sex and prevent HIV infection.

- Youth who are sexually active can reduce their risk of HIV infection by choosing to stop having sex. They can also limit their number of sex partners, not have sex with an older partner who may be more likely to already have HIV, and use a condom every time.

- All youth at risk (sexually active or injection drug users) need to be tested and know where to get a confidential HIV test. Testing is the first step to getting medical care and treatment that can improve health, save lives, and prevent the spread of HIV.

Young Gay And Bisexual Males At Greatest Risk For HIV

Most new HIV infections in youth (about 70%) occur in gay and bisexual males; most are African Americans.

Sexually active young gay and bisexual males

- Have higher risk for getting HIV if they are having sex with older or multiple partners, using drugs or alcohol, or not using condoms during every sexual encounter.

- Should get an HIV test at least every year. Those at greater risk could benefit from testing as often as every 3 to 6 months.

- Aren't always getting HIV prevention education that is accurate and effective.

HIV Affects Everyone.

- Risk for HIV

- not knowing the fact or personal risk

- having sex

- alcohol or drug use with sex

- sex with older partners who may be more likely to be infected

- injecting drugs

- no condoms

- not tested

- not treated

What Can Be Done

Youth Can

- Get the facts about HIV and understand their risk.

- Get tested for HIV. Contact 1-800-CDC-INFO or text your zip code to Knowit (566948) or go to http://HIVtest.cdc.gov for more information and testing locations.

- Talk with parents, doctors, and other trusted adults about HIV, sexual health, and concerns about depression, drugs or alcohol.

- Resist pressure to have sex or inject drugs. Do not pressure others to engage in risky behaviors.

- Sexually active youth can reduce their risk by choosing to stop having sex, limiting their number of sex partners, not having sex with an older person who may be more likely to already have HIV, and using a condom every time. Don't have sex while using drugs or alcohol.

- Participate in HIV prevention programs, share HIV prevention information with friends and partners, and support other youth in protecting themselves against HIV.

- If you have HIV, get support, seek treatment, and stay in care to remain healthy and prevent passing the virus to others.

Parents And Families Can

- Talk with youth about HIV prevention.

- Ask your doctor about HIV testing and prevention for your youth, and ask your insurer if HIV screening is available without a co-pay, as required by the Affordable Care Act for most health plans.

- Engage in HIV education programs and support safe environments in schools for all youth.

- Make sure your community offers testing for HIV and sexually transmitted infections (STIs) as well as treatment for youth needing it.

Health Care Providers Can

- Follow current HIV testing and treatment guidelines and test youth at risk for HIV. Sexually active young gay and bisexual men should be tested at least once a year. People in communities with more HIV infections may benefit from being tested more often.

- Educate parents and youth about sexual development, what puts youth at risk, and how to prevent HIV.

- Provide HIV prevention services tailored for youth and protect patient confidentiality.

Everyone Can

- Get the facts about HIV and understand your risk. Get tested for HIV and other STIs. If you have HIV, get treatment and stay in care to remain healthy and prevent passing the virus to others.

- Engage in community and web-based education and other effective programs to prevent HIV and STIs among youth, particularly youth at highest risk.

- Combat the stigma and discrimination that keep young people, particularly young gay and bisexual males, from prevention and treatment services.

Chapter 58

HIV Testing Among Adolescents

What Schools And Education Agencies Can Do

Routine HIV testing for adolescents and adults aged 13–64 years is one of the most important strategies CDC recommends for reducing the spread of HIV. HIV testing is also an integral part of the *National HIV/AIDS Strategy* to prevent the spread of HIV and improve health outcomes for those who are already infected. Because youth spend a significant part of their day in school, education agencies and schools can play key roles in supporting HIV testing.

Why HIV Testing Is Important For Adolescents

Many young people in the United States remain at risk for HIV infection.

In 2010,

- Youth aged 13–24 years accounted for 7% of the estimated 1.1 million persons living with HIV infection.

- 26% (about 1 in 4) of the estimated 47,500 new HIV infections were among youth aged 13–24 years: 57% among blacks/African Americans, 20% among Hispanics/Latinos,* and 20% among whites.

Adolescents engage in behaviors that put them at risk for HIV infection. Among U.S. high school students in 2013,

- 47% have had sexual intercourse at least once.

- 34% are currently sexually active.

About This Chapter: Information in this chapter is excerpted from "HIV Testing Among Adolescents," Centers for Disease control and Prevention (CDC), July 2014; and information from "Special Populations," Centers for Disease control and Prevention (CDC), June 4, 2015.

- 41% of currently sexually active students did not use a condom the last time they had sexual intercourse.

- 15% have had four or more sex partners.

- 6% had sexual intercourse for the first time before age 13.

Knowing one's HIV status is one of the most important parts of prevention. Studies show that people who know they are infected are far less likely to have unprotected sex than those who do not know. Early diagnosis of HIV infection and linkage to care enable people to start treatment sooner, leading to better health outcomes and longer lives, and reducing the risk of spreading HIV to others.

CDC recommends routine HIV testing for adolescents and adults, with repeat testing at least annually for those at higher risk.

How Schools And Education Agencies Can Support HIV Testing

Collect And Use Health Risk Behavior Data.

CDC's national Youth Risk Behavior Survey (YRBS), a school-based survey that monitors health risk behaviors among high school students, measures the percentage of students who have been tested for HIV infection. According to the 2013 national YRBS, only 13% of 9th–12th grade students had ever been tested for HIV.

Although the national YRBS data are useful for characterizing HIV testing trends nationwide, state and local data are also needed to examine local trends in testing behaviors, identify disparities in testing for certain groups, and determine whether young people at high risk are being tested. Starting in 2015, the state/local standard questionnaire will include a question measuring HIV testing.

Teach Students About HIV And Other Sexually Transmitted Diseases.

Educating students about HIV and other sexually transmitted diseases (STDs) could increase students' likelihood of being tested. According to an analysis of YRBS data, HIV testing was more common among students who had ever been taught in school about AIDS or HIV infection (13%) than among those who had not (10%). The CDC's 2006 School Health Policies and Programs Study found that nationwide, in required health education courses, 85% of high schools taught students how HIV is spread and 77% taught students how HIV is diagnosed and treated. High schools can strengthen their HIV prevention curricula by including information on locations and procedures for obtaining free, or low-cost, confidential HIV testing.

Support Student Access To HIV Counseling And Testing Services.

Schools can play a critical role in facilitating access to HIV testing. A school-based referral program can help connect students to adolescent-friendly community health care providers. Some schools may be able to offer on-site testing in conjunction with a school-linked or school-based clinic or in partnership with mobile (e.g., van-based) testing programs.

Promote Communication Between Parents And Adolescents.

Effective communication between parents and adolescents about HIV is important. Approximately 60% of adolescents aged 15–19 years report that they have not had a conversation with their parents about how to prevent HIV infection. Schools can encourage activities shown to promote parent-child communication, such as assigning sex education homework assignments to be completed with a parent or trusted adult, or providing multi-session parent-child sex education programs.

Chapter 59

Pubic Lice ("Crabs")

What Are Pubic Lice?

Also called crab lice or "crabs," pubic lice are parasitic insects found primarily in the pubic or genital area of humans. Pubic lice infestation is found worldwide and occurs in all races, ethnic groups, and levels of society.

What Do Pubic Lice Look Like?

Pubic lice have three forms: the egg (also called a nit), the nymph, and the adult.

Nit: Nits are lice eggs. They can be hard to see and are found firmly attached to the hair shaft. They are oval and usually yellow to white. Pubic lice nits take about 6–10 days to hatch.

Nymph: The nymph is an immature louse that hatches from the nit (egg). A nymph looks like an adult pubic louse but it is smaller. Pubic lice nymphs take about 2–3 weeks after hatching to mature into adults capable of reproducing. To live, a nymph must feed on blood.

Adult: The adult pubic louse resembles a miniature crab when viewed through a strong magnifying glass. Pubic lice have six legs; their two front legs are very large and look like the pincher claws of a crab. This is how they got the nickname "crabs." Pubic lice are tan to grayish-white in color. Females lay nits and are usually larger than males. To live, lice must feed on blood. If the louse falls off a person, it dies within 1–2 days.

About This Chapter: Information in this chapter is excerpted from "Pubic "Crab" Lice," Centers for Disease control and Prevention (CDC), September 24, 2013.

Where Are Pubic Lice Found?

Pubic lice usually are found in the genital area on pubic hair; but they may occasionally be found on other coarse body hair, such as hair on the legs, armpits, mustache, beard, eyebrows, or eyelashes. Pubic lice on the eyebrows or eyelashes of children may be a sign of sexual exposure or abuse. Lice found on the head generally are head lice, not pubic lice.

Animals do not get or spread pubic lice.

What Are The Signs And Symptoms Of Pubic Lice?

Signs and symptoms of pubic lice include

- Itching in the genital area

- Visible nits (lice eggs) or crawling lice

How Did I Get Pubic Lice?

Pubic lice usually are spread through sexual contact and are most common in adults. Pubic lice found on children may be a sign of sexual exposure or abuse. Occasionally, pubic lice may be spread by close personal contact or contact with articles such as clothing, bed linens, or towels that have been used by an infested person. A common misconception is that pubic lice are spread easily by sitting on a toilet seat. This would be extremely rare because lice cannot live long away from a warm human body and they do not have feet designed to hold onto or walk on smooth surfaces such as toilet seats.

Persons infested with pubic lice should be examined for the presence of other sexually transmitted diseases.

How Is A Pubic Lice Infestation Diagnosed?

A pubic lice infestation is diagnosed by finding a "crab" louse or egg (nit) on hair in the pubic region or, less commonly, elsewhere on the body (eyebrows, eyelashes, beard, mustache, armpit, perianal area, groin, trunk, scalp). Pubic lice may be difficult to find because there may be only a few. Pubic lice often attach themselves to more than one hair and generally do not crawl as quickly as head and body lice. If crawling lice are not seen, finding nits in the pubic area strongly suggests that a person is infested and should be treated. If you are unsure about infestation or if treatment is not successful, see a health care provider for a diagnosis. Persons infested with pubic lice should be investigated for the presence of other sexually transmitted diseases.

Although pubic lice and nits can be large enough to be seen with the naked eye, a magnifying lens may be necessary to find lice or eggs.

Treatment

A lice-killing lotion containing 1% permethrin or a mousse containing pyrethrins and piperonyl butoxide can be used to treat pubic ("crab") lice. These products are available over-the-counter without a prescription at a local drug store or pharmacy. These medications are safe and effective when used exactly according to the instructions in the package or on the label.

Lindane shampoo is a prescription medication that can kill lice and lice eggs. However, lindane is not recommended as a first-line therapy. Lindane can be toxic to the brain and other parts of the nervous system; its use should be restricted to patients who have failed treatment with or cannot tolerate other medications that pose less risk. Lindane should not be used to treat premature infants, persons with a seizure disorder, women who are pregnant or breast-feeding, persons who have very irritated skin or sores where the lindane will be applied, infants, children, the elderly, and persons who weigh less than 110 pounds.

Malathion* lotion 0.5% (Ovide*) is a prescription medication that can kill lice and some lice eggs; however, malathion lotion (Ovide*) currently has not been approved by the U.S. Food and Drug Administration (FDA) for treatment of pubic ("crab") lice.

Both topical and oral ivermectin have been used successfully to treat lice; however, only topical ivermectin lotion currently is approved by the U.S. Food and Drug Administration (FDA) for treatment of lice. Oral ivermectin is not FDA-approved for treatment of lice.

How to treat pubic lice infestations: (Warning: See special instructions for treatment of lice and nits on eyebrows or eyelashes. The lice medications described in this section should not be used near the eyes.)

- Wash the infested area; towel dry.

- Carefully follow the instructions in the package or on the label. Thoroughly saturate the pubic hair and other infested areas with lice medication. Leave medication on hair for the time recommended in the instructions. After waiting the recommended time, remove the medication by following carefully the instructions on the label or in the box.

- Following treatment, most nits will still be attached to hair shafts. Nits may be removed with fingernails or by using a fine-toothed comb.

- Put on clean underwear and clothing after treatment.

- To kill any lice or nits remaining on clothing, towels, or bedding, machine-wash and machine-dry those items that the infested person used during the 2–3 days before treatment. Use hot water (at least 130°F) and the hot dryer cycle.

- Items that cannot be laundered can be dry-cleaned or stored in a sealed plastic bag for 2 weeks.

- All sex partners from within the previous month should be informed that they are at risk for infestation and should be treated.

- Persons should avoid sexual contact with their sex partner(s) until both they and their partners have been successfully treated and reevaluated to rule out persistent infestation.

- Repeat treatment in 9–10 days if live lice are still found.

- Persons with pubic lice should be evaluated for other sexually transmitted diseases (STDs).

Special instructions for treatment of lice and nits found on eyebrows or eyelashes:

- If only a few live lice and nits are present, it may be possible to remove these with fingernails or a nit comb.

- If additional treatment is needed for lice or nits on the eyelashes, careful application of ophthalmic-grade petrolatum ointment (only available by prescription) to the eyelid margins 2–4 times a day for 10 days is effective. Regular petrolatum (e.g., Vaseline)* should not be used because it can irritate the eyes if applied.

Prevention And Control

Pubic ("crab") lice most commonly are spread directly from person to person by sexual contact. Pubic lice very rarely may be spread by clothing, bedding, or a toilet seat.

The following are steps that can be taken to help prevent and control the spread of pubic ("crab") lice:

- All sexual contacts of the infested person should be examined. All those who are infested should be treated.

- Sexual contact between the infested person(s) and their sexual partner(s) should be avoided until all have been examined, treated as necessary, and reevaluated to rule out persistent infestation.

- Machine wash and dry clothing worn and bedding used by the infested person in the hot water (at least 130°F) laundry cycle and the high heat drying cycle. Clothing and items that are not washable can be dry-cleaned OR sealed in a plastic bag and stored for 2 weeks.

- Do not share clothing, bedding, and towels used by an infested person.

- Do not use fumigant sprays or fogs; they are not necessary to control pubic ("crab") lice and can be toxic if inhaled or absorbed through the skin.

Persons with pubic lice should be examined and treated for any other sexually transmitted diseases (STDs) that may be present.

Chapter 60

Trichomoniasis

Trichomoniasis or "trich" is a sexually transmitted infection (STI) caused by a parasite. The parasite is spread most often through vaginal, oral, or anal sex. It is one of the most common STIs in the United States and affects more women than men. It is treated easily with antibiotics, but many women do not have symptoms. If left untreated, trichomoniasis can raise your risk of getting HIV.

What Is Trichomoniasis?

Trichomoniasis is an STI caused by a parasite. It is one of the most common STIs in the United States.

Who Gets Trichomoniasis?

Trichomoniasis is more common in women than men. It affects more than 2 million women ages 14 to 49 in the United States.

Trichomoniasis affects more African-American women than white and Hispanic women. The risk for African-American women goes up with age and lifetime number of sex partners.

How Do You Get Trichomoniasis?

Trichomoniasis is spread through:

- Vaginal, oral, or anal sex. Trichomoniasis can be spread even if there are no symptoms. This means you can get trichomoniasis from someone who has no signs or symptoms.

About This Chapter: Information in this chapter is excerpted from "Trichomoniasis," Office on Women's Health (OWH), August 31, 2015.

- Genital touching. A man does not need to ejaculate (come) for trichomoniasis to spread. Trichomoniasis can also be passed between women who have sex with women.

What Are The Signs And Symptoms Of Trichomoniasis?

Most infected women have no signs or symptoms. If you do get signs or symptoms, they might appear five to 28 days after exposure and can include:

- Irritation and itching in the genital area
- Thin or frothy discharge with an unusual foul odor that can be clear, white, yellowish, or greenish
- Discomfort during sex and when urinating
- Lower abdominal pain (this is rare)

If you think you may have trichomoniasis, you and your sex partner(s) need to see a doctor or nurse as soon as possible.

How Is Trichomoniasis Diagnosed?

To find out whether you have trichomoniasis, your doctor or nurse may:

- Do a pelvic exam
- Use a cotton swab to take a fluid sample from your vagina to look for the parasite under a microscope
- Do a lab test, such as a DNA test or a fluid culture. A culture tests uses urine or a swab from your vagina. The parasite then grows in a lab. It takes up to a week for the parasite to grow enough to be seen.

> A Pap test is *not* used to detect trichomoniasis.

If you have trichomoniasis, you need to be tested for other STIs too.

How Is Trichomoniasis Treated?

Trichomoniasis is easily cured with one of two antibiotics:

- Metronidazole
- Tinidazole

These antibiotics are usually a pill you swallow in a single dose.

If you are treated for trichomoniasis, your sex partner(s) needs to be treated too. Do not have sex until you and your sex partner(s) finish taking all of the antibiotics and have no symptoms.

What Can Happen If Trichomoniasis Is Not Treated?

Most people with trichomoniasis have no symptoms and never know they have it. Even without symptoms, it can be passed to others.

If you have trichomoniasis, you are at higher risk of getting HIV (the virus that causes AIDS) if you are exposed to HIV. If you are HIV-positive, having trichomoniasis also raises your risk of passing HIV to your sex partner(s). The Centers for Disease Control and Prevention recommends that women with HIV get screened for trichomoniasis at least once a year.

What Should I Do If I Have Trichomoniasis?

Trichomoniasis is easy to treat. But you need to be tested and treated as soon as possible.

If you have trichomoniasis:

- **See a doctor or nurse as soon as possible.** Antibiotics will treat trichomoniasis.

- **Take all of your medicine.** Even if symptoms go away, you need to finish all of the antibiotics.

- **Tell your sex partner(s)** so they can be tested and treated.

- **Avoid sexual contact until you and your partner(s) have been treated and cured.** Even after you finish your antibiotics, you can get trichomoniasis again if you have sex with someone who has trichomoniasis.

- **See your doctor or nurse again if you have symptoms that don't go away** within a few days after finishing the antibiotics.

How Does Trichomoniasis Affect Pregnancy?

Pregnant women with trichomoniasis are at higher risk of premature birth (babies born before 37 weeks of pregnancy) or a low-birth-weight baby (less than 5 1/2 pounds). Premature birth and a low birth weight raise the risk of health and developmental problems at birth and later in life.

The antibiotic metronidazole can be used to treat trichomoniasis during any stage of pregnancy. Talk to your doctor about the benefits and risks of taking any medicine during pregnancy.

Can I Take Medicine For Trichomoniasis If I Am Breastfeeding?

You can take the antibiotic metronidazole if you are breastfeeding. Your doctor may suggest waiting 12 to 24 hours after taking metronidazole before breastfeeding. Do not take tinidazole if you are breastfeeding.

How Can I Prevent Trichomoniasis?

The best way to prevent trichomoniasis or any STI is to not have vaginal, oral, or anal sex.

If you do have sex, lower your risk of getting an STI with the following steps:

- **Use condoms.** Condoms are the best way to prevent STIs when you have sex. Because a man does not need to ejaculate (come) to give or get trichomoniasis, make sure to put the condom on before the penis touches the vagina, mouth, or anus. Other methods of birth control, like birth control pills, shots, implants, or diaphragms, will not protect you from STIs.

- **Get tested.** Be sure you and your partner are tested for STIs. Talk to each other about the test results before you have sex.

- **Be monogamous.** Having sex with just one partner can lower your risk for STIs. After being tested for STIs, be faithful to each other. That means that you have sex only with each other and no one else.

- **Limit your number of sex partners.** Your risk of getting STIs goes up with the number of partners you have.

- **Do not douche.** Douching removes some of the normal bacteria in the vagina that protects you from infection. This may increase your risk of getting STIs.

- **Do not abuse alcohol or drugs.** Drinking too much alcohol or using drugs increases risky behavior and may put you at risk of sexual assault and possible exposure to STIs.

The steps work best when used together. No single step can protect you from every single type of STI.

Can Women Who Have Sex With Women Get Trichomoniasis?

Yes. It is possible to get trichomoniasis, or any other STI, if you are a woman who has sex only with women.

Talk to your partner about her sexual history before having sex, and ask your doctor about getting tested if you have signs or symptoms of trichomoniasis.

Chapter 61

STDs And Pregnancy

Women who are pregnant can become infected with the same sexually transmitted diseases (STDs) as women who are not pregnant. Pregnant women should ask their doctors about getting tested for STDs, since some doctors do not routinely perform these tests.

Can Pregnant Women Become Infected With STDs?

Women who are pregnant can become infected with the same sexually-transmitted diseases (STDs) as women who are not pregnant. Pregnancy does not provide women or their babies any additional protection against STDs. Many STDs are 'silent,' or have no symptoms, so women may not know they are infected. A pregnant woman should be tested for STDs, including HIV (the virus that causes AIDS), as a part of her medical care during pregnancy. The results of an STD can be more serious, even life-threatening, for a woman and her baby if the woman becomes infected while pregnant. It is important that women be aware of the harmful effects of STDs and how to protect themselves and their children against infection. Sexual partners of infected women should also be tested and treated.

How Do STDs Affect A Pregnant Woman And Her Baby?

STDs can complicate pregnancy and may have serious effects on both a woman and her developing baby. Some of these problems may be seen at birth; others may not be discovered until months or years later. In addition, it is well known that infection with an STD can make it easier for a person to get infected with HIV. Most of these problems can be prevented if the

About This Chapter: Information in this chapter is excerpted from "STDs During Pregnancy - CDC Fact Sheet," Centers for Disease Control and Prevention (CDC), July 10, 2013.

mother receives regular medical care during pregnancy. This includes tests for STDs starting early in pregnancy and repeated close to delivery, as needed.

Should Pregnant Women Be Tested For STDs?

Screening and treating pregnant women for STDs is a vital way to prevent serious health complications to both mother and baby that may otherwise happen with infection. *The sooner a woman begins receiving medical care during pregnancy, the better the health outcomes will be for herself and her unborn baby.* The Centers for Disease Control and Prevention's 2010 STD Treatment Guidelines recommend screening pregnant women for STDs. The CDC screening recommendations are incorporated into the recommendations below.

Pregnant women should ask their doctors about getting tested for these STDs. It is also important that pregnant women discuss any symptoms they are experiencing and any high-risk sexual behavior that they engage in, since some doctors do not routinely perform these tests. Even if a woman has been tested in the past, she should be tested again when she becomes pregnant.

Table 61.1. CDC Screening Recommendations

Disease	CDC Recommendation
Chlamydia	Screen all pregnant women at first prenatal visit; 3rd trimester rescreen if younger than 25 years of age and/or high risk group
Gonorrhea	Screen all pregnant women at risk at first prenatal visit; 3rd trimester rescreen women at continued high risk Risk factors include: women younger than 25 years, living in a high morbidity area, previous GC infection, other STDs, new or multiple sex partners, inconsistent condom use, commercial sex work, drug use
Syphilis	Screen all pregnant women at first prenatal visit; during 3rd trimester rescreen women who are at high risk for syphilis or who live in areas with high numbers of syphilis cases, and/or those who were not previously tested or had a positive test in the first trimester
Bacterial Vaginosis	Test pregnant women who have symptoms or are at high risk for preterm labor
Trichomoniasis	Test pregnant women with symptoms
Herpes (HSV)	Test pregnant women with symptoms
HIV	Screen all pregnant women at first prenatal visit; rescreening in the third trimester recommended for women at high risk for getting HIV infection

Table 61.1. Continued

Disease	CDC Recommendation
Hepatitis B	Screen all pregnant women at first prenatal visit Retest those who were not screened prenatally, those who engage in behaviors that put them at high risk for infection and those with signs or symptoms of hepatitis at the time of admission to the hospital for delivery Risk factors include: having had more than one sex partner in the previous six months, evaluation or treatment for an STD, recent or current injection-drug use, and an HBsAg-positive sex partner
Human Papillomavirus (HPV)	There is not enough evidence to make a recommendation
Hepatitis C	All pregnant women at high risk should be tested at first prenatal visit

Can STDs Be Treated During Pregnancy?

STDs, such as chlamydia, gonorrhea, syphilis, trichomoniasis and BV can all be treated and cured with antibiotics that are safe to take during pregnancy. STDs that are caused by viruses, like genital herpes, hepatitis B, hepatitis C, or HIV cannot be cured. However, in some cases these infections can be treated with antiviral medications or other preventive measures to reduce the risk of passing the infection to the baby. If a woman is pregnant or considering pregnancy she should be tested so she can take steps to protect herself and her baby.

How Can Pregnant Women Protect Themselves Against Infection?

Latex male condoms, when used consistently and correctly, can reduce the risk of getting or giving STDs and HIV. The surest way to avoid STDs and HIV is to abstain from vaginal, anal, and oral sex or to be in a long-term mutually monogamous relationship with a partner who has been tested and is known to be uninfected.

Part Seven
If You Need More Information

Resources For Additional Information About Sexual Development And Sexually Transmitted Diseases

Adolescent AIDS Program Children's Hospital at Montefiore Medical Center
111 East 210th St.
Bronx, NY 10467
Phone: 718-882-0232
Fax: 718-882-0432
Website: www.adolescentaids.org
E-mail: info@adolescentaids.org

Advocates For Youth
2000 M St. N.W., Ste. 750
Washington, DC 20036
Phone: 202-419-3420
Fax: 202-419-1448
Website: www.advocatesforyouth.org

American Academy of Family Physicians
11400 Tomahawk Creek Pkwy
Leawood, KS 66211-2672
Phone: 913-906-6000
Toll-Free: 800-274-2237
Website: www.aafp.org
E-mail: fp@aafp.org

American Academy of Pediatrics
141 N.W. Pt. Blvd.
Elk Grove Village, IL 60007-1098
Phone: 847-434-4000
Fax: 847-434-8000
Website: www.aap.org

About This Chapter: Information in this chapter was compiled from many sources deemed reliable; inclusion does not constitute endorsement. All contact information was verified and updated in December 2015.

American Board of Obstetrics and Gynecology
2915 Vine St.
Dallas, TX 75204
Phone: 214-871-1619
Fax: 214-871-1943
Website: www.abog.org
E-mail: info@abog.org

American College of Nurse-Midwives
8403 Colesville Rd. Ste. 1550
Silver Spring, MD 20910-6374
Phone: 240-485-1800
Fax: 240-485-1818

American College of Obstetricians and Gynecologists (ACOG)
409 12th St. S.W.
Washington, DC 20090-6920
Phone: 202-638-5577
Website: www.acog.org

American Pregnancy Association
1425 Greenway Dr. Ste. 440
Irving, TX 75038
Phone: 972-550-0140
Website: www.americanpregnancy.org
E-mail: info@americanpregnancy.org

American Psychological Association
750 First St., NE
Washington, DC 20002-4242
Phone: 202-336-5500
Toll-Free: 800-374-2721
TDD/TTY: 202-336-6123
Website: www.apa.org

American Social Health Association
P.O. Box 13827
Research Triangle Park, NC 27709
Phone: 919-361-8400
Fax: 919-361-8425
Website: www.ashastd.org
Teen-oriented website: www.iwannaknow.org

Association of Reproductive Health Professionals (ARHP)
1901 L St., N.W. Ste. 300
Washington, DC 20036
Phone: 202-466-3825
Fax: 202-466-3826
Website: www.arhp.org

Breastcancer.org
7 E. Lancaster Ave. 3rd Fl.
Ardmore, PA 19003
Website: www.breastcancer.org

Boys Town
14100 Crawford St.
Boys Town, NE 68010
Phone: 402-498-1300
Toll Free: 800-448-3000
Website: boystown.org

Center for Adolescent Health Johns Hopkins Bloomberg School of Public Health
615 N.Wolfe St. Rm. E4612
Baltimore, MD 21205
Phone: 410-614-3953
Website: www.jhsph.edu/adolescenthealth

Center for Young Women's Health
333 Longwood Ave., 5th Fl.
Boston, MA 02115
Phone: 617-355-2994
Fax: 617-730-0186
Website: www.youngwomenshealth.org

Centers for Disease Control and Prevention
1600 Clifton Rd.
Atlanta, GA 30333
Toll-Free: 800-232-4636
Website: www.cdc.gov

Childhelp National Child Abuse Hotline
Toll-Free: 1-800-4-A-CHILD (1-800-422-4453)

The Cleveland Clinic
9500 Euclid Ave.
Cleveland, OH 44195
Toll-Free: 800-223-2273
TTY: 216-444-0261

Endometriosis Association
8585 North 76th Pl.
Milwaukee, WI 53223
Phone: 414-355-2200
Fax: 414-355-6065
Website: www.endometriosisassn.org

Endometriosis Research Center
630 Ibis Dr.
Delray Beach, FL 33444
Phone: 561-274-7442
Toll-Free: 800-239-7280
Fax: 561-274-0931
Website: www.endocenter.org
E-mail: askerc@aol.com

Alan Guttmacher Institute
125 Maiden Ln., 7th Fl.
New York, NY 10038
Phone: 212-248-1111
Toll-Free: 800-355-0244
Fax: 212-248-1951
Website: www.guttmacher.org
E-mail: info@guttmacher.org

GLBT National Help Center
2261 Market St., PMB #296
San Francisco, CA 94114
Toll-Free: 888-843-4564 (National Hotline)
Toll-Free: 800-246-7743 (Youth Hotline)
Website: www.glnh.org
E-mail: help@GLBThotline.org

Hormone Foundation
8401 Connecticut Ave. Ste. 900
Chevy Chase, MD 20815-5817
Toll-Free: 800-HORMONE
Fax: 301-941-0259
Website: www.hormone.org
E-mail: cclerkley@endocrine.org

Henry J. Kaiser Family Foundation
2400 Sand Hill Rd.
Menlo Park, CA 94025
Phone: 650-854-9400
Fax: 650-854-4800
Website: www.kff.org

National Campaign to Prevent Teen and Unplanned Pregnancy
1776 Massachusetts Ave., N.W. Ste. 200
Washington, DC 20036
Phone: 202-478-8500
Fax: 202-478-8588
Website: www.thenationalcampaign.org

National Cancer Institute
NCI Public Inquires Office
6116 Executive Blvd. Ste. 300
Bethesda, MD 20892-8322
Toll-Free: 800-4-CANCER (800-422-6237)
TTY: 800-332-8615
Website: www.cancer.gov

National Cervical Cancer Coalition (NCCC)
P.O. Box 13827
Research Triangle Park, NC 27709
Toll-Free: 800-685-5531
Website: www.nccc-online.org
E-mail: nccc@ashasexualhealth.org

National Family Planning and Reproductive Health Association
1627 K St., N.W., 12th Fl.
Washington, DC 20005
Phone: 202-293-3114
Website: www.nfprha.org
E-mail: info@nfprha.org

National Human Genome Research Institute
National Institutes of Health
Bldg. 31, Rm. 4B09
31 Center Dr., MSC 2152
9000 Rockville Pike
Bethesda, MD 20892-2152
Phone: 301-402-0911
Fax: 301-402-2218

National Institute of Allergy and Infectious Diseases
NIAID Office of Communications and Public Liaison
6610 Rockledge Dr., MSC 6612
Bethesda, MD 20892-6612
Toll-Free: 866-284-4107
Fax: 301-402-3573
TDD: 800-877-8339
Website: www.niaid.nih.gov

National Institute of Arthritis and Musculoskeletal and Skin Diseases (NIAMS)
Information Clearinghouse
National Institutes of Health
1 AMS Cir.
Bethesda, MD 20892-3675
Phone: 301-495-4484
Toll-Free: 877-22-NIAMS (226-4267)
Fax: 301-718-6366
TTY: 301-565-2966
Website: www.niams.nih.gov
E-mail: NIAMSinfo@mail.nih.gov

National Institute of Child Health and Human Development (NICHD)
31 Center Dr., Bldg. 31 Rm. 2A32, MSC 2425
Bethesda, MD 20892-2425
Toll-Free: 800-370-2943
TTY: 888-320-6942
Website: www.nichd.nih.gov

National Kidney Foundation

30 E. 33rd St.
New York, NY 10016
Phone: 212-889-2210
Toll-Free: 800-622-9010
Fax: 212-689-9261
Website: www.kidney.org
E-mail: info@kidney.org

National Kidney and Urologic Diseases Information Clearinghouse

3 Information Way
Bethesda, MD 20892-3580
Phone: 800-891-5390
Fax: 703-738-4929
TTY: 866-569-1162
Website: kidney.niddk.nih.gov
E-mail: nkudic@info.niddk.nih.gov

National Prevention Information Network

P.O. Box 6003
Rockville, MD 20849-6003
Toll-Free: 800-458-5231
Fax: 888-282-7681
Website: cdcnpin.org
E-mail: info@cdcnpin.org

National Research Center for Women & Families

1701 K St. N.W., Ste. 700
Washington, DC 20006
Phone: 202-223-4000
Fax: 202-223-4242
E-mail: info@breastimplantinfo.org

National Teen Dating Abuse Helpline

Toll-Free: 866-331-9474
TTY: 866-331-8453

National Women's Health Information Center U.S. Department of Health and Human Services

200 Independence Ave., S.W. Rm. 712E
Washington, DC 20201
Phone: 800-994-9662
TDD: 888-220-5446
Website: www.womenshealth.gov/
Pregnancy

Nemours Foundation

Website: www.kidshealth.org
E-mail: info@kidshealth.org

Office on Women's Health Department of Health and Human Services

200 Independence Ave., S.W. Rm. 712E
Washington, DC 20201
Phone: 202-690-7650
Fax: 202-205-2631

Planned Parenthood Federation of America

434 West 33rd St.
New York, NY 10001
Phone: 212-541-7800
Toll-Free: 1-800-230-PLAN (7526)
Fax: 212-245-1845
Website: www.plannedparenthood.org

Sexuality Information and Education Council of the United States (SIECUS)

90 John St. Ste. 402
New York, NY 10038
Phone: 212-819-9770
Fax: 212-819-9776
Website: www.siecus.org
E-mail: siecus@siecus.org

Social Health Education

7162 Reading Rd., Ste. 702
Cincinnati, OH 45237
Phone: 513-924-1444
Fax: 513-924-1434
Website: www.socialhealtheducation.org

STD Services Group Inc.

10 S. Riverside Plaza Ste. 1800
Chicago, IL 60606
Phone: 877-242-8710
Website: www.tstd.org
E-mail: info@tstd.org

U.S. Department of Health and Human Services (HHS)

200 Independence Ave., S.W.
Washington, DC 20201
Phone: 202-619-0257
Toll-Free: 877-696-6775
Website: www.hhs.gov

U.S. Food and Drug Administration (FDA)

10903 New Hampshire Ave.
Silver Spring, MD 20993-0002
Toll-Free: 888-INFO-FDA (463-6332)
Website: www.fda.gov

Index

Index

Page numbers that appear in *Italics* refer to tables or illustrations. Page numbers that have a small 'n' after the page number refer to citation information shown as Notes. Page numbers that appear in **Bold** refer to information contained in boxes within the chapters.